European Revolutions,
1492–1992

THE MAKING OF EUROPE
Series Editor: Jacques Le Goff

The Making of Europe series is the result of a unique collaboration between five European publishers – Beck in Germany, Blackwell in Great Britain and the United States, Critica in Spain, Laterza in Italy and le Seuil in France. Each book will be published in all five languages. The scope of the series is broad, encompassing the history of ideas as well as and including their interaction with the history of societies, nations and states to produce informative, readable and provocative treatments of central themes in the history of the European peoples and their cultures.

Published

The European City
Leonardo Benevolo

Europe and the Sea
Michel Mollat du Jourdin

European Revolutions, 1492–1992
Charles Tilly

In preparation

Migration and Culture
Klaus Bade

Women in European History
Gisela Bok

Literacy in European History
Roger Chartier

Nature and the Culture of Europe
Robert Delort

The European Identity
Josep Fontana

The Enlightenment
Ulrich Im Hof

The Industrialization of Europe
Jordi Nadal

The Peasantry of Europe
Werner Rösener

Divided Christendom
Peter Brown

The Romantic Movement
Maurice Cranston

Europe and the Perfect Language
Umberto Eco

The Individual in European History
Aaron Gurevitch

The Culture of Food
Massimo Montanari

The First European Revolution, 900–1200
R. I. Moore

Democracy in Europe
Maurice Agulhon

European Revolutions, 1492–1992

Charles Tilly

BLACKWELL
Oxford UK & Cambridge USA

First published in 1993 by Blackwell Publishers and simultaneously by four other
publishers: © 1993 Beck, Munich (German); © 1993 Critica, Barcelona (Spanish);
© 1993 Editions du Seuil, Paris (French); © 1993 Laterza, Rome and Bari
(Italian).

Reprinted 1993, 1994

Blackwell Publishers
108 Cowley Road
Oxford OX4 1JF, UK

238 Main Street
Cambridge, Massachusetts 02142, USA

British Library Cataloguing in Publication Data
A CIP catalogue record for this book is available from the British Library.

Library of Congress Cataloging-in-Publication Data
Tilly, Charles.
European revolutions, 1492–1992 / Charles Tilly.
p.   cm.
Includes bibliographical references and index.
ISBN 0-631-17398-6
1. Revolutions—Europe—History.   2. Europe— History— 1492–1992
I. Title.
D214.T54   1993
940.2—dc20   92–39019
                                                                         CIP

Typeset in 11 on 12½ pt Garamond by TecSet Ltd, Wallington, Surrey
Printed in Great Britain by T. J. Press (Padstow) Ltd, Cornwall

This book is printed on acid-free paper

TO CHRIS, KIT, LAURA AND SARAH
once my children, now my friends

Contents

Figures

Tables

Series Editor's Preface

Europe is in the making. This is both a great challenge and one that can be met only by taking the past into account – a Europe without history would be orphaned and unhappy. Yesterday conditions today; today's actions will be felt tomorrow. The memory of the past should not paralyse the present: when based on understanding it can help us to forge new friendships, and guide us towards progress.

Europe is bordered by the Atlantic, Asia and Africa, its history and geography inextricably entwined, and its past comprehensible only within the context of the world at large. The territory retains the name given it by the ancient Greeks, and the roots of its heritage may be traced far into prehistory. It is on this foundation – rich and creative, united yet diverse – that Europe's future will be built.

The Making of Europe is the joint initiative of five publishers of different languages and nationalities: Beck in Munich; Blackwell in Oxford; Critica in Barcelona; Laterza in Rome; and le Seuil in Paris. Its aim is to describe the evolution of Europe, presenting the triumphs but not concealing the difficulties. In their efforts to achieve accord and unity the nations of Europe have faced discord, division and conflict. It is no purpose of this series to conceal these problems: those committed to the European enterprise will not succeed if their view of the future is unencumbered by an understanding of the past.

The title of the series is thus an active one: the time is yet to come when a synthetic history of Europe will be possible. The books we shall publish will be the work of leading historians, by no means all European. They will address crucial aspects of European history in every field – political, economic, social, religious and cultural. They will draw on that long historiographical tradition which stretches back to Herodotus, as well as on those conceptions and ideas which have transformed historical enquiry in the recent decades of the twentieth century. They will write readably for a wide public.

Our aim is to consider the key questions confronting those involved in Europe's making, and at the same time to satisfy the curiosity of the world at large: in short, who are the Europeans? where have they come from? whither are they bound?

Jacques Le Goff

Preface

When Jacques Le Goff invited me to write a book on European revolutions, I gladly accepted. I had just finished a book on European states and an essay on the changing character of European revolutions: what could be easier and more enjoyable than to draw on the one and expand the other? Rod Aya, Jack Goldstone, Michael Kimmel and James Rule had recently made the task seem more manageable by publishing important critiques and syntheses of the literatures on revolution, rebellion and related processes. I therefore imagined an expedient job resembling the undergraduate course one might teach on the subject: general theories of revolution, state of the question on major European revolutions, rapid summaries of the events, provocative comparisons, tentative conclusions, suggestions for further inquiry.

The design was very seductive. Alas, I reckoned without conscience and curiosity. Although I had written about various revolutions for thirty years and had occasionally strayed into conceptualizing revolutionary processes, I had never really tried to formulate a general theory – or, for that matter, a general history – of revolutions. I discovered my incapacity to write this book without at least thinking about what such generalizations entail. The result was enjoyable and educational, but far from easy. I ended up sceptical about all efforts to formulate single models of revolution. I also missed the deadline, made more urgent by the European Community's consolidation in 1992 and 1993.

As a specialist historian, I have worked chiefly on France from the seventeenth century to the present and on Great Britain during the century after 1750. For the rest, I have relied on scholarly syntheses that were available in my customary libraries. The book's bibliography identifies the kinds of works I have consulted. Although with varying degrees of ease I can make my way through English, German, Russian, most of the Romance languages and other languages closely connected with them, I have favoured works in English and have completely ignored works in Turkish, Finnish, Hungarian or Arabic. As a result, the only 'facts' in this book that will surprise specialists in the various eras and areas it covers are no doubt my factual errors. Approaching a continent's history over half a millennium, I have surely misidentified persons, places and processes, mistaken causes, and made incorrect links among events. In those portions of the scholarship I know well, this book's new interpretations all have plenty of predecessors; they present new versions of old arguments. Surely that will also turn out to be the case in literatures I know less well, such as studies of the Balkans. Let me ask specialist historians not to spare my errors, but to ask, before they reject the entire analysis, whether the errors vitiate the book's general comparisons.

A few passages in the book adapt materials from earlier publications: 'State and Counterrevolution in France', *Social Research* 56 (1989), 71–97; 'Changing Forms of Revolution', in E. E. Rice (ed.), *Revolution and Counter-Revolution*, pp. 1–25 (Oxford: Blackwell Publishers, 1991); 'Conclusions', in Leopold Haimson & Giulio Sapelli (eds), *Strikes, Social Conflict and the First World War. An International Perspective*, pp. 587–98 (Milan: Feltrinelli, 1992). However old the ideas, all of the remaining text is new.

I have received acute criticism of various sections in earlier drafts and oral presentations from Rod Aya, Karen Barkey, Perry Chang, Randall Collins, Rafael Cruz, Jeff Goodwin, Michael Hanagan, Robert Jervis, Nikki Keddie, Sadrul Khan, Roy Licklider, Gloria Martinez Dorado, Tony Pereira, Ariel Salzmann, Theda Skocpol, Jack Snyder, Michele Stoddard, Sidney Tarrow, Wayne TeBrake, Bridget Welsh, Harrison White and Viviana Zelizer. (Tarrow and TeBrake urged major changes in the book's structure that I was ultimately unable to make, which gives them the right to an I-told-you-so if readers misconstrue the argument. Both, fortunately, have related books in progress that will allow them to correct my errors.) Carol Stevens helped generously with Russian sources. The New School's proseminar on state formation and collective action and a special seminar convened by Harrison

White at the Center for the Social Sciences, Columbia University, both vetted important parts of the manuscript expertly. Laura Kalmanowiecki and Hong Xu provided indispensable assistance with sources, while Brigitte Lee edited the manuscript impeccably. Adele Rotman gave me crucial advice on how to organize and finish the book. None of these helpful friends has seen the final draft, and none therefore bears the blame for my mistakes. I will take the rap.

New York City

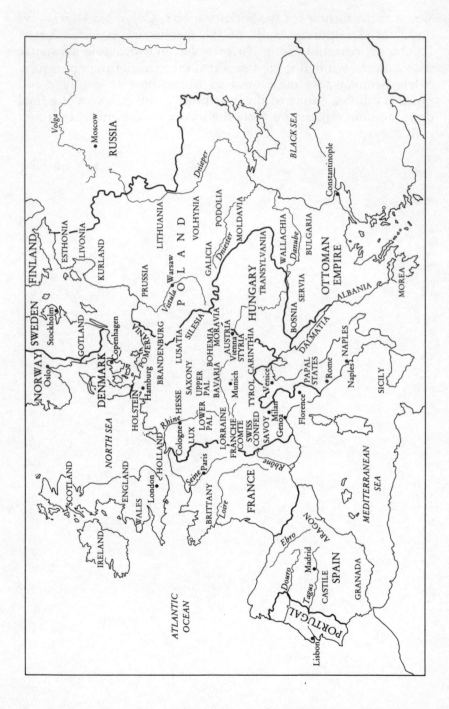

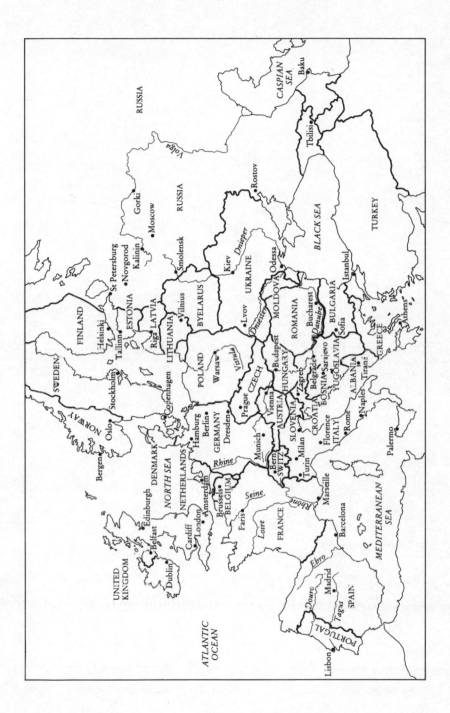

1

Conflict, Revolt and Revolution

Revolution's Return

History hates hubris. In 1989, French scholars and francophiles heralded the great French Revolution's bicentennial with requiems for revolution. Historical gadfly François Furet declared that the French Revolution begun in 1789 had at last ended, since the institution of a popularly elected president and a constitutional council had finally limited the national assembly's powers, since the Catholic Church was making its peace with democratic political parties, and – not least! – since the Communist Party, heir of the Jacobins, was disappearing as a major political force. Elsewhere in Western Europe and in Latin America, Furet continued, Marxism was dissolving as people discovered the 'risks of revolutionary maximalism' (Furet 1989: 28).

In the preface to a best-selling dictionary of the Revolution published that same year, Furet and Mona Ozouf propounded a paradox of French politics: a *coup d'état* healed the Revolution that had for almost 200 years remained an open wound. De Gaulle's seizure of power as French nationalists rebelled against decolonization put an end to the revolutionary myth: 'de Gaulle apparently hit on the key to creating a monarchical republic that after two hundred years has reconciled Ancien Régime and Revolution' (Furet & Ozouf 1989: xxi). The Revolution had passed away; France could finally go about the political business the unfortunate events of 1789 had so rudely interrupted. Most Europeans, French or otherwise, shared the sense that the age of revolution had vanished. In Western Europe, people seemed too prosperous and self-interested for revolution. In Eastern Europe, on the other hand, governments looked too repressive and citizens too fragmented for revolution.

In 1988, speaking of the West in general and of France in particular, Jacques Denoyelle declared that the experience of authoritarian socialism and the advent of democratic individualism 'joined to make violent rebellion a leftover from the past, a utopia stripped of its greasepaint' (in Gambrelle & Trebitsch 1989: II, 306). In a time of consumerism and powerful states, after all, it hardly seemed that dissidents within European countries could do much more than plant bombs, scrawl graffiti, mumble curses or give up. Reform or repression, perhaps; revolution, never. Hadn't the pitiful parodies of revolutionary programmes in 1968 taught as much?

In 1989, however, the people of Eastern Europe vigorously vitiated any analysis that implied an end to rebellion. They made their own revolutions. What is more, their dominant state, the Soviet Union, helped them unwittingly. During the years after coming to power in 1985, the Soviet Union's Mikhail Gorbachev had made it clear that as he trimmed burdensome military expenditure he would try not only to make peace with the United States and NATO but also to curb the Soviet military's intervention in other states' domestic affairs. The Soviet Union's expensive and demoralizing stalemate in Afghanistan – its most direct big confrontation with American military power in years – had sapped the Soviet military's prestige and raised doubts about the policy of military parity with the United States. Gorbachev's programme of non-interference and demilitarization extended to Eastern Europe's Soviet satellites.

With the Soviet Union reducing its military presence and expenditure, citizens of other Eastern European states began to recognize that their own rulers were now less likely to receive Soviet military support in the face of domestic challenges. Inside the Soviet Union, residents of non-Russian regions began to draw the same inference. Repression's relaxation encouraged the public making of long-silenced claims.

Challenges came quickly, if variously, in Poland, Hungary, Czechoslovakia and East Germany. In the first three, different sorts of opposition had been forming for ten years or more; they greatly expanded in the post–1985 thaw. In June 1989, Poles voted

99 out of Solidarity's 100 anti-communist candidates into a democratically elected upper house. In the lower house, the electoral law had restricted Solidarity to 35 per cent of the seats, but in August 1989 the Peasant Party bolted its forty-year alliance with the communists to give Solidarity a majority and the country a non-communist prime minister, Tadeusz Mazowiecki. The Soviets sat and watched. A similar, if slower, disestablishment of the Communist Party was then proceeding in Hungary; by the end of the year the formerly hegemonic Hungarian Socialist Workers Party had disbanded while a national referendum had overwhelmingly endorsed the dismantling of Party cells in factories, the dissolution of the Party's militia and the disclosure of the former Party's assets.

Czechoslovakia's leaders continued to use force for the repression of demonstrations until November. The flow of East German exiles through their country, the condemnation of the 1968 invasion of Czechoslovakia by two of its participants (Hungary and Poland), and the visibly vital transformation of the country's formerly communist neighbours nevertheless increased pressure on the regime. In mid-November, mass demonstrations in Prague and elsewhere brought government to a standstill, fostered the formation of a public opposition in Civic Forum, and incited a series of political improvisations that ended with the long-banned Alexander Dubcek speaker of Parliament and the recently imprisoned Václav Havel president of the republic. Irony triumphed.

East Germans, unlike their neighbours, had previously offered little overt resistance to their communist regime. During the autumn of 1989, however, Czech, Polish and Hungarian authorities allowed thousands of East Germans (ostensibly in their countries as fraternal tourists and holiday-makers) to pass into West Germany. The non-intervention of Soviet forces and the incapacity of the East German regime to stop the haemorrhage signalled even more dramatically that times had changed. East Germans at home began demonstrating for democratic reform and against their mediocre living conditions. When Prague's Soviet Embassy received a delegation from Czechoslovakia's dissident Civic Forum respectfully instead of rebuffing it, opposition leaders throughout Eastern Europe took note. Soon, in varying manners and degrees, popular rebellions in Romania, Bulgaria and Albania had also driven their communist leaders from power.

What is more, demands for independence or autonomy gathered strength in regions of Yugoslavia, Czechoslovakia and the Soviet Union itself. The Soviet Union began an unravelling that undid it entirely by the end of 1991. The Soviet Union's changed position also precipitated major shifts of power outside of Europe: in Mongolia, Ethiopia, Somalia and elsewhere. A number of African states that the Cold War had hardened into tyrannies began to melt toward democracy or anarchy. Not all of these struggles, by any means, counted as revolutions. Yet all of them demonstrated the revolutionary potential of populations long thought to be fragmented and docile.

Which European events of 1989 actually qualify as revolutions? It depends on how broadly we define the term. If we insist narrowly that a revolution closely resemble France's struggles between 1789 and 1799 or Russia's between 1917 and 1921, none of 1989's turmoil in Eastern Europe wins the medal. We will be hard put to find any equivalents of the Estates General, the Soviets, Robespierre, Lenin or the Civil Constitution of the Clergy. If, on the other hand, we include any abrupt, wide-reaching, popular change in a country's rulers, most Eastern European countries experienced revolutions that year.

A narrow definition has the advantage of hewing to the *Communist Manifesto*'s idea of a rare event, possible only under exceptional conditions, that alters an entire people's history; since Marx and Engels, so many militants have organized theory and practice around such an idea of revolution that it has a claim to special treatment. A broad definition, however, has the advantage of drawing attention to important problems that the narrow definition obscures: to what extent and in what ways do great revolutions conform to the regularities of non-revolutionary politics? In particular, how do broad changes in the organization of states impinge on revolutions? Applied to Europe between 1492 and 1992, the two questions motivate this book.

Historians have studied the relations between states and revolutions for centuries. During the last few decades, historians such as R. R. Palmer, Perez Zagorin, Roland Mousnier, Peter Blickle and Yves-Marie Bercé have even dared to write general histories of rebellion and revolution for limited periods of European history (see Palmer, 1959, 1964; Zagorin, 1982; Mousnier, 1967; Blickle, 1988; Bercé, 1980). We do not lack historical accounts. Nor do we lack broad theories of revolution (for examples, summaries and critiques, see Amann 1962; Arendt 1963; Aya 1990; Baechler 1970; Brinton 1938; Dunn 1989; Friedrich 1966; Goldstone 1986; Hobsbawm 1986; Kimmel 1990; Laqueur 1968; Rule & Tilly 1972; Trotsky 1932). What we lack is a systematic, historically grounded analysis of revolutionary processes that connects them firmly to our accumulating knowledge of state formation and routine political contention. For the last 500 years of European history, this book takes up that challenge.

The book before you relates European revolutions of the last five centuries to changes in the character of states, and in relations among states. It offers a general account of Europe's revolutions, their causes and their effects, while paying special attention to connections between alterations in state power and shifts in the nature, locus and outcome of revolutions. Furthermore, although it spotlights the English, French and Russian Revolutions, the book worries less about the common properties of great revolutions than about their place in Europe's long-term political transformations. In so doing, it links past, present and future.

The succeeding pages inspect European revolutions, broadly defined, from three angles. First, they ask how forcible transfers of state power have changed in character as a function of transformations in European social structure, especially the organization of states and relations among states. Second, they ask how changes in revolution connect with alterations in non-revolutionary conflict and collective action. Third, they ask how revolutions work, and whether the regularities within revolutions have changed systematically over the five centuries under review. All three angles intersect at a single apex, the observation that:

> whatever else they involve, revolutions include forcible transfers of power over states, and therefore
> any useful account of revolutions must concern, among other things, how states and uses of force vary in time, space and social setting.

The possibility and character of revolution changed with the organization of states and systems of states; they will change again with future alterations of state power. Revolutions are no longer what they were because states are no longer what they were. Whatever else they involve, revolutions obviously include taking of power over states, and therefore vary in likelihood and character as a function of the prevailing system of states.

The point is not merely that the organization of any particular state affects its propensity to revolution. It is also that relations *among* states affect the locus, likelihood, character and outcome of revolution. Take the Russian Revolutions of 1905 and 1917: in both cases a lost war discredited the state – literally as well as figuratively, since both times the state's bankruptcy contributed mightily to its political collapse. By defeating Russian armies, Japan helped make the revolution of 1905, as Germany helped make the Russian Revolutions of 1917. Wars generally had a strong influence on the prospects for revolution in Europe. War does not result from the actions of a single state, however aggressive; it results from interactions among states, from alignments in the state system as a whole. How other states react to a state's internal struggles, furthermore, strongly affects those struggles' outcomes; ask any citizen of today's Lebanon or Afghanistan about outside influence! To know which states are liable to revolution, we must examine not only their domestic politics, but also their locations in the prevailing set of relations among states.

Not that revolutions take place in an isolated realm of state power, independent of surrounding social organization. On the contrary, social processes in a state's environment profoundly affect the prospect and character of revolution. But they do so indirectly, in three main ways: (1) by shaping the state's structure and its relation to the subject population; (2) by determining who are the major actors within any particular polity, as well as how they approach political struggle; and (3) by affecting how much pressure bears upon the state and from which directions. The transition from an agrarian to an industrial economy, for example, both changes the character of the state and diminishes the importance of landlords, peasants or landless rural labourers in struggles for power. Hence revolutions take very different forms in agrarian and industrial settings. Again, in the absence of expanding production and increasingly effective collection of state revenues, prolonged population growth weakens the capacity of any state to carry on its activities, including warfare and repression of domestic opponents. All else equal, a weakened state is more liable to revolution than a strong one. If we focus on changes in state structure, we must often turn to examine transformations of the social settings in which states change and revolutions unfold.

This book's broad conception of revolution argues that great revolutions do not develop *sui generis*, subject to laws that separate them entirely from more routine forms of political change. Take the difference between solar eclipses and traffic jams. Revolutions do not resemble eclipses of the sun, which because of the regularities of celestial motion repeat on a precise schedule under specifiable and perfectly comprehensible conditions – those conditions and no others. Instead revolutions resemble traffic jams, which vary greatly in form and severity, merge imperceptibly into routine vehicular flows, develop from those flows, and happen in different circumstances for a number of different reasons. Yet traffic jams do not happen randomly; they occur according to strong regularities in the timing of traffic, response of drivers to weather conditions, patterns of highway maintenance and construction, locations of automobile accidents and breakdowns, and a number of other factors, each of which is somewhat independent of the others but relatively predictable on its own. The coincidence of these factors is so complex as to seem almost a matter of chance. Dense fog, for example, is a likely sufficient condition for traffic jams in one kind of setting, a stalled car in another, opening of a drawbridge in yet another.

Once begun, traffic jams display recurrent patterns such as the efforts of those on the periphery to exit from the scene and of those in the middle to compete fiercely for small advantages. They also have variable but significant consequences, not only for daily schedules of people caught in them but also for the condition of their vehicles, pollution of the nearby environment, use of public transportation, deployment of police, incidence of new traffic accidents, and much more.

Taken separately, each of the causal mechanisms – response of drivers to weather conditions, highway maintenance and so on – displays substantial, comprehensible regularities. Both traffic policemen and theorists of traffic flows have codified the regularities better than students of revolution have codified theirs. With allowances for unpredictable events such as a traffic policeman's sudden sickness and for the emergence of chaos in some combinations of factors, one could even model their interaction on a computer. It would be easier to work out a standard model for a special case, for example the spectacular pile-up of dozens of cars on a motorway in the event of a sudden snowstorm. Neither for traffic jams nor for revolutions, however, is a general theory specifying necessary and sufficient conditions, standard internal sequences or invariant consequences conceivable. In both cases, furthermore, not just one but a number of different conjunctions of settings and causal mechanisms all produce the critical outcomes: revolutions or traffic jams. That is why each time someone proposes a unique and general model of revolution someone else soon comes up with cases that do not 'fit', proposing modifications to the theory or even a new theory.

If it is impossible to state the invariant necessary and sufficient conditions of revolution for all times and places, it is nevertheless quite possible to show that similar causal mechanisms come into play within a broad range of revolutionary situations, such mechanisms as the dramatic demonstration that a previously formidable state is vulnerable and the partial dissolution of existing state powers that commonly occurs in post-war demobilizations. I am wagering, and hoping to show, that the same sorts of mechanisms underlie the broad range of events I will call revolutions, indeed a wide variety of conflicts that do not issue in revolution. I also hope to show that variation in the character and incidence of revolutions results from variation in those recurrent mechanisms. Finally, I hope to show that the mechanisms chiefly concern the routine operation and transformation of states. Just as the regularities in traffic jams spring from uniformities in the ways that vehicles flow on streets and highways – how passers-by respond to traffic accidents, how traffic lights change, how lorry drivers park for deliveries, how working hours and train timetables generate commuter driving and so on – regularities in revolutions spring from features of states that underlie the operation of states outside of revolutions. My analyses of European revolutions start from that working hypothesis.

Let us therefore dare a more precise definition of revolution. Consider a revolution to be a forcible transfer of power over a state in the course of which at least two distinct blocs of contenders make incompatible claims to control the state, and some significant portion of the population subject to the state's jurisdiction acquiesces in the claims of each bloc. The blocs may be single actors, such as the class of great landlords, but they often consist of coalitions among rulers, members and/or challengers. In a revolution, the polity stops behaving as before; the distinctions among rulers, members and challengers blur, then change. In the course of a revolution, furthermore, non-contenders often mobilize and become contenders; once power over the state comes under serious challenge, every interest that depends on state action is at risk. Given some minimum of routine organization and connection among members of a population, having visibly shared interests suddenly at risk provides any population with strong incentives to mobilize.

Note the elements: two or more power blocs having significant support, incompatible claims on the state, transfer of state power. A full revolutionary sequence thus runs from a sundering of sovereignty and hegemony through a period of struggle to re-establishment of sovereignty and hegemony under new management. The course of struggle and change from the opening to the termination of multiple sovereignty constitutes the revolutionary process. In order to avoid strictly momentary seizures of governments, let us add the stipulation that the new regime must hold power for a significant period – say at least a month. In order to ignore strictly local challenges to state power, let us also stipulate that the smaller bloc must control at least one major subdivision, geographic or administrative, of the state.

Nothing in the definition precludes distinguishing the traditional subclass of great revolutions, in which divisions are profound, struggles massive, transfers of power sweeping, consequent transformations of social life extensive and enduring. Later chapters will actually single out the famous English, French and Russian Revolutions for close scrutiny. But my discussion will follow the broad definition, in an effort to differentiate the conditions under which great revolutions, small revolutions, civil wars and other violent transfers of power occur. Under such a definition, unsuccessful rebellions, bloodless coups and top-down social transformations do not quite qualify as revolutions, but remain their close kin. We could in fact expand or contract the definition's range somewhat without seriously affecting the analysis. The book will assert repeatedly and illustrate abundantly that the close kin have many characteristics in common with events included by the definition, that they all belong to the same continuous field of variation.

Revolutionary Situations

According to this definition, a revolution has two components: a revolutionary situation and a revolutionary outcome. A revolutionary *situation* – the idea comes directly from Leon Trotsky's conception of dual power – entails multiple sovereignty: two or more blocs make effective, incompatible claims to control the state, or to be the state. That happens when the members of a previously subordinate polity (e.g. Lithuania within the Soviet Union of 1990) assert sovereignty, when non-ruling contenders mobilize into a bloc successfully exerting control over some portion of the state (e.g. the coalitions among intellectuals, bourgeois and skilled workers that formed widely in 1848), and when an existing polity fragments into two or more blocs, each exercising control over some significant part of the state (e.g. the splitting of English gentry into Roundheads and Cavaliers after 1640). In a revolutionary situation, three proximate causes converge:

1 the appearance of contenders, or coalitions of contenders, advancing exclusive competing claims to control of the state, or some segment of it;
2 commitment to those claims by a significant segment of the citizenry;
3 incapacity or unwillingness of rulers to suppress the alternative coalition and/or commitment to its claims.

These causes are only proximate; a full explanation of any revolution requires us to explain in turn why coalitions of contenders appeared, why a significant number of citizens accepted their claims, why rulers were unwilling or unable to repress their opposition.

Why each of these occurs, and how conditions for them changed, will occupy much of this book. We will have to ask, for example, why the contenders have sometimes been patron–client networks, sometimes social classes, sometimes local communities, sometimes religious congregations, sometimes ethnic groups. Rather than uniformity, we will confront variability in the broader circumstances in which the proximate causes occur. The regularities will inhere not in the general conditions for revolution, but in the mechanisms that combine at times into ineffectual protest, at other times into civil wars, more rarely into political splits producing thorough transformations of social life.

Enumerating proximate causes of revolutionary situations resembles naming the components of a traffic jam. The causes follow inevitably from the definition of revolution as a forcible transfer of power involving a break of the polity into at least two blocs. They are tautologically true. Such truisms have the advantage of specifying exactly what must be explained and thereby of guiding the search for longer-term and more contingent causes. They also make clearer that revolutionary situations consist in the convergence of variable political conditions – exclusive claims to the state, commitment to such claims, state unreadiness to suppress opposing coalitions and claims – that appear widely outside of revolutions.

The crucial causal mechanisms in revolutions group under the three headings: those that cause the emergence of rival claims to the state, those that cause commitment to such claims, those that make the holders of state power unready to suppress opposing coalitions and claims. The first set, for example, includes the mobilization of connected populations whose shared identities state action threatens and the spread of beliefs that the state is newly vulnerable. The same mechanisms combine in some circumstances to produce non-revolutionary contention for power and in others to produce revolutionary situations. Our task is both to understand those mechanisms in general and to single out the conditions in which they combine to form revolutionary situations.

Larger revolutions generally contain not one but a succession of revolutionary situations. Challengers change, rulers change, claims change, commitment of citizens to the claims changes, and capacity of rulers to suppress challengers changes. In long, complex revolutions the depth and character of revolutionary situations similarly fluctuate, with some moments in which most citizens are aligned on one side or the other and neither side exercises routine control of the state followed by other moments in which one coalition has seized effective control of the whole state apparatus. For just these reasons, it is debatable whether the French Revolution of 1789 to 1799 consists of one continuous series of revolutionary situations or a half-dozen revolutionary situations separated by temporary consolidations of state power.

Revolutionary situations drive to the extreme a political condition that is more common and equally crucial outside of revolutions: a shift in power over the state that threatens every group
having a stake in the existing structure of power at the same time as
it offers new opportunities to every group – including existing
power-holders – having the capacity to enhance its interests by
acting quickly. While the acuteness of the conjunction between
opportunity and threat sets off full revolutionary situations from
their cousins, it is precisely this conjunction that helps us recognize
their kinship. Ends of lost wars, disintegrations of empires and
cycles of protest may occur with or without open splits in polities,
but they all have some recognizable traits of revolutions.

Even in the absence of open splits in the polity, ends of wars
often have this quality. Almost every state makes more commitments in the course of mobilizing for war than it can fulfil at the
war's end; the commitments take the form of accumulated public
debt, promises to organized workers, capitalists, office-holders or
ethnic contenders who have muted their claims to cooperate with
the war effort, responsibility for veterans and their families, and so
on. Furthermore, states commonly erect extraordinary controls
over economic and social life in wartime only to start dismantling
those controls at the war's end, just as they are demobilizing
military production and reintegrating former warriors into civilian
economic life. The more capacity and credibility the state has lost
during the war (utter defeat by an occupying power being the
extreme condition) the greater the overload.

These circumstances threaten old rights and make the state
vulnerable to new claims. Consider the situation at the end of
World War I, where every belligerent state including the late-
entering United States faced major challenges from political actors
who had earlier collaborated with the war effort. The seriousness
of each state's challenges varied directly with the country's losses
in the war. Only Russia and Germany, badly battered by war
losses, opened fully revolutionary situations. But Italy's post-war
politics, with major strikes, mass occupation of factories and rapid
increase of fascist activism, soon reached the edge of revolution.
Meanwhile France, Great Britain and the United States, in that
order, faced lesser challenges to the established order. Elsewhere in
Europe, Ireland, the Netherlands and the states of the exploding
Ottoman and Austro-Hungarian Empires had their own varying
brushes with revolutionary situations.

Disintegrations of empires, coalitions and federations, indeed, share properties with revolutionary situations. The unpunished defection of one visible member sends a whole barrage of signals: the very possibility of defection, the decreasing capacity of the central executive to maintain its commitments and keep others in line, the opportunity to seize assets formerly under central control, the chance for cooperation with other defectors and the probable increased costs of loyalty to the centre. Once Estonia, Latvia and Lithuania escaped from his Soviet Union with strong Western encouragement, Mikhail Gorbachev tasted that bitter logic. So, decades or centuries before, had earlier rulers of Burgundian, Habsburg, Ottoman and Austro-Hungarian Empires as possessions fled their control with the collusion, and usually to the profit, of rival powers.

Revolutionary situations similarly have something in common with cycles of protest in polities that survive them without fundamental change. As Sidney Tarrow (1989) points out, social movements (sustained challenges to public authorities in the name of wronged populations) often come in waves: witness the student–worker protests of 1968 in much of Europe and America. During such waves, one set of demands seems to incite another, social-movement organizations compete with each other for support, and demands become more extreme for a while before subsiding. As this happens, activists often experiment with new ways of organizing, framing their demands, combating their enemies and holding on to what they have. At the end of the cycle, some new actors have typically gained at least a modicum of power, some polity members have lost power, the framing of public issues has altered somewhat, and prevailing repertoires of contention have changed at least slightly.

In cycles of protest, early demands do two crucial things. First, they demonstrate the vulnerability of authorities to such demands, which signals immediately to other contenders that the time may be ripe for their own demands. Second, they inevitably challenge the interests of other contenders, either because the distribution of benefits to one group will diminish the rewards available for another, or because the demands directly attack the interests of an established group. The parallels to revolutionary situations are obvious. Indeed, the multiplication of revolutionary situations in adjacent states, as in Europe's many revolutions and near-revolutions of 1848, shares many characteristics with more contained cycles of protest (Tarrow & Soule 1991). The demonstration that one important state is vulnerable to revolutionary demands signals the possibility of making similar demands elsewhere, makes available transferable revolutionary expertise and doctrine, and reduces the likelihood that the state undergoing revolution will intervene to shore up neighbouring old regimes.

Political crises at the ends of wars, the disintegration of empires, federations or coalitions, and cycles of protest have similar proximate causes to revolutionary situations: (1) appearance of contenders, or coalitions of contenders, advancing strong claims on the state, or some segment of it; (2) commitment to those claims by significant segments of the citizenry; and (3) incapacity or unwillingness of rulers to suppress the alternative coalitions and/or commitment to their claims. The difference lies especially in the extent and exclusiveness of claims on the state. So long as all major participants are treating the state as an actor that will continue to act and that ought to respond to their interests, a revolutionary situation has not arisen. When one or more participants other than incumbent rulers begin to make exclusive claims for control of the state itself, routine claim-making has passed over into a revolutionary situation.

Revolutionary Outcomes

A revolutionary *outcome* occurs with transfer of state power from those who held it before the start of multiple sovereignty to a new ruling coalition – which may, of course, include some elements of the old ruling coalition. Given a revolutionary situation, a revolutionary outcome is more likely to occur if substantial coalitions form between challengers and existing members of the polity (that is, if some members or even some rulers defect from the existing government) and if the revolutionary coalition comes to control extensive armed force. More generally, the proximate causes of revolutionary outcomes are defections of polity members, acquisition of armed force by revolutionary coalitions, neutralization or defection of the regime's armed force and control of the state apparatus by members of a revolutionary coalition. When all of these have happened rapidly, a revolutionary transfer of power has occurred. The causes again follow tautologically from the definition of revolution as a forcible transfer of power over a state involving a break in the polity, and again serve chiefly to orient the search for longer-term causes.

Few revolutionary situations have revolutionary outcomes; in many cases, the old holders of state power reconquer their challengers; power-holders often co-opt some new claimants and check the rest; sometimes civil war leads to the polity's permanent division. At times revolutionary outcomes – major transfers of state power – occur either so gradually or so instantaneously that multiple sovereignty never appears. Only in the minority of instances where new power-holders emerge from multiple sovereignty can we properly speak of full-fledged revolution.

By such a definition, nevertheless, many civil wars and succession struggles qualify as revolutions, just so long as power eventually changes hands after a forcible break in sovereignty. So do some military seizures of power, if an open fissure appears in the polity. So, too, do victorious, violence-wielding independence movements. The British revolutions of 1640–60 and 1687–9 clearly qualify, although the defeated Paris Commune of 1871, lacking a durable transfer of power, does not. By this definition, no fundamental alteration of social structure need occur – although in general the greater the change in the ruling coalition wrought by a revolution, the greater is the transformation of other aspects of social life. In short, this conception of revolution takes in a wider range of events than great revolutions but still a much narrower range than civil violence, protest, transfer of power or rebellion.

The distinction of revolutionary situations from revolutionary outcomes makes it easier to see the relations among several types of political action that have revolutionary elements. Figure 1.1 lays some of them out schematically. A great revolution by definition entails both a basic split in the polity (a deep revolutionary situation) and a large transfer of power (a serious revolutionary outcome). A civil war certainly includes a deeply revolutionary situation, but does not necessarily lead to a revolutionary outcome, a major transfer of power. A top-down seizure of the state can involve a substantial transfer of power (a revolutionary outcome) but not a major split in the polity (a revolutionary situation). These are all, in any case, matters of degree and timing: revolts merge into great revolutions, coups run wild to become important transfers of power. But all these circumstances have some revolutionary features.

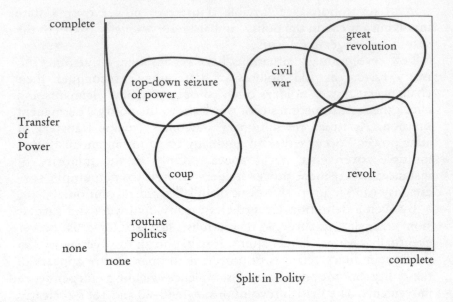

Figure 1.1   Types of revolution as a function of revolutionary situations and outcomes.

This broad definition of revolution poses an empirical question: why do forcible transfers of state power have such amazingly varied outcomes, from deep alterations of social life to restorations of the *status quo ante*? It suggests the necessity of answering the question by looking closely at the interaction among the nature of the coalition that comes to power, the process by which the polity split and the revolutionary process itself.

Prospect

One thing about the analysis of revolution should already be clear: in order to understand how revolutionary situations and revolutionary outcomes combined in full-fledged revolutions, we must follow them somewhat separately. The history of revolutionary situations draws us into examination of many struggles that ended without substantial transfers of power, just as the study of revolutionary outcomes compels us to consider how control over states changed in general. To trace those distinct strands, then to knot them together, is this book's object. Because previous writings have so emphasized the determinants of revolutionary outcomes, the book compensates by focusing on the opening of revolutionary situations and on revolutionary processes as such.

The book also seeks to avoid one of the besetting sins in analyses of revolution: teleology. Historians of England's seventeenth century, France's eighteenth century or Russia's nineteenth and early twentieth centuries suffer a great temptation to treat their periods as preparations for the great revolutions they contained. Everything converges on 1640, 1688, 1789, 1799, 1905 or 1917. As a result, earlier events lose their contingency, cause and effect reverse, the possibility of other outcomes than the revolution that actually occurred disappear. Although a teleology-finder will no doubt detect backward causal reasoning here and there in the pages that follow, they generally treat history as an opening and closing of possibilities, as a process of selection strongly constrained by previous history.

To the extent that their explanations invoke causal generalizations, the analyses to come concern social mechanisms that operate and interact on the small scale rather than grand standard sequences, unilinear changes of vast social structures or universal historical forces. I claim, for example, that the relation between a form of taxation and its ambient economy (e.g. the imposition of excise taxes in highly commercialized vs. subsistence economies) strongly influences not only its financial effectiveness but also the extent of popular resistance the tax incites and the sort of governmental organization its pursuit generates. I will never, on the other hand, suggest that a given kind or level of taxation reliably promotes revolutionary situations in every sort of state and social setting. The crucial mechanism consists of the generation of popular resistance by certain combinations of fiscal strategy and economic setting. Whether such resistance feeds a revolutionary situation, however, depends on other circumstances that appear independently of fiscal policy – such circumstances as the presence or absence of support for rebels from outside powers.

Again, I will often emphasize how in early modern Europe the recruitment of heads of state by inheritance within royal lineages combined with the international marriage strategies of those lineages to make them vulnerable to crises at times of succession. Dynastic regimes ran the risk of revolutionary situations when the heir (or, even more, the heiress) was very young or incompetent and when two or more lineages had defensible claims to the throne. Yet it would be ridiculous to argue that the succession of incompetents is a necessary or sufficient condition for revolution in the Europe of our own time; would that it were! The form of taxation and the organization of royal succession affect the operation of government in a wide variety of states. But only in certain delimited conditions do they promote or inhibit revolution. History's regularities appear not in repeated sequences, replicated structures and recurrent trends on the large scale but in the causal mechanisms that link contingent sets of circumstances.

I am not arguing for a moment that everything is particular, that no regularities lie behind the ebb and flow of revolutionary situations and revolutionary outcomes. On the contrary, succeeding chapters will show repeatedly how, in different combinations, the character of taxation, the availability of powerful allies for popular rebels, the forms of succession, the vulnerability of monarchies to disputed successions and a number of other mechanisms promoted or inhibited revolutionary processes; these mechanisms varied systematically with broad changes in European economies, states and systems of states. Historical regularities exist; they lie in the operation of those mechanisms.

Alas, the following chapters will fall short of proving my arguments beyond a shadow of a doubt. By my own standards of historical research and writing, the book contains no more than illustrations of its main theses. I have worked selectively in relevant British national archives dealing with the decades from the 1750s to the 1830s and in French national, regional or local archives from 1600 to the 1980s; otherwise, my accounts depend entirely on an incomplete reading of other historians' published reports and syntheses. I do not command equally all the languages and historical literatures necessary to undertake comprehensive research on European revolutions between 1492 and 1992 – the thought boggles the mind! Although some day a single polymath, research team or computer may pack all the critical evidence into a connected bundle, in the meantime all an individual scholar can do is either to take up a small piece of the problem, or dare a provisional synthesis. I have spent much of my scholarly life doing the former. Here I am trying the latter.

Chronologies of wars and revolutionary situations identify what is to be explained in most of the following chapters; those chronologies come from standard compilations such as Jack S. Levy's *War in the Modern Great Power System, 1495–1975* and Evan Luard's *War in International Society*, modified by information drawn from the national histories I have consulted. As a rule of thumb, I have included as revolutionary situations sequences of events in which these accounts indicate that for a month or more some major segment, region or city within a previously existing state lived under the rule of an opponent, or set of opponents, to the established ruler. I have kept myself honest, and therefore vulnerable to criticism, by listing in chronologies the major events to be explained. I have no doubt missed many relevant events and misclassified others. Before specialists in one country or another dismiss the chronologies, hence the book's arguments, out of hand, I would ask them to consider whether the errors vitiate my general conclusions about trends and differences. If doubts about the arguments stimulate informed critics to research and rebuttal, I can only encourage them. I have written this book not to close an inquiry, but to open it.

If a coherent account of changes and variations in the character of European revolutions emerges from this book, as I hope it will, observers of other parts of the world will have reason to pay attention. Theoretically, accounts of revolution everywhere in the world have borne disproportionate weight from European revolutions; the French and Bolshevik Revolutions continue to provide models of what revolution could entail in Latin America or Asia. Moreover, because of the commanding position of European states, European revolutions influenced political change far beyond the continent, as when Toussaint l'Ouverture and his allies took advantage of the French Revolution to establish a free black republic in the French colony of Haiti. Today's renewal of European economic power practically guarantees that past, present and future European revolutions will continue to make a difference elsewhere. Finally, the state system that prevails in today's world as a whole originated in Europe and still bears European stigmata; we have good reason to believe that a proper understanding of relations between revolution and the changing European state system will aid our understanding of present and future revolutions outside of Europe.

In pursuit of that general understanding, the book proceeds to a general sketch of social and political change in Europe and its impact on revolutionary situations between 1492 and the present (chapter 2), a preliminary comparison of revolutionary situations in the Low Countries, Iberia and the Balkans since 1492 (chapter 3), closer examination of the revolutions in the British Isles, especially during the seventeenth-century upheavals (chapter 4), France, with special reference to the century after 1750 (chapter 5), and Russia, notably in the twentieth century (chapter 6), followed by comparisons among revolutions and concluding reflections (chapter 7). The central chapters magnify centuries containing the major revolutionary struggles in the Low Countries (1550–1650), the British Isles (1600–1700), France (1750–1850) and Russia (1900–92). By the end we should at least be able to place the Eastern European revolutions of 1989 and thereafter firmly in the context of 500 revolutionary years.

2

Transformations of Europe

Change since 1492

Let us begin our inquiry a half-millennium ago, in 1492. The starting point is arbitrary, but not nonsensical. The end of the fifteenth century brought a watershed in European economies and polities. Columbus' explorations of 1492 began the definitive integration of the Americas into the orbit of Europe. Soon Spaniards were extending to the Caribbean experiments in plantation cultivation of such tropical crops as sugar that they and their Portuguese neighbours had been conducting on closer Atlantic islands such as the Canaries, and were buying African slaves to do the heavy labour. In counterpart to the European flora and fauna (e.g. dandelions, horses and measles) that spread across the Americas, mainland American products soon became mainstays of European life. To its fifteenth-century American adventure Europe owes not only Coca Cola, tango and jazz, but also maize, potatoes, tobacco and perhaps syphilis.

That reaching out to the Americas constituted only one part of Europe's successful bid to become the world's economic centre. Until the fourteenth century, Europe had lived as the north-western periphery of a vast economic system extending into the Pacific and pivoting on the Mongol-dominated territories of Central Asia. Before then, empires rose and fell in Europe, notably around the Mediterranean and the Black Sea, but only the Roman Empire occupied as much as half of the European space and incorporated it firmly into the Eurasian system of trade, politics and culture. Neither the thin, wavering strands of commerce nor the scattered pockets of productive agriculture could sustain enough extraction to support large armies, priestly hierarchies, elaborate bureaucracies or sumptuous royal courts. In North-western Europe, not even daring, rapacious Norsemen could assemble a substantial empire.

As Byzantine, Persian, Arab and then Muslim Empires displaced the Romans and once again subordinated Europe's south-eastern half to the silk-trading Baghdad–Hangchow axis, the rest of Europe fragmented and peripheralized. Nevertheless, from the tenth to the thirteenth centuries, the whole Eurasian system ran so energetically that much of Europe prospered: commerce flourished, population expanded and cities grew, especially in those sections of the continent most strongly connected to the great belts of Eurasian trade. In the year 1000, the world's largest cities were probably Constantinople, Córdoba, Kaifeng, Sian, Kyoto, Cairo and Hasa; in that ranking, Europe's Seville, Palermo and Kiev lagged far behind. At the Millennium, then, the world's largest cities lay largely outside of Europe, while Europe's largest cities spun in the orbit of Islam.

By 1300, the list began with Hangchow, Peking, Cairo and Canton, with Paris, Granada, Constantinople, Venice, Milan and Genoa now among the top twenty. Around 1500, the world's largest cities were very likely Peking, Vijayanagar, Cairo and Hangchow – two in China, one in India, one in Muslim Africa – with Paris, Constantinople, Adrianople and Naples leading the European hierarchy, but still much smaller than their Asian counterparts. Although in 1700 Japan's Edo probably led the globe, for the first time three of the world's ten largest cities were European: Constantinople, London and Paris (Chandler & Fox 1974: 308–21). A clear shift of the hierarchy toward northern Europe occurred between AD 1000 and 1700, especially after 1500.

What happened during those 700 years? Over the two centuries following 1300, the Black Death intermittently severed the connection between Europe and Asia, fragmentation of the Mongol Empire placed formidable barriers on overland trade routes, China withdrew from its previously expansive maritime trade, sailing vessels of Atlantic powers began to press the galleys that had previously dominated the Mediterranean, Europeans started to use the gunpowder that had come from Asia, and the Ottoman capture of Constantinople in 1453 (the first and exemplary major deployment of siege artillery in Europe) defined the confrontation of Christendom with Islam while cementing a love–hate relationship between Muslim Turkey and Orthodox Russia. All these changes made Europe more of a connected, autonomous unit than it had ever been before. Europe and adjacent sections of the vast complex took a century or more to recover from the demographic devastation wrought by the Black Death. After having maintained a fast pace between the tenth and thirteenth centuries, then having collapsed halfway through the fourteenth, population growth only accelerated again during the sixteenth century. Soon the whole Eurasian system began to grow again. Henceforth, Europe occupied a far more prominent position in relation to the rest of the world than ever before, more prominent than during the Roman Empire.

Not that Europe passed the golden gate into today's world in or around 1492. The political texture of 1492 differed wonderfully from our own. At that point, the Kingdom of Aragon, powered by Catalan seafaring, extended from the Iberian mainland to Sardinia and Sicily. The Catholic Pope ruled one of Italy's major states. An enormous Kingdom of Poland exercised superficial sovereignty over much of Eastern Europe, while the territory we now call Russia fragmented into zones controlled by the Prince of Moscow, the Republic of Pskov, the Golden Horde, the Krim Tatars and many another conqueror from the Eurasian steppe. Much of 'Germany' lay nominally under Habsburg suzerainty, but actually consisted of nearly independent bishoprics, free cities, duchies and other tiny jurisdictions.

Nor did Europe dominate the world. In 1492 China wielded formidable weight in the East. The lands and seas of Islam lay astride the world's central commercial and cultural connections, and Islamic influence was still expanding between South-east Asia and Africa. On the Indian Ocean and the overland routes to Asia, Europeans long followed or compacted with Muslim merchants before they started to displace them. Columbus' search for a westerly route to 'the Indies' was no idle fancy, but an enterprise with visibly substantial payoff if it worked. By 1492 European ships were fending off the expansive Ottoman Empire and breaking into the Muslim commercial space of the Indian Ocean. By 1498, Vasco da Gama had reached India from Portugal. Portuguese, then Spanish, then Dutch traders and sailors started to dominate non-European seas. In 1500–1, Pedrálvarez Cabral's fleet sighted Brazil before circling east to India and then returning to Portugal. Between 1519 and 1522, one ship of Ferdinand Magellan's fleet circumnavigated the globe, despite leaving Magellan himself dead in the Philippines.

From the world's perspective, Europe was becoming a major pole of economic and political activity. From a narrowly European viewpoint, the late fifteenth century initiated a shift in the commercial centre of gravity from the South-east to the North-west, from the Mediterranean and Black Seas to the Atlantic. Although Iberian states led that reorientation, it soon involved French ports, the Low Countries, the Baltic and then the British Isles. In 1496, for example, Flanders and England signed the *Intercursus Magnus*, a commercial treaty according mutual privileges and recognizing the importance of the wool and textile trade that already linked them. The Atlantic, long a far edge of peripheries, was coming into its own.

In 1492 the dual monarchy of Castile and Aragon – the linked but not merged inheritances of Ferdinand and Isabella – completed the conquest of Granada. The conquest eliminated the last substantial vestige of once great Muslim Empires from Iberia as, under threat of death, those Spanish Jews who did not convert, at least nominally, to Catholicism began their diaspora across Europe and around the Mediterranean. Responding in part to the threat of a united Spain, France began a fateful military invasion of Italy only two years later. Spain sent competing forces into Italy almost immediately, and the previously contentious but relatively autonomous Italian city-states found themselves pawns of great power politics.

That French bid for Italian hegemony initiated the era of wars on a European scale. The French Valois and Spanish Habsburgs alone waged war with each other eleven distinct times between 1494 and the 1559 Treaty of Cateau-Cambrésis. As of 1492, the character of warfare and the international system were changing rapidly. During the wars of Burgundy in the 1470s, Swiss infantry massed into pike-squares had demonstrated its ability to defeat skilled cavalry. That strategic shift plus the widening use of extensive fortifications in defence against siege artillery greatly increased the financial and manpower requirements of armies, not to mention the demand for military architects and Swiss mercenaries. Those wars, in their turn, shaped the European state system, constructed the platform for European conquests outside of the continent, and helped form the sorts of centralized, differentiated, autonomous and bureaucratic states that eventually came to predominate in Europe and then in the world as a whole.

At the same time, the expansion of European trade along the sea lanes of Atlantic, Pacific and Indian Oceans offered a powerful stimulus to capital accumulation, which in turn gave war-making states growing wealth on which to build their armed force. What Immanuel Wallerstein calls the capitalist world-system, centred on Europe, began to take shape. Events of the great year 1492 did not, of course, cause all those momentous processes. Yet the rapid change in Iberia's position and the breakthrough across the Atlantic, for which 1492 was critical, pushed them vigorously. Starting the analysis of changing states, economies, political conflicts and revolutions in 1492, then, permits a long look at the entire period in which something like a coherent European system of states existed.

On the map of 1492, we might claim to recognize England, Ireland, Scotland and France in something approaching their contemporary boundaries, but that would require us to ignore large subsequent eastward conquests by France, not to mention the troubled formation of what we now call, with some exaggeration, the United Kingdom. Altogether, some 200 state-like units, many of them overlapping in territory and many of them comprising patchworks of semi-autonomous governments, divided up the European map of 1492.

By 1992, despite the Soviet Union's disintegration, those 200 had consolidated into about thirty-five sovereign states, of which only Andorra, Liechtenstein, Luxembourg, Monaco, San Marino and the Vatican recalled the enclave mini-states that had been common five centuries earlier; even the recognition of every major claim for independence within the former limits of the Soviet Union and Yugoslavia would not return Europe to anything resembling the political fragmentation of 1492. Indeed, in 1992 many signs point instead toward the increasing consolidation of European states into large entities including or resembling the European Community. While regions and nationalities will very likely acquire greater autonomy vis-à-vis today's states, sovereignty is actually drifting upward to conglomerates of states. If the

Community creates its own unified armed forces, the drift of sovereignty will become an inverted avalanche.

What is more, in 1992 the entire world's system of states is undergoing deep alterations: the Soviet Union has disintegrated, the bipolar confrontation of blocs led by the Soviet Union and the United States has ceased to dominate world politics, the power of militarily weak but capitalistically strong states such as Japan and Germany is continuing to expand, and multinational capital as represented by traffic in drugs, arms, electronics, publishing, oil or corporate ownership is coming to wield great power and mobility in partial independence of the states whose residents created and accumulated the capital. In short, 1492 does not offer a threshold for entry of the kinds of European states that have prevailed in recent centuries; it provides a baseline for enormous subsequent changes in state structure.

More changed than states. The whole of European life took on a different texture after 1492. Remember Europe in the late fifteenth century: with India and East Asia, it was already one of the world's three great regions of productive agriculture, hence of dense settlement and substantial cities. Around the Alps and along the littorals of Mediterranean, Atlantic, Baltic and Black Seas threaded a well-connected network of mercantile cities, most of them having substantial hinterlands that combined small-scale manufacturing with commercial farming. The rest of Europe divided into two kinds of regions: those of warrior-landlords (some of them churchmen as well) who extracted their revenues from peasant households, and other regions in which smallholding farmers, fishermen and foresters coexisted with merchants, soldiers, priests and officials. Hungary exemplifies the first, Scandinavia the second.

After 1492, that various but increasingly connected Europe showed to an amazed world an unprecedented burst of industrialization, urbanization, proletarianization and population growth. Not right away and not all at once, of course; if the sixteenth century, broadly defined, brought substantial urbanization and population growth, the seventeenth century marked a lull in both regards; after 1750 both accelerated as never before, only slowing well into the twentieth century. In fact, the demographic experience spanned Eurasia, with widespread population growth during the sixteenth and early seventeenth centuries, a century of demographic recession, more growth beginning the eighteenth century, insufficient food production and rising prices during periods of rapid growth (Goldstone 1991: 355).

Nevertheless, population growth had significantly different effects in the various segments of Eurasia. In China and Japan, the state managed to contain landlords and capitalists, diverting a significant share of their rents and profits to officialdom. In Europe, no empire existed that could check landlords or capitalists at a continental scale; there, rising prices and cheapening labour worked to the benefit of both landlords and capitalists, allowing the two to ally or even merge in many parts of the continent. Where markets for their crops were readily at hand, landlords, their large tenants and the more substantial landholding peasants became spear-holders of agricultural capitalism, promoting the multiplication of the landless wage-labourers in their midst. Merchants then led the way to industrial capitalism.

Industrialization is harder to date than urbanization or population growth because industrial production expanded first in rural households and small, scattered shops where people commonly divided their years – or even their days – among manufacturing, trade and cultivation. Roughly speaking, nevertheless, we can think of the seventeenth and eighteenth centuries as periods featuring massive growth of dispersed, small-scale manufacturing in towns and countryside around poles of capital such as Liège and Zürich, the nineteenth and twentieth centuries as the time of implosion: capital, workers and manufacturing concentrating increasingly in cities as the countryside became more exclusively agricultural. During the twentieth century, furthermore, manufacturing began to stabilize as a share of labour force and production while service industries – government, transportation, banking, education, health and so on – continued to grow at the expense of agriculture, forestry and fishing.

As a consequence of changing productive organization, the European population proletarianized. Proletarianization consists of an increase in the dependence of households on wage-labour and/or a decline in their control over the means of production. Despite the nineteenth-century image of 'proletarians' as grimy factory workers, until well into that century most European proletarianization took place in the countryside and in small towns; landless agricultural labourers, part-time weavers and other

Table 2.1   European proletarianization, 1500–1990

| | Millions of persons, including dependants | | | |
	1500	1800	1900	1990
Total population	56	150	285	800
Non-proletarians	39	50	85	200
Proletarians in cities	1	10	75	450
Rural proletarians	16	90	125	150

workers by the hour, the day, the month, the year, the task or the piece multiplied among the landlords, merchants, peasants and artisans. A speculative estimate of the change is shown in table 2.1 (adapted from Tilly 1984: 36). These are orders of magnitude, not precise numbers. Figures for 1990 involve even more guesswork than those for earlier years. The formation of state socialist regimes after 1917, ironically, makes the estimates for proletarians more problematic just as the quality of statistics improves; were members of collective farms, for example, proletarians? Yet the general point is clear: before 1800, rapid increase of rural proletarians; during the nineteenth century, large shifts toward urban proletarianization; since 1900, a near-stabilization of rural proletarians while the urban proletariat grew much faster than the general population.

These transformations meant that the *dramatis personae* of political conflict, collective action and revolutions changed fundamentally between 1492 and 1992. Many new actors, such as factory workers and industrial capitalists, entered the scene. Even those whose designations remained nominally the same, such as priests, peasants and landlords, bore only faint resemblances to their predecessors. Moreover, the social situations that faced rulers, their clients, their allies and their challengers altered deeply; a world of urban wage workers creates an entirely different sort of politics from a predominantly rural world of merchants and cultivators. In the midst of such changes, revolutions and related political processes could hardly stay constant. The more so because states, the targets of revolution, also underwent deep transformations.

From Segmented to Consolidated States

For millennia, the essential histories of states throughout the world flowed from the interaction of war, the various kinds of organizations that made war, and the diverse populations that bore the costs of war. Only in recent centuries have states grown so muscular that they reach daily – and nightly – into the lives of most of their citizens. The recent expansion of states began with the inflation of war and its costs after 1750 by the creation of large, well-equipped and publicly financed standing armies drawn from states' own populations. Massive struggles entailed by the inflation of war then transformed the state into a powerful instrument that could serve more than one end. Once it had such power, indeed, large segments of the population made claims on it for their own (mostly non-military) ends. Through a century or more of struggle, states took on burdens of economic infrastructure, education, welfare, even economic management. Today's thick, exigent, capacious Western states therefore give little idea of the thin, capricious, if often deadly, apparatuses of states before the last few hundred years.

Earlier European states were not mere miniatures of their successors, pygmy elephants anticipating mastodons; the period after 1492 wrought massive changes in the anatomies of European states. Those changes concentrated during the century beginning in 1750, although some parts of Europe anticipated them before the eighteenth century, and despite the fact that state expansion continued apace after 1850. In the course of the crucial transition, the mercenary troops and freebooting military entrepreneurs that had dominated European war-making for several centuries practically disappeared from the European scene; military forces fell subordinate to civilian administrators as never before; the division between armies and police (the former committed chiefly to fighting other armed organizations, the latter dealing with the civilian population) grew much sharper; states created extensive and relatively uniform field administrations at the level of community and region; central bureaucracies (both those servicing the military and, increasingly, those oriented to civilian activities) expanded and regularized; systems of taxation and public finance became massive divisions of the state; and representative institutions (however elitist) bulked larger in national power struggles as a popular politics oriented to influencing both those representative institutions and the central executive came into being.

Driven by military reorganization, larger European states generally underwent a shift from indirect to direct rule. Instead of relying on largely autonomous intermediaries such as great landlords, churchmen, city councils and merchants to govern on their behalf, rulers created state apparatuses that reached down into communities, even into individual households, by means of taxation, conscription, population registration, public education and other forms of control. Agents of central governments involved themselves as never before in promoting the priority of a single version of national culture in the form of language, communication, the arts, education and political belief. They circumscribed the resources – capital, labour, commodities, money, technologies – within their national boundaries, controlling their movement over frontiers defined with increasing precision by geographers, generals and politicians, devising national policies to affect their employment, coordinating their uses and asserting the priority of the state's claims on these resources over all competing claims.

The French Revolution and Empire performed the most sweeping of these transformations but (partly as a consequence of French conquest and/or example, partly in response to the huge increase of armies and navies occasioned by the French wars) most other European states moved in the same directions. In the process, they created broader, more active, more equal definitions of citizenship: strong mutual obligations of inhabitants and of state agents on the basis of authorized residence alone. With obvious, powerful variations from a noble-ridden Russia to a fragmented and disputatious Switzerland to a class-divided but partly democratic Great Britain, rulers generally augmented the power of their states at the cost of extensive bargaining with their national populations.

The actual trajectories of these changes differed dramatically from one region and era to another. At various times after 1492, city-states, empires, federations, republics, centralized kingdoms, loosely knit elective monarchies and many variants on them all prospered somewhere in Europe. All of them were *segmented* to some degree: either they consisted of a single small segment such as a city-based bishopric and its immediate hinterland, or they contained a composite of different sorts of unit, each enjoying considerable distinctness and autonomy. The largest differences depended on the relative concentrations of capital and of coercive means in the environments of various states. Where great concentrations of capital appeared – especially in the urban band extending from northern Italy around the Alps into the Low Countries – merchants and financiers played central roles in the formation and transformation of states. In those regions, capitalists facilitated the financing of state activities, especially war, but set strong barriers to the creation of major standing armies, durable bureaucracies or powerful central executives. As a result, influential but organizationally exiguous city-states and federations such as Genoa, Dubrovnik, Switzerland and the Dutch Republic predominated in the urban regions. They followed a *capital-intensive* path.

In Europe's zones of herding and subsistence agriculture, capital long remained slight and dispersed, magnates choked cities and trade, conquest and dynastic politics set the order of the day, and the only way rulers built up their states' strength was by seizing or co-opting the private armies formed by great landlords. In those regions, the effort to create massive, centralized armed force, if successful, brought into being the paradoxical combination of large, privileged nobilities and substantial state bureaucracies. Russia, Hungary, Poland, Portugal and Castile illustrate different versions of this *coercion-intensive* path.

In between lay those regions that combined some concentrated capital with substantial armed force in the hands of autonomous landlords – areas to which historians of the Middle Ages have most comfortably applied the word 'feudal', and those of the seventeenth and eighteenth centuries the word 'absolutist'. They typically interlaced networks of trading cities with large agricultural areas that produced surpluses (including domestic manufactures) for the urban market. In such environments, rulers could often expand their power by pitting the bourgeoisie against the nobility only to fuse them eventually in service to the crown. As warfare became extremely expensive after 1700 or so, such states became more capable than their capital-intensive and coercion-intensive neighbours to recruit, equip and finance large standing armies from the resources and manpower of their own populations.

As a result, from a military and diplomatic point of view, they eventually became Europe's dominant states. England, France and Prussia best illustrate this path of *capitalized coercion*.

The organization of war made a fundamental difference to the character of states, and therefore of revolutions. How did war matter? After a few seventeenth-century experiments with national armies, notably in Sweden and Russia, the eighteenth century saw the definitive decline of mercenary armed forces. They gave way to large standing armies and navies recruited or even conscripted almost entirely from national populations and financed chiefly by taxes on those same populations; the French *levée en masse* of 1793 marked a major moment in that change. Except where invasion loomed, ordinary people resisted press gangs and conscription fiercely. Nevertheless, agents of states beat down their resistance. Once France, Prussia and a few other powers were fielding massive armies and navies in this way, the market for mercenaries collapsed in most of Europe; every state that claimed a military presence then followed the great-power suit.

The formation of such vast military forces in this peculiar way had a whole series of unintended but fundamental consequences: involving rulers in extended struggle and bargaining with their subject populations; expanding definitions of citizenship; forwarding ideas and practices of popular sovereignty; generating enforceable claims of subjects on states in such forms as rights to petition and associate; reinforcing various kinds of representative institutions; inflating central state bureaucracies; moving states from indirect toward direct rule; extending state controls over stocks and flows of labour, capital, commodities and money within and across increasingly well-defined national borders; enlarging state obligations to military veterans and their families; constituting veterans as collective political actors; and forwarding shared experience through military service itself. In Great Britain, for example, the war years from 1792 to 1815 saw not only massive increases in armed forces and taxation, substantial growth and centralization of the national state, and a large increase in the powers of parliament, but also a great mutation of popular collective action toward associational bases, national issues and claims on parliament (Tilly 1982, 1991a, 1991b).

These multifarious changes fell into three overlapping categories: (1) circumscription, (2) control, (3) obligation. As never before states circumscribed the capital, labour, commodities, technology and money within their territories – inhibiting their movement across increasingly well-defined frontiers, earmarking them for uses within the frontiers for the benefit of the state and (sometimes) of its citizens. All states exercise priority within relatively well-defined territories; that is one way we know they are states, not lineages, gangs, churches, corporations or something else. Nevertheless, they vary widely with respect to how contiguous and sharply bounded those territories are and in regard to how deeply they exercise control at and within their boundaries. In eighteenth-century Europe, larger states generally maintained lax controls over ill-defined and enclave-ridden borders; within those borders, furthermore, either they did not penetrate very deeply or they left that penetration to largely autonomous intermediaries. Migrant workers, merchants, goods and money confronted many bandits and tollgates, but otherwise moved easily and without state monitoring within and across frontiers.

Few states, furthermore, maintained effective systems of registration for property or persons; witness the rarity of national tax assessments and the surprise occasioned by the results of nineteenth-century censuses. Even obligatory military service, where it occurred during the eighteenth century, depended on local knowledge of the eligible males and was therefore highly vulnerable to mystification. With the creation of national standing armies and their attendant infrastructure, however, European states took up the work of circumscription with a vengeance. They mapped boundaries, negotiated them with neighbours, staked them off with guards, inspected goods and people who crossed them, issued or refused passports and visas for people on either side of them, mythologized them as natural, proper, even predestined.

Within those frontiers, states also began exerting much more extensive controls over populations, resources and activities – taxing, conscripting, commandeering, regulating, policing, erecting systems of surveillance. With the growth of massive national armed forces and the attendant growth of state budgets, almost all states erected wider, deeper, more direct systems of control. Central control extended, obviously, to property, production and political activity; rulers stopped relying on highly autonomous magnates and pressed toward direct rule, toward the creation of administrations extending directly from the central power down to individual communities and households. It emphatically included cultural control, the designation or creation of a single linguistic, historical, artistic and practical tradition to take priority over all those previously present within the national territory. States began as never before to create national educational systems, to impose standard national languages, to organize expositions, museums, artistic subventions and other means of displaying cultural production or heritage, to construct communications networks, to invent national flags, symbols, anthems, holidays, rituals and traditions.

As a result, national populations did finally become less polyglot, even though few of them ever approximated the homogeneity of the ideal nation-state; the homogenizing effect extended to such profound matters as demographic behaviour (Watkins 1990; Winter 1986). National bourgeoisies and intelligentsias commonly collaborated in the effort, which in its early phases often discredited the exclusiveness and self-interest of the aristocracy, sometimes of the crown as well; after all, before the nineteenth century, aristocrats and kings had often spoken different languages from the mass of the population they governed. Once begun, the process perpetuated itself, for the advantages of speaking a national language and adopting a national style rather than continuing to live within a shrinking, stigmatized pool became more and more evident to members of national minorities.

In the process, unprecedented obligations came to bind states to citizens and, especially, citizens to states; as a result of coercion, struggle and bargaining over the means of war, the residents of a national territory fell increasingly under the obligation to yield labour, goods, money and loyalty to the state, but also acquired rights of redress, voice and compensation. That process broadened popular politics and created the opportunity for interest groups to demand services and protections from the state in the form of economic infrastructure, policing, courts of law, education, welfare and much more. With the expansion of those two-sided obligations, Europeans created a kind of citizenship that extended to most of the population rather than to its small ruling classes alone. Citizenship began to acquire something like the meaning today's Europeans assign to it: a set of rights and obligations with respect to the state that apply more or less equally to the broad mass of people born within its territory or 'naturalized' to it.

Although many other sorts of state, all of them segmented in one way or another, flourished in Europe at various times before 1800, from the eighteenth century onward a special variety of state consequently began to prevail. We might call it the consolidated state: large, differentiated, ruling heterogeneous territories directly, claiming to impose a unitary fiscal, monetary, judicial, legislative, military and cultural system on its citizens. The consolidated state's appearance constituted an extraordinary historical event; it made almost all previous states look puny in comparison. China's intermittently centralized empires were the most notable predecessors of the European consolidated state; even the powerful but segmented Japanese state did not then match its European counterparts.

Many observers called this new type of state the nation-state. Until I saw how much mischief the word caused, I myself called it the 'national' state. The term nation-state is misleading; it expresses a programme, not a reality. The phrase national state lends itself to almost as much confusion. Although many consolidated states claimed to contain homogeneous citizenries drawn from a single connected people, few actually qualified: perhaps Sweden and Norway after their separation in 1905 (if we ignore the peoples of Lapland), Finland after the finnicization of the 1920s and 1930s (also forgetting the peoples of Lapland), Denmark after the collapse of its empire, Ireland and the Netherlands if we discount Protestant–Catholic cleavage, Hungary after its post-1866 Magyarization and its shrinkage in the settlement of World War I, and not many more (Østergard 1992). Certainly Belgium, Switzerland, the United Kingdom, Spain, France and Prussia never came close to having culturally homogeneous populations. Nevertheless, the claim represented two crucial realities: first, an unprecedented effort by rulers to impose uniform languages, educational systems, cultural practices and loyalties; second, new legitimation of the principle that if a coherent, connected, homogeneous population *did* exist, it had the right to distinct political position, even to its own state. Those became two vital principles of nationalism.

Struggle Changes

The long transformations of European states, economies and cultures deeply affected the character of struggle, including revolution. Let us think about various kinds of popular claim-making: visible statement of demands, threats, entreaties, attacks and other calls for action or acknowledgement. We can concentrate on forms of claim-making that are *contentious* (i.e. they threaten someone else's interest), *collective* (i.e. individuals concert their claims), and by or on behalf of relatively *powerless* people. Under what conditions do ordinary people make such claims? Recent work on the question has moved us far from the once dominant vision of 'collective behaviour' as a separate, largely non-political, domain produced by the dissolution of conventional social controls and characterized by performances that flout conventional rationality (see, e.g., Aya 1990; McPhail 1991; Rule 1989). Although plenty of controversy attends every current discussion of claim-making, on the whole recent analyses treat it as an eminently political process based on articulated interests and relatively organized populations.

Ordinary people make collective claims, according to the emerging account, when they have common interests, shared organization, mobilized resources and some security against repression, while perceiving an opportunity or threat with respect to their common interests. Claims become more likely and more pressing, most analysts concur, when the people in question have a salient social identity and internal organization that reinforces it, when well-established rights or privileges attach to the identity, and when the people share grievances against well-defined enemies or rivals. Sustained claim-making (far from being the speciality of disorganized individuals or uprooted groups) only occurs in the presence of relatively dense social organization. Claims, furthermore, always involve not just group action, but group *inter*action. At a minimum they link claimants to an object of their claims. More often they constitute only one part of a continuous give-and-take among multiple actors. Thus accounts that purport to explain 'protest' by referring to the condition of the protesters alone always miss at least half the story. Such accounts usually come from authorities or their sympathizers.

We cannot get much more specific than these very abstract stipulations without historicizing the problem. In the case of Europe since 1492, historicizing means (1) paying attention to the great social transformations of the continent, which provided the context for changing forms of claim-making, and (2) examining the history of those forms in their own right through the study of collective-action repertoires. A number of structural changes affected the character and incidence of claim-making: urbanization that accelerated after 1800, a shift from mercantile to industrial capitalism, quickening proletarianization of both rural and urban labour, vast population growth, mass emigration, increasing dominance of large, greedy, bureaucratic states. These processes provided the context for changes and variations in collective claim-making.

Among those changes, a historical approach to European claim-making since 1492 must stress Europe's master processes: the transformation of states and the development of capitalism. Both the transformation of states and the development of capitalism stimulated claim-making because they each entailed fundamental conflicts. First, states grew by extracting resources – men, money and goods – from their subject populations; to the extent that states succeeded, others who had rights to those resources lost out. Even if a substantial share were foreign mercenaries, when a state put the equivalent of 5 or 6 per cent of its whole population (men, women and children) in the armed forces, as did England around 1700, families, farms and shops felt the absence of their young men.

Second, consolidating states competed with other governments both inside and outside their territory for the allegiance and material support of those same populations. Where lords had large clienteles, they eventually lost them as states whittled away noble autonomy. Finally, groups within the state's orbit competed for the resources, facilities and benefits that were already under the state's control. Once it became clear that royal courts would and could actually enforce their decisions, lords, peasants and ecclesiastics competed to win lawsuits. All three varieties of conflict produced extensive claim-making: resistance to conscription or taxation, struggles between kings and great lords, demands that the state offer rewards or mete out punishments.

Similarly, the development of capitalism involved three fundamental conflicts: (1) between capital and labour; (2) between
capitalists and others having rights to land, labour and other means
of production; and (3) among competitors within the same
markets – markets for goods, markets for labour, markets for
capital itself. These varieties of conflict similarly generated claims:
strikes and workers' insurrections, struggles against enclosures,
attempts to defend job monopolies through violence against
outsiders. At times the state-oriented and capital-oriented conflicts
coincided, as when workers rebelled against states dominated by
capitalists.

Alternative paths and combinations of state transformation and
capitalism, however, significantly affected the timing, character,
social base and outcomes of collective claim-making. Massive
peasant rebellions, for example, occurred chiefly in bulky, poorly
capitalized, coercion-intensive states, while the struggles of guilds
for power and privilege concentrated in the territories of intense
commercial capitalism and capitalized states. In 1493, Alsatian
commoners being pressed into serfdom by ambitious landlords
raised a banner portraying a heavy peasant boot (a *Bundschuh*) as
their standard and declared a rebellion against their lords in the
name of godly justice (Blickle 1981: xiii). Within agrarian regions
of oppressive overlordship, as the German Peasants' War illustrates thirty years later, the *Bundschuh* was absolutely characteristic of its time. But by the seventeenth century, that time of deeply
religious, egalitarian peasant risings had disappeared in almost all
of Europe.

Patterns of conflict and rebellion changed dramatically as the
centuries passed. As economies and polities nationalized, all of
Europe shifted to some extent from local toward national claims,
from claims directed at or mediated by patrons toward direct
claims on regional and national power-holders, from claims made
in the names of compact, connected groups toward claims made in
the names of whole categories of the population. These transitions
were obviously never complete, but they constituted a large net
shift in the originators and objects of collective claims. Thus
workers moved at least part way from making demands on
particular masters to making demands on the owners of an entire
industry, or on a national state. The paths toward nationalization,

however, varied as a function of contrasting transformations in capital and coercive power.

Historical changes in collective-action repertoires crystallized the effects of capital and coercion. In any connected population, people dispose of a limited number of established ways to make claims, forms of action hammered out in the course of struggles over previous claim-making. Eighteenth-century English workers, for example, could petition, carry out shaming ceremonies, organize community-wide turnouts against masters, serve as claques (but not, of course, as voters) for parliamentary candidates, and make claims in a few other ways. But they did not have at their disposal the firm-by-firm strike, the organization of trade unions, the appeal to a political party, and a number of other actions that channelled the claim-making of their nineteenth-century successors. Each of the standard actions linked particular groups of workers to specific others: masters, fellow-workers, local gentry and so on. Together those ways of making claims on other actors, and the responses of the actors, constituted workers' repertoires of collective action. Prevailing repertoires varied from group to group, region to region, period to period.

Existing repertoires constrained the claim-making of workers and of all other potential claimants, rendering some kinds of claims and objects of claims easy to act on, and others nearly impossible; those eighteenth-century workers had very effective ways to sanction a strike-breaker, but almost no direct way to deal with an obnoxious Member of Parliament. Struggle itself brought new elements into repertoires, as claimants or power-holders innovated – usually by means of minor variants on established forms of action – and succeeded in imposing the innovations on their interlocutors. Struggle also eliminated repertoire elements, as repression or failure marked one form of action or another as ineffectual or too costly. The history of Rough Music or charivari in England and France shows us elements of both innovation and failure (Le Goff & Schmitt 1981; Thompson 1972). In the Old Regime forms of these routines, youths of a locality gathered to bang on pans, jeer, sing bawdy songs or otherwise make noisy nuisances of themselves outside the dwellings of wife-beaters, adulterers, cuckolds, old men marrying young women and others who had violated the local marital codes. During the early

nineteenth century, innovators extended the scope of that venerable form of aggressive mockery from domestic sins and local
arenas to the struggles of national politics; that political phase,
however, preceded its rapid decline as a means of stating collective
disapproval.

Similarly, the firm-by-firm strike displaced the turnout, in
which many members of a trade gathered at the edge of town,
deliberated, marched from shop to shop calling workers out,
marched back to the edge of town, formulated demands, and sent a
delegation to parley with the masters of their trade. Through much
of Europe a combination of example, deliberate organization and
local learning taught workers that their ability to face all masters
was declining as large shops and proletarianization displaced the
small-shop artisanal system. They moved to shutting down one
firm at a time. Eventually Europeans came to regard the single-
firm strike as normal, the strike of a whole trade as exceptional.

Sidney Tarrow and Sarah Soule point out an unusual new feature
of the nineteenth-century forms: they were *modular* (Tarrow &
Soule 1991). Their eighteenth-century predecessors adapted beau-
tifully to particular situations such as a struggle over the enclosure
of commons (where mass breaking of fences and use of the land
often occurred) or the shaming of a worker who laboured for less
than the going wage (where transporting the offender through
town on a donkey or a rail exposed him to jeers and missiles). But
they did not transfer easily from one kind of situation to another.
The nineteenth-century forms transferred easily from one issue,
group or locality to another, and thus often became standard on a
national scale. The public meeting, the demonstration and the
petition drive, for example, served a wide range of interests;
indeed, competitors and enemies became likely to use exactly the
same forms of claim-making in hopes of outscoring their opponents.

The development of capitalism and the transformation of states
intertwined to alter prevailing repertoires of claim-making, the
nature of claims being made, the claimants and the objects of
claims. In states combining a relatively capitalist economy with a
state having strong national representative institutions, for
example, the national social movement took shape during the
nineteenth century. The national social movement is the making of
sustained, explicit, public demands on national power-

holders – usually state officials – in the name of a whole disadvantaged segment of the population: all women, all Bretons, all workers, all Flemings and so on. It bears a strong resemblance to the electoral campaign. The most important differences are that a national social movement can last much longer than an electoral campaign, and that established parties rarely join the claim-making of social movements; they are more often objects of such claims. Although similar series of events occasionally took shape before 1800 in moments of temporarily fragmented sovereignty such as the English and French Revolutions, national social movements only became standard means of claim-making in Western Europe after the Napoleonic Wars.

The national social movement grew out of older sorts of organized challenges to political authorities. When states pressed their subject populations for greatly increased contributions (in the form of taxes, conscripts and requisitioning) to war-making efforts, political entrepreneurs discovered that they could turn the essentially conservative idea of ancient popular rights into a progressive doctrine of popular sovereignty. For that reason, the American, French Revolutionary and Napoleonic Wars provided a strong impetus toward the new form of claim-making. Despite significant changes in décor and tactics, the innovation endured into our own time. In France, governmental authorities themselves participated in the institutionalization of social movement practices; as police and troops battled street demonstrators and worked out new tactics of containment in the process, the national legislature elaborated laws under which police, troops and courts could collaborate in setting limits on claim-making in the street. But by the very acts of repressing, negotiating, containing and legislating, the authorities helped lock movement practice in place. Efforts at control, furthermore, altered the authorities' own organization. The creation of national police forces, for example, increased the effectiveness of crowd control and political espionage, but also put in place a bureaucracy and a set of commitments to the general population that could not easily be bypassed.

In both its nineteenth- and twentieth-century versions, the national social movement focuses on interaction between presumed spokespersons for disadvantaged people and representatives of the power-holders in question. Its characteristic means include marches, rallies, demonstrations, meetings, petitioning and distribution of literature – all of which bring out its parallels to electoral campaigns. Most often it does much of its work through social movement organizations, associations formed around a specialized interest and a well-defined (if sometimes shifting) programme; that fact has often misled analysts into treating the organizations as if they *were* the movement. The error is easier because social movement organizers have strong investments in presenting themselves as spokespersons for large, determined, durable, organized segments of larger, aggrieved populations. Social movement organizations often survive the movements themselves; between movements many of them concentrate on affirmations of identity, organizational maintenance and the exertion of routine political pressure.

National social movements commonly occur through coalitions of organizations and activist networks, with new organizations and pseudo-organizations forming as a result of efforts to mobilize people to make claims. Historically, the sorts of claim-making represented by social movements have been extremely rare. In reviews of revolutionary situations in different regions of Europe, before 1800 we will only encounter sustained popular making of claims on national authorities in such long, deep divisions as the German Peasants' War of 1524–6. Over the last 150 years, however, they have become standard ways for aggrieved people to make their grievances and demands known. Within limits, they have even been effective. They have promoted the broadening of suffrage, the enlargement of welfare benefits and the constitution of new political actors at one time or another in most European countries.

Claim-making, then, extends from subtle winks to social revolutions, from stifled forms of opposition in Fascist Italy to toppling of Russian power in Finland after World War I. Over the long run of 1492 to 1992, the largest shifts within Europe in these regards were nationalization of the divisions involved in major conflicts, multiplication of claims bearing directly on state power, proliferation of the associational bases for collective action, and increasing salience within collective action of the class divisions inherent in capitalism. All these changes stemmed directly from the growth of consolidated states and the expansion of capitalism.

Types of Revolutionary Situation

The same vast changes greatly altered the character of revolution. Revolutions occurred frequently in sixteenth-century Europe, and still occurred frequently in twentieth-century Europe, but by the twentieth century their nature had changed drastically. In a two-dimensional simplification, we might define distinct kinds of revolutionary situation by the sorts of revolutionary coalitions they involved. The types derive from crossing two dimensions: (1) the *basis of group formation*: territory vs. interest; (2) *directness of relations* among members: direct vs. indirect. Figure 2.1 summarizes the relationships.

These are of course continua, representing the relative directness of relations among group members and the relative weight of territory and interest. In patron–client revolutionary situations, for example, whole communities that were little connected to each other joined their patrons, who were great lords, in massive

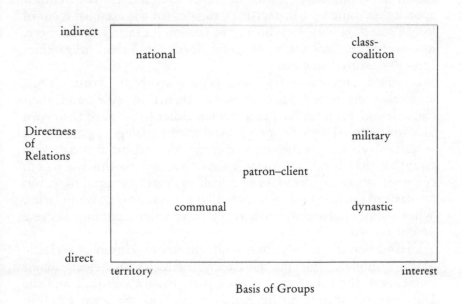

Figure 2.1   Types of revolutionary coalitions as a function of territory vs. interest and directness of relations among actors.

resistance to royal authority; they combined territorial and interest bases of connection. We will encounter many alliances of this sort during the sixteenth and seventeenth centuries, only to see them fade away in the eighteenth. Military juntas became more common during the nineteenth century in Iberia, the Balkans and several other parts of Europe, for reasons that we will explore. They usually bid for power in alliance with some dynastic faction or some fragment of the bourgeoisie, progressive or conservative. They involved a connected interest, but the connections among the different military units that did the dirty work of seizing power usually passed indirectly through ambitious officers.

The resistance of whole communities to tax collectors, which was common during military build-ups from the seventeenth century to the nineteenth, belongs in the communal lower left-hand corner: relatively simple in structure, unified largely by territory and the social ties it generated. In general, communal revolutions involved members of constituted communities, such as peasant villages, craft guilds and religious orders. Plenty of revolutionary situations took a communal form, but no purely communal revolutionary outcome ever occurred; the closest approaches came with successful struggles for the establishment of local Protestant churches during the sixteenth century. Even there, however, the protection of great lords or urban oligarchies typically assured success.

Dynastic revolutionary situations involved great lords, especially those who had dynastic claims to rule, and their clienteles. Great lords frequently acted either to forward their own bids for national power, or to protect their privileges against royal assault. Dynastic revolutions include the repeated succession struggles that beset European monarchies up to the eighteenth century; dynasties often lacked a well-defined territorial base, but maintained connections that spread far across national boundaries. When communal and dynastic revolutions combined, they became potent indeed.

Class-coalition revolutions conform more closely to classic Marxist models, but include many struggles in which major elements of the ruling classes took part; France's Fronde and the Dutch revolt against Spain qualify as well as the great English, French and Russian Revolutions. Finally, national revolutions had in common with communal revolutions that they relied on conti-

guous populations and the ties created by contiguity, but they
worked at a larger scale and with a more complex division of
labour among intellectuals, political entrepreneurs, military men
and common members of a putative nationality. Both class-
coalition and national revolutions became more common and
successful as time went on, due precisely to the fact that the
organization of states and the state system changed in ways that
facilitated them.

The two-dimensional scheme classifies coalitions that form
revolutionary *situations* rather than those that gain in revolutionary outcomes; it identifies the principal alignments among contenders, emphasizing challengers to established control of the state.
Outcomes often differed dramatically from the divisions with
which revolutions began, as in the Ottoman struggles of 1826; they
started with Janissary resistance to the sultan's restrictions on their
enormous power but ended with the massacre and dissolution of
the Janissaries. In the same way, the disbanding of the Soviet
Union in 1991 began with an attempted coup by centralizers,
defenders of the old bureaucratic state, only to end with one
national revolution after another.

Each era – or, rather, each distinctive conjunction of political,
economic and cultural conditions – generated its own kinds of
revolution, its own revolutionary actors and its own outcomes of
revolutionary action. During much of the sixteenth and seventeenth centuries, for example, the dependence of claims to state
power on single lineages and their clienteles made rulers vulnerable
to disruptions in inheritance (death of a king without an adult male
heir, rivalry among potential heirs), to competition for their
clienteles from other patrons (a would-be king offers new privileges), or resistance to rulers' excessive demands (opposition to
paying new taxes for the wars of kings who should be financing
their armies out of routine revenues). In any combination of these
circumstances, existing power-holders and their own clienteles
gained reasons to bid for state power, established communal
groups and their own clienteles gained reasons to deny royal
authority, and each gained reasons to ally with the other.

The seventeenth and eighteenth centuries, however, saw a
general consolidation of royal power through much of Europe.
During the period of rapid increase in the professionalism, scale
and expense of military activity, rulers sought to subordinate their

previously autonomous nobles and cities as well as seizing their armed force; rulers also strove to enlist financiers in lending them funds and collecting their revenues, and mercenaries despoiled the land, the cities and their people, as taxes rose precipitously. Each of these efforts threatened to incite collective resistance, especially if state demands outpaced available resources, either because the growth of per capita income slowed or because state demands increased rapidly and visibly. In these cases, a whole social class or a whole connected segment of the population was likely to feel the state's pressure simultaneously, and to rebel. Paradoxically but powerfully, the shift of states toward direct rule promoted a movement of revolutionary situations toward indirect connections among actors; at a national scale, only groups linked by brokers, entrepreneurs and coalitions had the capacity to seize state power.

Consolidation, Nationalism and Revolution

What about the relations of class-coalition and national revolutions to the consolidation of states? Where European states began creating large standing military forces recruited from their own national populations, as we have seen, the scope and bulk of the state itself expanded rapidly. Rulers circumscribed their national territories and the resources within them as never before, monitoring and intervening in stocks and flows of capital, labour, commodities and money. In collaboration with classes having their own interests in national identity, rulers also strove to homogenize their national populations by imposing standard languages, creating national educational systems, forming and publicizing a common cultural heritage.

The myth and then the partial reality of the nation-state formed, as other states and international compacts acted to reinforce the legitimation of states on the basis of shared identity. At the same time, the struggle over the construction of armed force led to bargains with major segments of the population, the broadening of citizenship and the displacement to the state of many activities, issues and disputes that had previously little concerned it. As a consequence of this expansion and homogenization, the advantages of those who controlled their own national state over those who did not increased dramatically and visibly. That was true of a wide range of interests, including regional power-holders who had served as brokers for distinctive cultural groups. Thus the incentives to demand a piece of state power or a separate state increased rapidly, and stimulated revolutionary mobilizations.

Two different phenomena acquired the name 'nationalism'. We might call one *state-led* nationalism, the other *state-seeking* nationalism. In state-led nationalism, rulers aggressively pursued a defined national interest while successfully making demands on a broadly defined citizenry in the name of the whole nation and in exclusion of other loyalties those citizens might have. In state-seeking nationalism, representatives of some population that currently did not have collective control of a state claimed a distinctive political status, or even a separate state. The two sometimes merged in irredentism, the demand that the territories occupied by related populations in adjacent states be attached to a putative mother state. In any case, the two phenomena linked in their insistence that states ought to correspond to homogeneous peoples, that homogeneous peoples had distinctive political interests, that members of homogeneous peoples owed strong loyalties to the states that embodied their heritage, that the world should therefore consist of nation-states having strongly patriotic citizenries.

European nationalism did not spring into life during the eighteenth century without precedents. The idea that the nation existed and should take precedence over other loyalties had a longer history, one rooted in critiques of existing states (Greenfeld 1990; C. C. O'Brien 1989). The question here, however, concerns how such an idea became a programme – or rather a set of competing programmes – that commanded support from millions and became the rationale of hundreds of European revolutionary situations.

During the sixteenth-century Protestant Reformation, claims for religious and political autonomy often coincided, notably in those zones of the Holy Roman Empire and of Habsburg power where municipalities or princes challenged their overlord by defying his ally, the Catholic Pope. In Russia, Serbia and Greece, established Orthodox churches promoted state power, just as national Protestant churches later fortified the states of England, Scotland, the Netherlands and Scandinavia. Religion continued to serve community solidarity and political rivalry within states. But as bases of

revolutionary claims, shared language, land and origin myth came
to count for much more than religion.

From 1789 onward, European rulers made larger and larger
demands on their citizens in the nation's name while insisting that
citizens themselves give their nation priority over other interests;
states commonly adopted programmes of normative indoctrina-
tion designed to homogenize their subject populations and to
activate their national commitments; cultural uniformity within
states increased; the cultural distinctiveness of states similarly
increased; and spokespersons for national minorities demanded
distinctive political treatment or separate states far more often than
before 1789. Although we think of the century and a half after 1789
as the age *par excellence* of class revolutions, for example, even
then the majority of forceful seizures of state power took place in
the name of oppressed, geographically concentrated populations
(Luard 1987: 54–8).

Why did nationalism flourish? Because in the face of wars that
demanded far more men, supplies and funds from national populations than ever before, those women and (overwhelmingly) men
who ran European states laid claim to and bounded a much wider
range of resources than previously, found it advantageous to
homogenize and commit their populations, took steps to do so,
allied with segments of the bourgeoisie that shared an interest in
advancing their own definitions of national identity over and
against parochial identities, diminished the leverage of cultural
brokers as such, and thus increased the difference in power
between those whose culture predominated in an existing state and
those whose culture did not.

This vast top-down process constituted state-led nationalism,
making it seem normal politics in a world that had only recently
witnessed a quite different politics of dynastic interest, indirect
rule, virtual representation, brokerage among multiple ethnicities
and extensive particularism. State-led nationalism activated the
formation, mobilization and claim-making of ethnic groups. It did
so by legitimating the potent principle of correspondence between
people and state, by greatly increasing the advantages to any group
of controlling its own state (not to mention the disadvantages of
not controlling its own state), by more frequently situating cultural
minorities within one state adjacent to cultural majorities in
neighbouring states, by diminishing state toleration of distinctive

cultural enclaves, and by attempts at forced assimilation of minorities, which in their turn threatened the positions of regional intelligentsias and bourgeoisies as cultural brokers. The exact modalities of mobilization and resistance varied with the national population's class composition, urbanity, extent and multiplicity of cultural cleavage and aggressiveness of attempts at assimilation. Throughout Europe, nevertheless, as those groups that controlled the state apparatus pursued campaigns of homogenization and assimilation, they faced not just widespread resistance but newly mobilized demands for political autonomy, even for independence. State-led nationalism generated state-seeking nationalism.

Collective Action, Contention and Revolution

The two forms of nationalism, then, became major bases of collective action and contention in Europe during the nineteenth and twentieth centuries. At the same time, the divisions produced by agrarian and industrial capitalism grew more salient as bases of claims, and various forms of specialized association became more prominent as political vehicles. As a result, both interest revolutions, national revolutions and combinations of the two crowded out the dynastic and communal revolutions of the sixteenth to eighteenth centuries.

Remember our working definition of revolution: forcible transfer of power over a state in the course of which at least two distinct blocs of contenders make incompatible claims to control the state, and some significant portion of the population subject to the state's jurisdiction acquiesces in the claims of each bloc. Recall also that we can distinguish two components of a full-fledged revolution: a revolutionary situation and a revolutionary outcome. The proximate conditions for each are :

Revolutionary Situation	*Revolutionary Outcome*
1 The appearance of contenders, or coalitions of contenders, advancing exclusive competing claims to control of the state, or some segment of it.	1 Defections of polity members.
	2 Acquisition of armed force by revolutionary coalitions.

Revolutionary Situation	Revolutionary Outcome
2 Commitment to those claims by a significant segment of the citizenry.	3 Neutralization or defection of the regime's armed force.
3 Incapacity or unwillingness of rulers to suppress the alternative coalition and/or commitment to its claims.	4 Control of the state apparatus by members of a revolutionary coalition.

Massive changes of European social organization between 1492 and 1992 altered the conditions for all of these proximate causes. In a day of dynastic states, for example, contenders advancing exclusive competing claims to control the state frequently appeared at the death of a sovereign; brothers, illegitimate sons, nephews, cousins and pretenders all staked claims on the crown. The question was whether any segment of the citizenry (especially, in this case, the nobility) would honour those claims, and whether supporters of a competing claim would strike them down. As the dynastic order declined, however, this source of revolutionary situations declined with it.

Again, the acquisition of armed force by revolutionary coalitions and the neutralization of a regime's armed force became much more difficult with the demilitarization of great lords, the abolition of mercenary forces, the disarmament of ordinary citizens and the creation of standing armies under central control; the possibility of a revolutionary power transfer came to depend increasingly on exceptional circumstances such as the end of a losing war; the defection of government troops became more crucial than ever to revolutionary situations. On the other hand, the rise of an urban industrial bourgeoisie and proletariat organized in mutual-aid societies, political clubs and other associations greatly increased the likelihood that some significant segment of the citizenry would make or support revolutionary claims. Each major change we have traced in economy, culture and political structure affected the likelihood and character of revolution.

Moreover, the same changes that affected the incidence of revolution reshaped popular struggles in general. One flowed into the other, as nationalists often demonstrated and sometimes created revolutionary situations, religiously mobilized peasants sometimes attacked their local lords and sometimes braved royal troops, organized radicals often met to denounce the regime and, once in a while, joined insurrections. By now, this should come as no surprise. Revolutions are part and parcel of collective contention. The same conditions that transform collective contention alter the conditions for revolutionary situations as well as revolutionary outcomes. The following chapter will document and compare those changes in three very different regions of Europe between 1492 and 1992, giving pride of place to the Low Countries (especially in their revolutionary struggles of 1550–1650), then contrasting them with Iberia and the Balkans.

3

Revolutions, Rebellions and Civil Wars in the Low Countries and Elsewhere

The Low Countries, Home of Bourgeois Revolution

In 1492, a visitor to the Burgundian Netherlands saw one of the world's most vivid vistas of commerce and culture. He also entered a major centre of political power – power of a peculiarly segmented sort. As in much of central and northern Italy, Switzerland and south Germany, municipalities and their hinterlands constituted the essential units of government, whatever broader political units theybelonged to in name. The Netherlands of 1492 belonged, at least nominally, to a composite empire called Burgundy. Before his death in combat at Nancy in 1477, duke Charles the Bold had made himself master not only of Burgundy and much of Lorraine, but also of Flanders, Brabant, Luxembourg, Holland, Zealand and Hainaut – the combined deltas of the Rhine, the Scheldt and the Meuse. Charles the Bold's domains in the Low Countries approximated the territory that we now know as Belgium, the Netherlands and Luxembourg, although with very important exceptions: while including a substantial chunk of what is now northern France, they lacked Friesland and Groningen as well as the independent enclave bishoprics of Overijssel, Utrecht, Liège, Tournai and Cambrai.

Today Benelux, despite recurrent struggles over language, social policy and immigration, has a peaceful reputation. As compared with, say, Yugoslavia, citizens of the three small, rich states seem inclined to resolve their differences without recourse to violence. Yet a longer look at the Low Countries reveals wars, rebellions and revolutions in abundance. The fifteenth-century Burgundian Netherlands already had a long experience of rebellion. Its next two centuries brought one of Europe's greatest revolutionary struggles, then both the eighteenth- and nineteenth-century histories of its successor states crackled with conflict. To be sure, the forms, circumstances and outcomes of revolutionary situations in the Low Countries changed greatly over the five centuries after 1492. That is the point of reviewing them carefully.

This chapter examines the chronology of the Low Countries' multiple revolutions between 1492 and 1992 before treating changes in revolution in two very different sections of Europe: Iberia and the Balkans. It therefore compares the evolution of revolution in a capital-intensive region (the Low Countries), a coercion-intensive region (the Balkans), and one of capitalized coercion (Iberia). In each region we witness the shift from communal, dynastic and patron–client to national and class-coalition revolutionary situations, but along trajectories and schedules differing significantly as a function of varying combinations between coercion and capital. In Iberia and the Balkans, if not in the Low Countries, we also see the conditions for extensive involvement of the professional military in revolutionary situations.

The chapter makes three essential points. First, the character of revolutions altered greatly over the 500 years in question, as a function of the same processes that eventually created consolidated states. Second, the organization and incidence of revolution varied substantially from one region of Europe to another, especially as a function of the relative predominance of capital and coercion in each region. Third, revolutions and other non-revolutionary political conflicts varied in parallel from region to region and period to period. The Low Countries' experience amply illustrates the connection of revolution to state formation and the change in revolution from period to period, but gives no more than hints of regional variation within Europe as a whole. To explore the latter, we will turn to comparisons with the Iberian and Balkan peninsulas.

With the Battle of Nancy, Charles the Bold's creation of a small empire ended; Swiss pikemen, allied with French armies, checked

Charles' cavalry and seized his artillery. His demise without a visibly viable male heir, furthermore, split his quasi-kingdom; Burgundy proper reverted directly to the French crown, while Lorraine regained its partial autonomy as a duchy of France and magnates of the coastal provinces rallied to Charles' daughter, Mary. In opposition to central authority, the provinces that Charles had brought together by force proved capable of demonstrating a solidarity that they were rarely able to muster for the purposes of positive cooperation. From this point on, the Low Countries' provinces discovered two contradictory desires: on one side, to have a sovereign whose international connections would protect them from invasion; on the other, to retain great freedom of action in commercial and regional affairs. During 1477, in the absence of a strong ruler, the Low Countries' States General assembled at their own initiative, enacted a Great Privilege asserting the rights of their constituent cities and provinces, created an ephemeral (if, in principle, representative) governing council, and decreed the use of Dutch in official proceedings. At the same time, they held Mary under polite but firm house arrest in Ghent.

Threatened by French invasion and under pressure from the States, nineteen-year-old Mary soon married Maximilian, heir to the Habsburg lands. Margaret of York (Charles the Bold's third wife and foster-mother to Mary of Burgundy) was sister of English king Edward IV; her intercession promoted a formal alliance with England in 1481. Thus a young woman's securing of her inheritance shaped the fates of nations. Wars with France and struggles with regional power-holders continued for fifteen years; Maximilian was already at war with Ghent and Bruges by 1483. Yet by 1492 the Habsburgs exerted control over most of the region through resident governors-general. The last great rebel, Philip of Cleves, abandoned his resistance and left for France in October of that year. For a few decades most of the Low Countries acquired a measure of distinctness and unity. If independent Burgundy had dissolved, the Burgundian Netherlands now lived as a relatively coherent segment of the Habsburg domains, and as a close associate of the Holy Roman Empire.

The segment was not only coherent, but also rich. Its workers wove wool from Spain and England, shipping their fabrics to much of the known world. Its merchants dominated the lucrative Baltic trade. They were starting to compete with their confrères from

Spain and Portugal for the Indian Ocean's commerce. When Hugo Grotius published his famous treatise on freedom of the seas in 1609, he subtitled it *The Right which Belongs to the Dutch to Take Part in the East India Trade*. Although they were just entering that trade as major participants, the Low Countries' cities already served as entrepôts for all the world.

A region of efficient, commercialized agriculture, extensive communications networks, speedy water-borne transportation and small-scale but well-connected textile production, the Low Countries epitomized the conjunction of capitalism and Renaissance. Who says Renaissance speaks chiefly of the urban regions extending around the Alps from northern Italy to the Low Countries. Over the fifteenth century, Renaissance vitality shifted northward. Toward 1492, after all, Hieronymus Bosch, Sebastian Brant, Hans Memling, Gerard David and Quentin Metsys were painting masterpieces in and around the cities of the Burgundian Netherlands. As is often revealed in their portraits of dignitaries and their insertions of donors in religious paintings as pious, kneeling figures, they drew their patrons from a wealthy, cultivated patriciate and bourgeoisie. Together, the Low Countries' landed nobility, substantial churchmen, urban oligarchs and, especially, mercantile burghers wielded great power in the European world of capital and commerce.

Through much of the region, for daily transactions ordinary people used dialects of what later consolidated into Dutch. In Flanders and southern Brabant, however, patricians commonly used French while their bourgeois neighbours and their kinsmen to the north were shifting from Latin to Dutch for the purposes of administration and intellectual discourse. South of a line running approximately from Aachen to Calais, ordinary people usually spoke variants of French, notably including Walloon. To linguistic geography corresponded a much stronger orientation to France, and a more intense political division over language, in the southern Netherlands. In Antwerp and further north, ties to England loomed larger; as Dutch–English trade expanded and dynastic connections with the English proliferated, those ties became more pivotal. Despite cleavages between north and south, the cities of all the Low Countries connected closely to each other through ample flows of commodities, capital, people and information. Their merchants, furthermore, commonly knew some French or English and were familiar with the low German that served as commercial *lingua franca* in the great triangle from the Low Countries to Scandinavia and southern Germany. They made the Burgundian Netherlands a great European junction.

Given the extensive trading networks and agricultural hinterlands they implied, as of 1492 European cities of 10,000 or more occupied prominent places in the continent's life; Europe as a whole had a little more than 150 of them. At the end of the century, the Low Countries' cities of 10,000 or more included Amsterdam, Antwerp, Bois-le-Duc, Bruges, Brussels, Delft, Dordrecht, Ghent, Gouda, Groningen, Haarlem, Leiden, Louvain, Liège, Lille, Maastricht, Mechelen, Mons, Nijmegen, Tournai, Utrecht, Ypres and perhaps Valenciennes. A century earlier, Ghent and Bruges had formed the core of a great trading system. Antwerp had more recently gained preponderance. Now to the north a cluster of cities around Amsterdam was growing even more rapidly. The Burgundian Netherlands as a whole crowded almost a sixth of Europe's cities into a zone containing a hundredth of the continent's land and a twenty-fifth of its population; 18.5 per cent of the region's population lived in cities of 10,000 or more, by far the highest proportion of any major European region (de Vries 1984: 39; see also Prevenier & Blockmans 1985: 392).

Political Struggle in the Netherlands

With that dense urbanization, we might expect the region's political sovereignty to be greatly fragmented, its bourgeoisie assertive and influential. So they were, despite the overlay of Burgundian administration. Burgundian burghers sought to extend their influence from their urban seats into the hinterland, but to resist more than provisional consolidations of power over their cities by higher authorities. They perfected a decentralized system of government in which municipalities and their dependencies, governed by local oligarchies, formed the essential units, provinces acted as federations of municipalities, and the regional state lived only a tenuous existence. At the provincial level, furthermore, the burghers of Holland (the north's dominant province) created a system of public finance by means of bonds (*renten*) secured by specific future tax revenues that became the basis of cheap, sure public credit through much of the Netherlands. Taxes on flourishing trade meant that the Dutch did not resort to the bankruptcy and debasement of currency that were the frequent expedients of such hard-pressed monarchies as France and Spain. The Dutch fiscal system permitted the Dutch to bankroll their wars speedily and efficiently; it served as the model for British public finance when William of Orange became king of England in 1689 (Tracy 1985; 't Hart 1989, 1990, 1991).

The only trouble was that outsiders like the dukes of Burgundy kept trying to seize and administer the prosperous region for their own dynastic purposes, while the burghers wanted no more than guarantees of major land powers to protect them from invasion and occupation. Furthermore, outside princes typically wanted to recruit and finance professional armies at local expense, while, except during invasions, burghers settled for their dual-purpose fleets and urban militias. Dynasts specialized in the organization and use of military force, merchants in the protection of trade. Princes and burghers worked at cross-purposes.

As a consequence, the mercantile region produced repeated rebellions, and a series of revolutions, between 1477 and 1847, only to settle into relatively contained, if contentious, liberal-bourgeois politics thereafter. The fifteenth and sixteenth centuries steamed with struggle. In 1484, for example, Maximilian tried to put pressure on his putative subjects by ordering all foreign merchants to leave the great centre of Bruges. The leaders of Bruges then aligned themselves with Maximilian's enemies. In 1488, rebel forces led by Philip of Cleves held Maximilian captive in Bruges for four months, forcing him to cede his governorship over Flanders to a regency council including regional dignitaries and his wife Mary.

That time, Maximilian regained power. From the 1490s, Flanders and the Burgundian Netherlands entered three decades of economic expansion and political reconstruction, with no major rebellions against Habsburg rule outside of Gelderland and Friesland, which were still zones of strongly contested sovereignty. Looking forward from 1492, an observer could plausibly have predicted the Low Countries' integration into yet another empire, the greatest Europe had seen since Roman times, a Habsburg Empire formed as much by marriage and inheritance as by conquest. Philip the Fair, son of Mary and Maximilian, married

Joanna, daughter of Ferdinand of Aragon and Isabella of Castile. Joanna spent much of her subsequent life incarcerated as insane, but not before she bore Charles of Luxembourg (also known as Charles of Ghent), who eventually became Holy Roman Emperor Charles V, head of all the Habsburgs. Charles did not establish his rule without resistance; in 1539, for example, the burghers of Ghent, with broad popular support, rebelled against the imposition of imperial taxes in lieu of military service to which they had not consented. They proposed, plausibly enough, to supply soldiers, not money.

Charles, however, wanted money so that he could rent his own army instead of relying on troops beholden to his reluctant subjects. He soon returned to the Netherlands from Spain in great train, bringing almost 5000 soldiers along to crush his opponents. Eventually Charles had nine rebels executed, revoked the city's privileges, removed its bell from the belfry, confiscated Ghent's artillery, broke down the gates, filled the moats, imposed a royal garrison . . . and collected his money. But Charles and his troops could not be everywhere at once; much of the time the emperor had to deal with resistance by means of negotiation.

In 1548, Charles annexed his Low Country provinces *en bloc* to the Burgundian Circle of the empire. Under Charles, a close female relative typically served as governor of the Netherlands, while in each province a lieutenant governor (a Stadhouder, literally *lieutenant* or state-holder) represented the central power. Born in the Netherlands and speaking Dutch as a native, Charles managed to control the region's nobles and bourgeois from Madrid until his abdication in 1555. Then his Spanish-born son Philip II assumed power, and new struggles began.

During Philip's reign, city-dwellers of the north, like their German neighbours earlier, converted massively to Protestantism, especially its Calvinist variant. Outside of Spain and Italy, one kind of Protestantism or another had great popular appeal through much of Catholic Europe; in Poland-Lithuania and Livonia, for example, many people converted during the early sixteenth century. But the durability of conversion depended on cooperation, or at least toleration, by authorities; in Polish and Livonian zones of influence, only Estonia and Finland remained predominantly Protestant. French people converted to Calvinism in large numbers during the sixteenth century, only to be driven or drawn back into

Catholicism during the seventeenth. If the Peasants' War of 1524–6 had not gone down in bloody defeat, more of south and central Germany would have ended up durably Protestant.

In Europe as a whole, successful popular Protestant breakaways from the Catholic Church occurred overwhelmingly in the overlapping zones of the Holy Roman Empire and of Habsburg power, although rulers in Scandinavia and England instituted their versions of state-church Protestantism as well. While Zwingli appealed to a distinct 'communalist' movement among independent peasant communities, on the whole Protestantism gained its greatest strength in cities and urban hinterlands where the landed nobility held relatively little sway: to that extent, it embodied a muffled revolution against the alliance of imperial and noble authorities (Blickle 1987; Wuthnow 1989: 52–82). In important parts of Central Europe, Lutheran, Zwinglian or Calvinist urban oligarchies allied with powerful popular movements (Brady 1985).

In 1967, Guy E. Swanson published a remarkable book on the Reformation. It disappeared almost immediately from scholarly discussion of the subject because no one knew what to do with it. Drawing on a theory strongly influenced by Emile Durkheim's ideas, Swanson reasoned that people's preferred religious conceptions depend strongly on the relations of authority within which they live. In earlier work, Swanson had examined the correspondence between theologies and authority structure in a wide variety of non-literate populations. In the 1967 book, he looked at forty-one regional jurisdictions in Europe including ten German states, thirteen Swiss cantons, most other major states of Catholic Europe, a few minor states, plus Highland and Lowland Scotland taken separately. His scheme of correspondences ran like this:

Type	Description	Expected religious outcome
commensal	**ruler directly represents body politic** (Appenzell, Florence, Fribourg, Glarus, Poland, Schwyz, Unterwalden, Uri, Venice, Zug)	Catholic
centralist	**ruler holds sole power** (Austria, Bavaria, Berg, France, Ireland, Jülich, Lucerne, Portugal, Highland Scotland, Solothurn, Spain)	Catholic

Type	Description	Expected religious outcome
limited centralist	**governor shares some power with other authorities** (Brandenburg, Denmark, England, Hesse, Prussia, Saxony, Sweden, Württemberg)	Anglican/ Lutheran
balanced	**balance of power between governor and representatives of constituents** (Bohemia, Geneva, Hungary, Lowland Scotland, Transylvania, Cleves, Mark)	Calvinist
heterarchic	**representative of special interests rule** (Basel, Bern, Schaffhausen, United Provinces, Zürich)	Calvinist

Authority structure essentially classifies the relations among chief executive, representative assemblies and constituted special interests. Swanson placed a political unit in a given religious category if it adopted that category as its official religion durably or (in the absence of an official religion) if at least 60 per cent of its population had chosen that religion as of the later eighteenth century. Swanson's criteria eliminated Protestantizing subdivisions of larger sixteenth-century political units (e.g. Estonia) that later become predominantly Protestant states as well as some major sixteenth-century states (e.g. Poland-Lithuania) where Protestantism made substantial inroads only to recede under official persecution. According to Swanson's placements, only Appenzell and Glarus (where a substantial majority of the population adopted Zwinglian or Calvinist beliefs despite the ruler's direct representation of the body politic) failed to match his theoretical expectations.

It is easy to quibble with Swanson's definitions and evaluations, and to criticize the heterogeneity of the units he compared. To what degree rulers held sole power, even as a matter of constitutional principle, in France, Ireland and Highland Scotland, for example, is quite debatable. Nevertheless, revised evaluations of the relations among chief executive, representative assemblies and constituted special interests would produce similar clusters of political units, and the differences in religious orientation among the categories would remain striking. Whatever we make of Swanson's Durkheimian *explanation* of the relationship between religion and regime, the *correlation* will remain impressive.

Let me suggest an interpretation of Swanson's findings. Autonomous urban oligarchies and strong monarchs held on to Catholic orthodoxy, monarchs who shared power with serious noble and bourgeois rivals opted for the financial and political leverage of royally controlled state churches, while those regimes in which the populace had a strong say – however indirect – moved to Calvinism and Zwinglianism. Rival Protestant faiths differed little in theology; the burning questions concerned who would govern churches, and how. The more radical forms of Protestantism, in short, had enormous popular appeal through much of Catholic Europe, especially in zones of commercial capitalism; whether countries actually became and remained Protestant depended on whether ruling classes blocked or collaborated with bourgeois and working-class demands. To that extent, a massive shift toward popular Protestantism resulted from a democratic impulse.

Philip II saw it clearly enough, declaring in 1559 that 'a change of religion doesn't occur except in the company of movement toward a republic, and often the poor, idlers, and vagabonds take on new colors to attack rich people's property' (van Kalken 1946: 241). The formula (strong city + weak nobility = Reform) works well for the geographic distribution of Protestantism in the Low Countries. To the south, the interacting combination of a stronger landed nobility, close ties of nobles to churchmen and more extensive imperial control restrained the opportunities for a durable artisan–bourgeois alliance in favour of Reform. Although Antwerp became a Calvinist stronghold in the 1540s, southerners generally remained within the Catholic fold. Despite Charles V's efforts to contain the assault on his religion, hence at least indirectly on his rule, the north moved massively toward Protestantism. In 1559 Philip II sought to fortify the Catholic position by multiplying the number of bishoprics and taking their nominations out of the hands of regional grandees, but that effort only incited resistance from Catholic lords and churchmen who would otherwise have been inclined to take his side against Protestants.

Battles continued. When governor-general Margaret of Parma (Philip II's natural sister) and her advisor Cardinal Granvelle decreed regular taxation to support the Spanish garrison, issued edicts against heretics and threatened to install the Inquisition, a league of nobles (the Compromise of Breda) spoke on behalf of regional liberties, while in the textile regions of Flanders, not to mention scattered areas as far north as Friesland, common people broke into Catholic churches, sacked them and smashed their sacred images. In 1567, Philip dispatched a Spanish army under the duke of Alba, who wasted little time in repressing opposition and executing great lords such as Egmont and Hoorn, despite the fact that they, too, had opposed the popular uprisings. Over the next two years, Alba's Council on the Disorders had almost 8000 suspects executed (van Kalken 1946: 251). Thus began the series of conflicts that the Dutch later called the Eighty Years War and that historians now call the Revolt of the Netherlands.

Another great lord, William of Orange, escaped as Alba arrived. He later invaded the Low Countries, but retreated before Alba's superior force. Then Alba's imposition of heavy new taxes to support the military establishment incited another rebellion allying nobles and bourgeois. When the rebel force of Sea Beggars captured Brill in 1572, resistance to Spanish rule spread through much of the Low Countries, especially the northern provinces. From that time forward, the maritime Dutch retained mastery of the nearby seas. On land, it was different; when their troops were fighting well, Alba and his successor Requesens were often able to defeat their enemies in the field and to capture rebel cities. But they faced a formidable problem: Spain did not send them enough money to pay and supply their armies. They therefore tried to extract the necessary funds and supplies from local populations, which engendered further resistance at the very moment when unpaid mercenaries were devastating cities and living off the land. In 1574, for example, Requesens' troops defeated those of rebels Louis and Henry of Nassau near Nijmegen, leaving both rebel generals dead, yet Requesens was unable to follow up the victory effectively because Spanish troops whose pay was twenty-eight months in arrears then mutinied.

After the Spanish sacking of Antwerp, Maastricht, Ghent and other places in 1576, all provinces joined in the Pacification of Ghent, which for the first time unified their efforts to drive out the Spaniards. Among other things, the Pacification established limited toleration for Protestants in fifteen provinces as well as Protestant hegemony in Holland and Zealand. However we describe the previous twenty years of war, by that time the Burgundian Netherlands had entered a deeply revolutionary situation. The province of Holland had engaged in open rebellion no later than 1572. Whether a revolutionary outcome would occur, however, still remained uncertain.

Requesens' successor Don John of Austria was unable to stem the rebellion, but the duke of Parma, governor from 1578 to 1592, simultaneously reconquered the southern provinces by force of arms and bought them off with promises to respect their old rights. That severing of the rebel alliance led to the northerners' formation of the Union of Utrecht in alliance with southern cities such as Bruges, Ghent and Antwerp (1579). The next steps were their rejection of Philip II's authority (1581) and their naming of a Stadhouder, the Calvinist William of Orange. The Stadhouder served essentially as a governor-general on behalf of a shadowy sovereign. Some said the sovereign inhabited the States General, some said the individual cities and provinces, some few said the people of the Low Countries at large. Since, despite abortive experiments with French and English royalty, the rebellious provinces were unable to recruit a nominal ruler who combined a powerful international position with willingness to accept their restrictive conditions, the political structure leaders fashioned during those crucial years came close to being a confederation of city-states coordinated by an executive whose rule remained contingent on proper performance: a kind of republic. The Stadhouder was no king.

Philip II still defined William of Orange, however contingent his power, as the enemy, so much so that in 1580 he banned William and declared his properties forfeit with the proviso that:

> So that this purpose may be achieved more promptly and our people may be delivered more quickly from this tyranny and oppression, and wishing to reward virtue and punish crime, we promise upon the word of a king and as a servant of God that if there be someone, either our subject or a foreigner, with such good will and so strong a desire for our service and the public good that he can enforce our said ordinance and rid us of this plague, delivering Orange to us dead or alive or even just killing him, we will give and furnish to him and to his heirs the sum of 25,000 gold crowns, in land or cash at his

choice, immediately after the accomplishment of the deed. If he has committed any crime or breach of the law whatever, we promise to pardon him as of now. Further, if he is not a nobleman, we grant him nobility for his valor. (Rowen 1972: 79)

Two men tried for the prize; after the first wounded William seriously in 1582, the second, Balthazar Gérards, assassinated him in Delft. That happened in 1584, four years after Philip's invitation to homicide.

Killing William did not defeat the Dutch. With English military assistance (the English smashing of the Spanish Armada in 1588 being a notable moment) and the advantage given by Spain's also being at war with France, Maurice of Nassau and his Dutch forces drove back the Spaniards until a truce of 1609 gave *de facto* independence to what had become known as the United Provinces. Well before then England and France, with malice aforethought, had recognized the provinces as an independent state. Not until the Treaty of Westphalia (1648), however, did the Dutch Republic gain official international recognition as an independent entity.

As is often the case, the winning coalition had trouble avoiding its own splits, especially when victory became more certain. Between the truce and the treaty, a deep division over the powers of the Calvinist church led to the trial and execution of Johan van Oldenbarnevelt, the chief officer of Holland's Estates, as well as the sentencing of Hugo Grotius, theorist of international law and adherent of Oldenbarnevelt, to life imprisonment. After the peace treaty of 1648 the Dutch Reformed Church, like its Anglican counterpart, became an official church in most provinces, with the two-thirds of the Dutch population that was Catholic, Jewish or Dissenter barred from high office.

Does the Eighty Years War, or some part of it, qualify as a revolution? Certainly control of the state changed hands through armed struggle in the course of which at least two distinct blocs of contenders made incompatible claims to control the state, and some significant portion of the population subject to the state's jurisdiction acquiesced in the claims of each bloc. By our criteria, the tumults of 1567 to 1648 clearly constituted at least one revolution. If there had been only one caesura and only two blocs of contenders, indeed, how simple the analysis of the Revolt of the Netherlands would be! Seventeen different formally autonomous sovereignties operated during the Revolt, each with a somewhat different relation to Spain and to its fellows. Revolutionary situations erupted like craters on Mars, while revolutionary outcomes occurred more than once in north, south and both together.

As late as 1618, the lethal division between Maurice of Nassau and Johan Oldenbarnevelt opened up yet another revolutionary situation. Some historians have even qualified the eighty-year struggle as a great revolution 'comparable to and deserving a place of priority in the list of great revolutions which have ushered in modern times' (Griffiths 1960: 452). The argument is straightforward and even credible: taken separately, the struggles of north and south look like an independence movement plus a failed revolt. Taken together, however, they amount to a deep transformation of the conditions of rule everywhere in the Low Countries. One could make a reasonable case that the Low Countries set the European model for bourgeois revolution.

From the Southern Netherlands to Belgium

Nor did revolution then disappear from the south. The Spanish Netherlands passed to the Habsburg's Austrian branch with the Treaty of Utrecht (1713), except that the bishopric-principality of Liège remained an independent segment of the Empire. As a result of the war just ended, the now Austrian Netherlands found themselves under Dutch occupation, with the obligation to pay 500,000 écus per year to support eight Dutch fortresses across the land, and with the Scheldt's mouth closed. Although the French forces against which it was aimed made the so-called Barrier of eight fortresses quite porous during the War of the Austrian Succession (1740–8), Dutch garrisons returned to the Austrian Netherlands at the end of the war. As the century wore on, the region went about its business under Austrian surveillance that was considerably closer than Spain had ever managed. Powerful nobles and churchmen generally collaborated with the imperial regime, while the bourgeoisie harboured dreams of their old authority. Except in an occasional uprising, the working classes had no say whatsoever.

In 1781 the new emperor Joseph II, the very model of an enlightened despot, made the first visit any nominal ruler had made to the southern Netherlands since 1559. He then followed up with a series of administrative reforms: weakening the church's power on one side, increasing central control on the other. In a move that commanded broad support, he completed the expulsion of Dutch forces from Austrian territory. His effort to reorganize the country's administrative geography, however, faced resistance from almost every entity within the slowly composed mosaic that had been the region's government – the Council of Brabant, the States of Brabant, individual municipalities and merchant guilds as well. The 'Revolution of Brabant' took a conservative turn, demanding the end of religious toleration and the restoration of provincial privileges while seeking outside support for its stand against the Empire. Yet it also had a populist side connected by widespread Freemasonry, which gained strength as neighbouring France entered its own revolution in 1789. That year, armed uprisings, supported by a Patriot army based in the Dutch Republic, drove Austrian administrators from Ghent, Bruges, Namur and Brussels. The *manifeste du peuple brabançon* issued at the time adapted and translated the 1581 declaration that had denied Philip II his authority on behalf of local and regional liberties (Kossmann 1978: 59). The bourgeois nucleus of the Netherlands' revolutionary movements became even more obvious.

In 1790 an assembly of delegates from all the southern provincial Estates except Luxembourg declared the creation of a United States *à l'américaine*, complete with Congress and Declaration of Independence. By then a split was opening between Statists and Democrats; the split almost broke into civil war. Before the end of 1790 Austrian troops had dispersed what remained of the revolutionary regime. Many Democrats fled to French territory, while Statists sought exile in England or Holland. Meanwhile, the Principality of Liège acted out its own version of the Parisian revolution, complete with taking of the local Bastille; occurring in an ecclesiastical state, the Liège revolution took a much more anti-clerical turn than its Belgian neighbour, with the result that its supporters got a cold shoulder from predominantly Catholic Belgium. When Austrian troops reoccupied Liège in 1791, few people resisted them. In both Belgium and Liège, reaction had gained by mid-1791.

Then the French took their turn; they soon chose the Low Countries as a battleground against Austria and their other enemies. When French general Dumouriez led his troops into Belgium in the autumn of 1792, he hoped to be greeted as a democratic liberator; while small numbers of Democrats did extend a fraternal hand to him, Statists treated him as a menace. Nevertheless, his Belgian supporters erected a political apparatus similar to that of the French Jacobins. Meanwhile, the Convention of Liège voted for union with France. In 1793, Austrian troops returned, retaking important parts of the southern Netherlands and making much of the rest a field of battle. French forces counter-attacked. By 1795 they controlled the Low Countries as far north as Amsterdam. In 1794 and 1795 the French occupiers undertook to integrate Belgium into their national political system, including secularization of many religious functions and imposition of French as the language of public life. From that point until 1814, Belgium existed as occupied territory, then as part of a satellite kingdom. A centralized state in the French image came into being. Belgians even had their own small Vendée, a broad rural movement of resistance to conscription in 1798.

The Bellicose Dutch

What about the north? In their very time of sixteenth- and seventeenth-century rebellion, the northern provinces were establishing themselves as a great commercial power on a world scale, for example through the founding of the Dutch East India Company in 1602. They made up a surprising state: an archipelago of bourgeois republics, each with its own militia, fiercely defending local privileges against the demands of the Stadhouder and even of their own creature, the States General. Nevertheless, the provinces and the States worked out a remarkably efficient division of labour, the provinces taxing and administering, the States waging war.

By the beginning of the seventeenth century, the United Provinces were conducting wars with England and other rivals for imperial power; they often won. Table 3.1 lists major wars directly engaging the Dutch. Of course, the dates given in the table have a spurious precision: in the Atlantic, Pacific and Indian Oceans, Dutch fleets fought almost continuously, while in Europe some seventeenth-century wars dragged on with relatively little combat

Table 3.1   Dutch wars of the seventeenth and eighteenth centuries

1567–1648	(intermittent) Dutch–Spanish war	1652–3	Dutch–Portuguese war in Indian Ocean and Atlantic
1605–6	Dutch–Portuguese war over Malacca	1652–5	Anglo-Dutch Naval War
1615–18	Venetian war against Uskoks, Austrian Habsburgs	1654–70	Dutch conquest in Sumatra
1611–28	Dutch conquest of Ceylon, entailing war with Portuguese forces	1654–60	Great Northern War
		1657–61	Dutch–Portuguese war
1616–19	Dutch conquest in Macassar	1661–2	Dutch–Chinese war over Taiwan
1619	Dutch conquest in Java	1663–7	Anglo-Dutch Naval War
1622	Dutch–Portuguese war over Macao	1669–81	Dutch intervention in Java
1624–54	(intermittent) Dutch–Portuguese wars over Brazil	1672–9	Dutch War of Louis XIV
		1679–80	Dutch war with Algiers
1628–9	Dutch–Mataram–Java war	1688–97	War of the League of Augsburg
1638–40	Dutch–Portuguese war over Ceylon and Goa	1701–14	War of the Spanish Succession
		1703–5	Dutch conquest in Java and Mataram
1640–1	Dutch–Portuguese war over Malacca	1715–26	Dutch war with Algiers
1641	Dutch–Portuguese war over Angola	1718–20	War of the Quadruple Alliance
1646	Dutch conquest in Moluccas	1740–48	War of the Austrian Succession
1648	Dutch–Portuguese war over Angola	1780–3	War of American Independence
1650–6	Dutch conquest in Amboyna	1795–	French Revolutionary War
1651	Dutch conquest in Ceram		

from one year to the next. Nevertheless, the seventeenth- and eighteenth-century records put the Dutch among the world's great war-makers. By this count, the Dutch were at war somewhere at least four years out of five during the seventeenth century. The chronology traces the entry of Dutch forces into the Mediterranean and Adriatic (where they joined that other great maritime power, Venice, in battling the Uskok raiders who enjoyed support from the Austrian Habsburgs), the long and partly successful struggle with Portugal for eminence on the high seas, and the enormous colonial effort put out before the United Provinces had achieved formal recognition as an independent power. After the War of the Spanish Succession, the Dutch withdrew to lesser military involvement; they did not play major parts in any European wars after 1715. Since the mercantile economy continued to expand, that military withdrawal is what historians generally have in mind when they speak of eighteenth-century Dutch 'decline'.

War had a side effect: it generally promoted the Stadhouder's political power. In times of war, furthermore, popular support for the Stadhouder – Orangism – commonly rose, inciting not only celebrations of the national leader but also attacks on the urban ruling classes (Dekker 1982: 41–5). On the other hand, war also increased the importance of fiscal support from the provinces for the central government, which gave the provinces and their municipalities leverage as well. In 1650, soon after independence, Stadhouder William II sought to capitalize on popular enthusiasm by seizing more durable princely power in Holland, but his failure reaffirmed the provinces' autonomy. For another century, his successors had to settle for a tenuous hold on government despite surges of wartime support.

Having married James II's daughter Mary in 1677, Stadhouder William III became king of England in the Glorious Revolution of 1688–9. At that point the Dutch and English enemies turned into military allies, as their ruling families intermarried, for almost a century. Although the Stadhouder gained greater power in matters and times of war, however, the provinces (especially Holland) commonly behaved as nearly sovereign states. Each province selected its own Stadhouder, or chose to have none at all; when he invaded England to lead the Protestant revolt in 1688, William III was not actually Stadhouder of the United Provinces as such, but elected Stadhouder in five of the seven Dutch provinces. When William died in 1702, all provinces but Groningen and Friesland (which had a different Stadhouder) left the office empty. Only in 1747, during the southern Netherlands' involvement in the War of the Austrian Succession and after a major rebellion, did the States General again designate a hereditary Stadhouder for the entire country. Even then he frequently faced opposition from one or more of the provinces.

During the 1780s, a Patriot Party mobilized opposition to the Stadhouder for the first time on a national scale; Dutch participation in the War of American Independence had encouraged opponents of the Stadhouder to believe in the possibility of ending arbitrary rule through popular collective action. Their conception of liberty centred characteristically on local autonomy and on rule by the propertied classes, a preference that eventually lost them considerable support from ordinary workers. Between 1785 and William V's summoning of Prussian troops in 1787, nevertheless, the Patriots executed bourgeois-democratic revolutions, including the formation of popular independent militias (Free Corps), in Holland and elsewhere. France supplied surreptitious financial and political support for the Patriots while Britain did the same for their Orangist enemies. The Prussian invasion snuffed out a revolutionary situation that was still unfolding.

Some Patriots returned to power when French invaders established the Batavian Republic (1795), and retained it under the satellite Kingdom of Holland, with Napoleon's brother Louis Bonaparte as king (1806–10). In both guises, the wealthy Netherlands paid substantial tribute to France. In 1810, after Louis abdicated rather than let Holland be drained of its resources for imperial expansion, Napoleon absorbed Holland directly into his decreasingly French Empire. By then, French administration had replaced the old federal structure with a bureaucratized central state similar to the one Belgium had been acquiring. Late in 1813, the son of the late Stadhouder re-entered the Netherlands as the French occupation disintegrated, leading a 'revolt' that consisted largely of taking over when the French withdrew. Within two weeks a commission was drafting a new constitution, and the prince of Orange was running a provisional state.

The victorious allies then soldered together the northern and southern provinces, now including Liège, in a new Kingdom of the

Netherlands resembling the old Burgundian Netherlands but shifted northward and incorporating the enclaves that had punctured its predecessor. William, prince of Orange, became king in a constitutional monarchy giving equal weight to north and south, despite the considerably larger population of the south. Governing in a French-style administration that long followed the *Code Napoléon* and the *Code pénal*, the king enjoyed considerable autonomy through his direct control of colonial revenues.

Conflict between south and north continued to 1839, and ended in a definitive separation of the two. In 1828 a Belgian Union of Oppositions formed to campaign against official candidates. It soon proposed a federalist reorganization of the Netherlands, south vs. north. In October 1830, a bourgeois–working class coalition followed the French Revolution of that year by demanding an autonomous administration, fighting off Dutch troops, and gaining outside intervention. After a year of international negotiations, the Belgians elected as their king Leopold of Saxe-Coburg – widower of the heiress-apparent to the British throne, thereby uncle and mentor of Victoria, who would herself become Britain's queen six years later. Belgium suffered a Dutch invasion when Dutch king William rejected the terms of settlement.

After a French counter-invasion and protracted occupation-cum-bargaining (in the course of which Leopold fortified his crown by marrying the daughter of France's new king Louis-Philippe) the Dutch finally reconciled themselves to an armistice in 1833 and to full recognition of Belgium in 1839. Meanwhile, the Belgians adopted a strikingly liberal constitution, which promoted further political mobilization. They also adhered to the political neutrality imposed by the international settlement of 1839. In 1847, Belgium's clerical–liberal governing coalition gave way to a party system in which bourgeois liberals predominated; the new regime anticipated the revolutions of 1848 by greatly expanding the franchise, drawing petty bourgeois and organized workers more fully into national politics. Similarly, bourgeois-led reform movements proliferated and gained in the Netherlands before the revolutions of 1848 took place elsewhere.

From the mid-nineteenth century until their twentieth-century wartime occupations, neither Holland nor Belgium passed through a truly revolutionary situation – that is, an open division of the polity into two or more blocs each exercising some effective power. By the middle of the nineteenth century, Belgium was rapidly creating one of Europe's great concentrations of heavy industry; the working class expanded accordingly. At something like the same rhythm, Belgium also began to create colonies in Africa. Belgian domestic politics divided sharply among Catholics, liberals and, eventually, socialists. Conflicts between organized Flemish speakers and better-off francophones repeatedly rocked Belgian politics. The line between Flemish and French marked not only a zone of political contention but also a great social divide; changes in fertility, for example, broke precisely at the linguistic frontier (Lesthaeghe 1977: 111–14).

Nevertheless, Belgium's nineteenth- and twentieth-century conflicts offered no greater threat to the state's continuity than the strike waves, mass demonstrations and turbulent electoral campaigns that were becoming the standard accoutrements of democratic politics in much of Europe. German forces occupied Belgium, and imposed their own regime, for most of World War I and again during World War II. After the Second World War, linguistic, religious, regional and class divisions compounded into intense and shifting struggles that stayed far short of revolution. The closest call came in 1950 with the abdication of Leopold III, the wartime king, when a referendum showed that he commanded majority support but faced wide opposition from francophones and anti-clericals, including many who thought in retrospect that he had cooperated too readily with Nazi occupiers.

Similarly, the northern Netherlands enacted top-down liberal reforms in the era of 1848, creating a politics crosscut by class and religion, if not by language. Although the Netherlands, with its mineral shortages and its already commanding position in world trade, never developed heavy industry on a Belgian scale, it did move more vigorously into manufacturing during the nineteenth century, using both oil and other products from its colonies to bolster its position in the European economy. The country maintained nervous neutrality during World War I, but was unable to hold off a German occupation during the Second World War. A revolutionary movement arose in 1918, but quickly lost strength. Although left and far right came to blows during the 1930s, those struggles similarly fell far short of a revolutionary situation.

The creation of an economic and diplomatic union among Belgium, the Netherlands and Luxembourg after 1950 opened the way toward participation of all three countries as a bloc in the European Community; their union further reduced the likelihood of revolutionary situations in any of the three by increasing the chances that two adjacent powers would intervene to support any regime suddenly stricken by weakness. While liberation movements such as the Provos (*provocateurs*) of the 1960s continued to flourish in the Netherlands, national politics travelled for the most part within the channels established by the liberal-democratic institutions of the nineteenth century. In both north and south, bourgeois revolutions had locked bourgeois politics into place.

Assaying the Low Countries' Revolutions

From 1477 to 1992, the Low Countries produced numerous revolutionary situations and a small series of revolutionary outcomes: the States General's seizure of autonomous power (1477), the temporarily successful rebellion of 1484–8, the Pacification of Ghent (1576), the rejection of Philip II as sovereign (1581), the establishment of the Dutch Republic (1609 and/or 1648), the Patriot and Brabantine Revolutions of the 1780s, the multiple transfers of power under influence of the French Revolution and Empire, the post-war creation of the Kingdom of the Netherlands and the Belgian Revolution of 1830. The Dutch Republic, which supplied a new king, also played its part in England's Glorious Revolution of 1688–9. During the twentieth century, German occupations entailed temporary revolutions of sorts, although most observers would give them other names.

Whether the sweeping sixteenth-century success of Calvinism in Antwerp and the north also constituted a revolution is more debatable; by the definition we are using here, it did not, despite its strong effect on subsequent struggles, revolutions and social life. The Belgian constitutional reforms of 1847 and the Dutch reforms of 1848 would also qualify as revolutionary under some definitions, but not by the criteria of this book. Nevertheless, the point is obvious: revolutionary situations and revolutionary outcomes abounded over the last five centuries of Dutch and Belgian history; at least a half-dozen times they coincided in durable revolutionary transfers of power. What is more, the region's changing but

Table 3.2   Revolutionary situations in the Low Countries, 1492–1992

1487–93	Rebellions of Ghent, Liège, Bruges, Louvain, Cleves vs. Burgundy
1498–1500	Renewed civil war in Friesland
1514–23	Burgundian-Guelders struggle for control of Friesland
1522–8	Broad resistance to Charles V's assertion of sovereignty in Low Countries
1532	Popular insurrection in Brussels
1539–40	Ghent rebellion
1566–1609	Revolt of the Netherlands (German, French, English intervention)
1618	Radical Calvinist seizures of power in many cities
1650	Failed coup of William II
1672	Orangist seizures of power in many towns
1702	Displacement of Orangist clients in Gelderland and Overijssel
1747–50	Orange revolt in United Provinces
1785–7	Dutch Patriot Revolution, terminated by Prussian intervention
1789–90	Brabant Revolution
1795–8	Batavian Revolution
1830–3	Belgian Revolution vs. Holland (French, British intervention)

continuously powerful bourgeoisie almost always weighed heavily in the character and outcome of revolutionary situations.

In general the Low Countries' revolutionary situations and outcomes took dynastic or communal forms from the fifteenth to the seventeenth centuries, with great lords and constituted municipalities playing the central parts. For that reason, civil wars, international wars, private wars and revolutions merged into each other indistinctly. Then both class-coalition and national revolutions succeeded the communal forms as the states in question became more substantial and demanding. At that point revolutionary situations and outcomes became much more distinct from wars, even when they involved armed struggle. Leaving aside the retroactive myth-making that treats the sixteenth-century rebellion as the righteous rising of a unified people, the Low Countries saw two major nationalist struggles, the first as Belgium wrested itself away from the Kingdom of the Netherlands in the 1830s, the second as within Belgium Flemings and Walloons fought for control of the state and, failing that, well-marked defences of their positions within it. The first involved a genuine, if limited, revolution; the second, a long series of battles and an incremental transformation of the polity, but no clear revolutionary situation.

The difference between the two great nationalist episodes in Belgium brings out another crucial point. The revolutions that occurred in each period shared many characteristics with the non-revolutionary politics of their time. Not that they were merely more of the same; revolutionary cleavages opened up, armed struggles took place and revolutionary transfers of power actually occurred because of exceptional incentives to mobilize against the holders of power and exceptional opportunities to overthrow them. In 1567, when the duke of Alba brought in his armies to fight well-connected nobles and well-mobilized cities hundreds of miles from reliable bases of supply, then sought to make the local populations pay for his extraordinary expenses, he heightened the regime's vulnerability at precisely the same time as he increased its threat to established rights and privileges; the combination deepened a revolutionary situation. Yet the actors, the interests and the struggles all had much in common with the region's turbulent politics over the previous ninety years, not to mention the century to follow.

The most valuable lesson of this brief review, however, is unexpected, if obvious in retrospect: revolutions that looked quite different when viewed from the standpoint of outcomes involved very similar elements and actors. The 'successful' sixteenth–seventeenth-century revolution in the north and the 'unsuccessful' revolution in the south sprang from essentially the same connected situation, the difference in outcome depending on the relative strength of the crucial actors in each of the zones. Similarly, the Brabant Revolution of the Austrian Netherlands and the Patriot Revolution of the Dutch Republic had many features in common, despite the apparently conservative cast of the first, as seen from the outcome, and the relatively liberal cast of the second up to the point at which Prussian troops crushed it. They even interacted, given the military and political base Brabant's revolutionaries set up in Breda, on Dutch territory, with Dutch Patriot assistance. The balance of forces again made a large difference in the revolution's apparent content and meaning. If the Low Countries were the home of bourgeois revolutions, the current position and alliances of the bourgeoisie varied substantially from one time and place to another; that variation produced very different manners of revolution.

As an extreme case of capital-intensive state formation, the Low Countries did not anticipate the experience of Europe in general. Elsewhere in Europe, for example, the sixteenth century featured large risings of peasants who were being threatened with enserf-ment by landlords who sought greater economic and political power; no such events occurred in the Low Countries. They did not happen there because agriculture was commercializing, peasant property was thriving and landlords held only limited political power in the presence of an expansive bourgeoisie. Not even in the 1780s, furthermore, did the northern or southern Netherlands see the mass revolutionary mobilizations that occurred in England during the 1640s or France during the 1790s. After the sixteenth century, finally, the scale of collective violence in the Low Countries did not approach that of Russia or Hungary. No doubt the bourgeois interest in order, the early elimination of private armies, the reluctance of urban militias to fire on their fellow-citizens and the relative weakness of the Low Countries' states all contributed to that outcome.

The prominence and autonomy of the region's patricians and burghers coupled with the great dependence of rulers on their financial support to bring out the salience of intermediaries for the successful exploitation of the Netherlands' wealth. Dukes, bishops and governors had little choice but to bargain with the rich men and the cities of their territories, if only because when rulers sought to have their way through the simple exercise of military force, a coalition of bourgeois and dissident nobles almost always formed. When rulers bargained effectively, their states did very well militarily, for the region's financiers could raise great sums rapidly at low rates of interest; ordinary citizens invested heavily in state securities. In the north, furthermore, the capitalist organi-zation of war-making created only exiguous, contingent state structure, while in the south rulers settled for indirect rule and shallow extraction of resources through most of the eighteenth century; in neither place did a build-up of bulky state bureaucra-cies occur before the Napoleonic occupation.

Consolidation of the state, furthermore, came to the Low Countries with large doses of outside intervention. Although the Patriots did attempt some liberalization of government and the Democrats' programme of popular sovereignty did entail considerable suppression of privilege, without France's example, occupation and deliberate reorganization of the two polities they would surely have carried much more fragmented and uneven forms of government into the nineteenth century. The French installed centralized, bureaucratized, uniform states in the Low Countries; those forms of organization, if not the particular states the French had imposed, survived France's defeat in 1815.

These lowland experiences all reflected the dominance of commerce and capital, the feebleness of concentrated coercive means. Where capital was thin and coercion was thick, very different kinds of states prevailed. Concentrated coercion generally meant noble power over land, peasants, commerce and the state itself. Eventually the organization of large national standing armies integrated nobles into states as dignitaries and military officers; the greater their prior power and autonomy, the more likely even then that they offered loyalty in return for large grants of fortified privilege within their own domains; Prussian Junkers served their king, receiving ratification not only as colonels but also as judges, administrators and privileged owners of grand estates. In such regions, only the specialization of expensive military forces and the expansion of capitalism in the nineteenth century moved states toward the consolidated type that was beginning to prevail throughout the continent. Those changes eventually, but only eventually, sapped the dominance of great landlords.

Different kinds of states, hence different patterns of revolution. At the coercion-intensive end of the European scale, revolutionary situations long took either the dynastic form, the communal form, the patron–client form or all three at once. Dynastic revolutions typically occurred when grandees resisted royal rule or factions of grandees fought to control the crown. Revolutionary situations of a dynastic type occurred frequently – notably at the deaths of monarchs – and ended fairly often with revolutionary outcomes, forcible transfers of power over the state. Communal revolutions typically occurred when peasants and artisans banded together to resist efforts of lords to extract greater revenues and services from them or to suppress the communities that gave them collective identities. Although local resistance to noble demands occurred every day, open revolutionary situations of a communal kind, with ordinary people commanding pieces of state apparatus or fabricating their own, were rare.

Revolutionary outcomes were even rarer. The fact that peasants, artisans and urban communities lacked arms while aristocrats accumulated them put commoners at a great disadvantage. Dynastic and communal revolutions sometimes combined, nevertheless, when dissident nobles aligned themselves with rebellious communities; then the blood-letting was likely to be terrible. The various alliances of Burgundian cities with duke Philip of Cleves, count Lamoral of Egmont and the princes of Orange – none of them merchants, all of them grandees in their own right – brought burghers into devastating open warfare with Spanish troops.

Class-coalition and national forms of revolution eventually supplanted dynastic, patron–client and communal forms in Europe's coercion-intensive regions, but only when partially independent bourgeoisies and proletariats had grown up to articulate demands for civil liberties, governmental reforms and regional autonomies. The creation of state bureaucracies, national educational programmes and extensive systems of communication contributed to these changes, but the fundamental conditions were the expansion of capitalist production, the proliferation of trade and the growth of cities – which is to say a decline in the coercion-intensiveness, a rise in the capital-intensiveness, of these regions. By 1848, bourgeois-led revolutions on behalf of class and nation were occurring in such former bastions of coercion as Hungary and Sicily.

To mention Hungary (then part of the Habsburg Empire) and Sicily (then part of the Kingdom of the Two Sicilies) is to recall emphatically that the territories of most European states were much more composite and shifting than my simple schematism implies. These are matters of degree and period. Even within the Low Countries we have seen considerable heterogeneity and frequent changes in the social compositions of different states as a consequence of new boundaries and governments. A comparison with two very different regions of relatively concentrated coercion – first Iberia, then the Balkans plus Hungary – will bring out the importance of the contrasting paths by which states formed and reformed.

Iberian Revolutions

The Iberian peninsula, for all its crucial connections with the Low Countries, had a fundamentally different encounter with revolution. The region's politics showed the effects of four influences: (1) the legacy of a long struggle against Muslim overlords, in the course of which both nobles and municipalities acquired exceptional rights vis-à-vis the crown, especially the crown of Castile; (2) the contrast between a landlord-dominated interior devoted to a pastoral-subsistence economy and coastal regions heavily involved in world trade; (3) rule by families having broad imperial interests and resources; (4) adjacency to a France that was building a large military machine and a centralized monarchy. All four factors shaped Iberian revolutions directly from the fifteenth century to the eighteenth, leaving their traces in the repeated violent transfers of power that occurred thereafter.

Economically, Iberia long maintained an odd relationship to the rest of the world: in the interior, a mosaic of subsistence economies overlaid with vast movements of cattle (especially the sheep from which Spanish lords sent wool into the world textile trade); around the exterior, ports and capitals strongly connected to commercial and political empires. For 300 years after 1492, both Portugal and Spain were sustaining their crowns through revenues from colonies and international trade, although their local economies did not benefit enormously from those revenues. Royal borrowing from foreign lenders, purchasing abroad and re-exporting commodities or silver drawn from colonies resembled the twentieth-century situation of many small oil-producing states in which the rich get richer and the powerful more powerful but the mass of residents (many of them non-citizens) remain outside circuits of prosperity.

Within Iberia, the power of large landlords and urban patricians in the interior reinforced the peninsula's ambivalent relationship to world markets, slowed economic innovation and maintained the emphasis on local autarky. In the case of Spain, declining revenues from Latin America and then the rebellion of almost all Latin American colonies during the Napoleonic Wars reduced the crown's independence before opening the way to the country's slow agricultural and industrial commercialization after 1815. Portugal, for its part, formed almost a dual monarchy with its rich colonies, especially Brazil, until 1820, then shrank like Spain into a diminished international role.

Iberian states long operated as essentially patrimonial organizations. As of 1492, four major political entities occupied the peninsula: Portugal, Castile, Navarre and Aragon. Navarre, a land-locked kingdom populated largely by Basques and held by the French royal family, spanned the Pyrenees; in 1516, Ferdinand of Aragon would annex its Iberian segment, leaving a tiny French kingdom to survive until it came directly to the crown with Henry of Navarre when he became Henry IV. Portugal and Aragon were maritime powers centred on Lisbon and Barcelona respectively, while Castile drew much more of its strength from the export of its interior's wool. If Portuguese and Catalan merchants waxed strong in their own territories as they dealt widely overseas, their Genoese counterparts controlled a significant part of Castile's trade through ports such as Seville and Cadiz. Indigenous Castilian merchants enjoyed little power.

The royal families of all four regions had frequently intermarried, so much so that the peninsula's political alignment could easily have ended up (Portugal + Castile) vs. (Aragon + Navarre) or all four united under a single crown. It could also have fragmented, since at times nobles of royal blood plotted for autonomous realms in Andalusia and Valencia. The 1469 marriage of Ferdinand and Isabella, heirs respectively to the crowns of Aragon and Castile, had precipitated a civil war with those who lost out, aided by the ever-watchful French. Yet it laid the foundation of an empire. Ferdinand and Isabella strengthened their own power in a standard imperial way: by confirming the privileges and exploitative means of grandees and municipalities who collaborated with their dynastic, military and fiscal programmes. By 1492, a strengthened dual monarchy was conquering Granada, the last Muslim stronghold on the peninsula, expelling Jews who did not convert to Catholicism, while following independent Portugal into the Atlantic and Indian Oceans. Soon Aragon and Castile were competing with France for power in Italy and expelling unconverted Muslims from their own territories.

By 1516 a united crown had passed to Charles I of Ghent, become Charles I of Spain, who already ruled the Low Countries (to the degree that they were ruled collectively at all) and who won election as Holy Roman Emperor (now as Charles V) in 1519. In 1580, Charles' son Philip II enforced his contested claim to the recently vacated Portuguese crown by means of an invasion that drove off his competitors. Without dissolving either as a distinct political entity or as a commercial and imperial power, Portugal then became a Spanish fief for sixty years, until the successful Portuguese rebellion of 1640. Thereafter, Portugal and Spain survived as distinct states within relatively constant borders. Their distinctness and constancy as states was, however, only relative: Spain remained only one element of a composite set of European family holdings until the Napoleonic invasions; both states seized and lost large colonial empires outside of Europe; Spain took the Iberian portion of Navarre from France between 1512 and 1516, and ceded Cerdagne and Roussillon definitively to France in 1659; and the French occupied and reorganized much of the peninsula temporarily under Napoleon. As in Belgium and Holland, that French reorganization had a durable impact on governmental institutions. While retaining more than the average share of patrimonial arrangements, Spain and Portugal began to approximate consolidated states.

The coercion-intensive path of change in Iberia marked the peninsula's revolutions. Table 3.3 chronicles revolutionary situations in the peninsula between 1492 and 1992, including some marginal cases such as the expulsions of Jews, Moriscos and Jesuits, where underground organization was extensive but concerted public resistance was minimal. Two features of Iberian revolutions immediately catch the eye: the long survival of dynastic struggles, and the extraordinary succession of revolutionary situations from the French wars to the 1930s. Although Portugal and Spain followed their own timetables, both countries experienced royalist risings well past 1850 and crackled with civil war repeatedly for over a century.

With respect to breadth and intensity of division, the chief revolutionary epochs were no doubt the struggles of the Comuneros and Germanias (roughly 1519–22), the revolts of Portugal and Catalonia that began in 1640, the War of Spanish Succession (1701–14), the multiple civil struggles precipitated by war with France (1793–1814), the repeated contests for control of both states between 1820 and 1932 and the Spanish Civil War (1936–9). After

Table 3.3   Revolutionary situations in Iberia, 1492–1992

1499–1500	War with Moors	1843	Coalition deposes Espartero; Narvaez president to 1851
1509–11	War with Moors	1846–50	Portuguese civil wars
1519–22	Rebellions of Germanias and Comuneros in Valencia, Castile	1854–6	Spanish revolution led by O'Donnell and Espartero
1568–71	Revolt of Moriscos	1866	Failed insurrection of General Juan Prim
1580	Philip enforces inheritance of Portuguese throne through invasion	1868	Pronunciamento of Admiral Juan Topete, generalization of insurrection; deposition of queen, establishment of liberal regime
1591	Rebellion of Aragon	1873–4	First Spanish Republic, Carlist risings
1609	Expulsion of Moriscos	1874	Military coup, continuation of Carlist wars to 1876, then another coup on behalf of Alfonso, son of deposed queen Isabella
1640–59	Catalan revolt		
1640–68	Revolt of Portuguese		
1667	Seizure of power as Portuguese regent by Pedro, brother of king Afonso	1889–1908	Sporadic revolts, strikes and conspiracies in Portugal
1701–14	War of the Spanish Succession, including invasions of Spain and Portugal, civil war, ending with loss of Spanish Netherlands, integration of Catalonia and Valencia into Castilian regime	1890	Anarchist 'outrages' in Spain
		1909	Catalan general strike, insurrection
		1910	Insurrection in Lisbon; proclamation of republic
1758	Conspiracy of the Tavoras in Portugal	1912	Lisbon general strike
1759	Expulsion of Jesuits from Portugal	1915	Portuguese insurrection of General Pimenta de Castro, followed by democratic revolt
1793–1814	Intermittent war with France, including invasion, eventual dismemberment, rebellions in Latin America	1917	Uprising and seizure of power by General Sidonio Paes (assassinated 1918); defeated general strike
1801	War of the Oranges, Portugal vs. Spain		
1807	Uprising against Goday (Aranjuez)		

1808	Popular insurrection in Spain, partial withdrawal of French
1820	Mutiny of Spanish troops under Colonel Rafael Riego, generalizing revolution to 1823, termination by French invasion
1820	Revolution at Oporto, Portugal
1822–3	Royalist rising in Spain
1823–4	Portuguese civil war
1827	British landing in Portugal, supporting constitutionalists
1827	Revolt of Malcontents in Spain
1828	Portuguese coup d'état by Dom Miguel, followed by Miguelite wars to 1834
1833–9	Carlist war in Spain
1834–53	Frequent insurrections in Portugal
1836	Progressist insurrection in Andalusia, Aragon, Catalonia and Madrid, ending in constitution of 1837
1840	Revolt of General Baldomero Espartero, who seized power in Spain
1841	Spanish coup on behalf of Queen Cristina, defeated
1842	Rising in Barcelona, temporary declaration of republic, crushed by Espartero
1919	Royalist uprising in northern Portugal
1923	Mutiny of Barcelona garrison, outbreak of separatist movement, coup d'état of Primo de Rivera
1925	Attempted coup in Portugal
1926	Successful coup in Portugal
1926	Attempted coup in Catalonia
1927	Failed insurrection against Portuguese military regime (by 1930, Salazar in power)
1930	Mutiny of garrison at Jaca, demanding republic
1931	Spanish elections with large majority for Republicans; Alfonso leaves; new constitution
1932	Revolt of General Jose Sanjurjo
1933	Barcelona risings of anarchists and syndicalists
1934	Working-class insurrection in Asturias, general strike and insurrection in Catalonia
1936–9	Spanish Civil War
1974	Coup d'état in Portugal
1981	Attempted coup in Spain

that, the relatively peaceful transitions at the deaths of Franco and Salazar (despite *coups d'état* in their two capitals and guerrilla warfare in Spain's Basque country) come almost as anticlimaxes.

Rebellions of the Comuneros and the Germanias both occurred as Charles V and his Flemish entourage sought to establish tighter fiscal control over his Spanish territories and finance his election as Holy Roman Emperor. The Comuneros consisted essentially of Juntas that took over Castilian cities and their hinterlands in a refusal to supply funds to the king unless he would dismiss his foreign advisors, respect their liberties and live in Castile; when the Juntas were not battling each other, they drove out royal representatives, formed popular armies and fought the king's troops. In many towns, ordinary people attacked the rich and the nobility. The Germanias referred literally to the brotherhoods, or guilds, of Valencia, who spearheaded assaults on nobles and their Morisco vassals after many of the wealthy had fled town during a plague epidemic. Both the Comuneros and the Germanias became more anti-noble as the prudent nobility aligned themselves clearly with the crown. When popular forces met royal troops in the field, they lost massively. The king's representatives ostentatiously executed rebel leaders; 150 died in Valencia, 200 in Mallorca. By 1522, Charles could safely return to Spain with his German army.

Although Charles' son Philip II faced serious rebellions by half-converted Moriscos, enforced his claim to the Portuguese crown by force of arms, and snuffed out a serious revolt in Aragon as well, the next great Iberian revolutionary crisis did not arrive until the Thirty Years War. The renewal of war with France in 1635 greatly increased the crown's demand for financial support from all its segments. By 1639, Philip IV's minister Olivares was pressing Catalonia hard for men and funds to combat the French, who had taken the Pyrenean fortress of Salses. Olivares sought to billet a royal army in Catalonia and use it to force support for the military effort, but thereby generated vast resistance. In June 1640, a crowd of harvest workers in Barcelona killed the viceroy, the count of Santa Coloma. Soon Castilian troops were advancing on Catalonia, while Catalan leaders were negotiating aid from the French. The leader of the Catalan *diputació*, the canon Pau Claris, saved its authority by declaring Catalonia an independent republic. The struggle lasted until 1659, when the Catalans reentered the empire with essentially the same liberties they had enjoyed before separating themselves from it, although without the Roussillon and Cerdagne their French allies had managed to snatch from Spain.

During the Catalan revolt, Olivares ordered the duke of Braganza and the Portuguese nobility, who had not lost their hopes of recapturing ancient autonomy, to aid the Castilian assault on the Catalans. But that order precipitated a conspiracy in Lisbon, which led to seizure of the royal palace, the execution and expulsion of royal agents and the proclamation of Braganza as king John IV. For almost thirty years, Spanish armies tried unsuccessfully to subdue the Portuguese, but in 1668, Spain finally recognized the independence of Portugal (subject to a *coup d'état* in the preceding year by king Afonso's brother Pedro) as an independent power. In 1648, at the Treaty of Westphalia, Spain had also acknowledged the definitive loss of the northern Netherlands.

The War of the Spanish Succession (1701–14) next rent Iberia, as Louis XIV's ultimately successful effort to place a Bourbon on the Spanish throne bloodied the peninsula by inciting civil wars among the supporters of rival candidates for the crown. It also had the effect of integrating Catalonia and Valencia into the Castilian regime, while separating Spain entirely from the Netherlands, whose southern provinces passed to Habsburg Austria. During the eighteenth century, Bourbon kings tried repeatedly to bring the military under their control, but the availability of colonial revenues ironically undermined their efforts: in good times, kings did not struggle with their own subjects for income to the degree that their French cousins did. They therefore never created autonomous civilian bureaucracies that contained the military. In bad times, they turned to quick financial expedients that fragmented their power, obligated them to regional power-holders and allied generals with the grandees or municipalities that supported them. Spain's *capitanes generales* swaggered in their eminence and autonomy.

After the War of the Spanish Succession, neither Portugal nor Spain entered major revolutionary situations for the next ninety years. Unlike the Low Countries, Iberia resonated very little to the revolution of the 1790s in neighbouring France. Nevertheless, Spain joined the international military effort against revolutionary France in 1793–5. Then the Napoleonic Wars created one of the peninsula's greatest revolutionary crises.

Spain soon shifted sides. Under the direction of its virtual dictator, Godoy, Spain first allied itself with Napoleon against Portugal, but Napoleon quickly conceived the project of making Spain his satellite. In 1808, an aristocratic-popular insurrection on behalf of the king's heir-apparent Ferdinand (the Tumult of Aranjuez) forced out both Godoy and his king. The new king Ferdinand VII, however, soon accepted Napoleon's demand of abdication in favour of Napoleon's brother Joseph. (To be precise, Ferdinand ceded the crown back to his father, who surrendered it to Bonaparte.) Popular insurrections against French rule quickly generalized into civil war, guerrilla-style, with many local authorities joining the anti-French resistance to keep it under control. In Saragossa, for example, the great aristocrat Palafox – no revolutionary democrat, he! – accepted designation as rebel Captain General.

French advance into Spain, resistance against the French and the spread of liberal ideas among the resistants combined to facilitate widespread independence movements in colonial Latin America. They also moved the Spanish opposition to formulating a plan for a constitutional monarchy. As the British under Wellington were driving the French out of the peninsula, liberals in Cadiz were assembling to adopt an advanced constitution. At the return of Ferdinand VII from his French captivity in 1814, conservative officers collaborated with the king in an anti-liberal *coup d'état*. But that only started a struggle that zigzagged across the next sixteen decades.

The subsequent centrality of the military in Spanish resistance recapitulated, to some degree, the acquisition of privilege by nobles and municipalities during the Reconquista a half-millennium earlier: led by disputatious, ambitious nobles and little beholden to civilian officials, the army operated as a distinct political force – or rather as a cluster of distinct political forces, each with its own patron. The great autonomy and power of Spanish armies during the Napoleonic Wars then set a precedent for post-war politics, in which soldiers repeatedly seized the state in the name of the nation. A conservative-clerical-royalist bloc faced a liberal-anti-clerical-constitutional bloc, each with its own supporters in the army. The alignment led to a progressive dispossession of the church, a mild advance of liberal institutions and almost unceasing armed struggle. Serious divisions, with military seizures of power, opened up in 1820–3, 1833–9, 1840–3, 1854 and 1868–76, after which general strikes, anarchist attacks and insurrections abounded, but no full transfer of power occurred again until 1917.

Then followed six more uncertain years, a 1923 coup by Primo de Rivera, another eight years of militarized control and military insurrection and, in 1931, a relatively peaceful expulsion of the king and the military regime in national elections; the republic established at that point lasted five years before the outbreak of open civil war, although not without major rebellions from left and right alike. Meanwhile, Portugal lived a similar turbulent history: coups, civil wars and rebellions, up to the establishment of a republic in 1910, sixteen more years of intermittent revolutionary situations, and then the consolidation of power by Oliveira Salazar during the late 1920s. Salazar kept the Portuguese lid on for more than forty years.

Francisco Franco was to hold on to his Spanish regime for three decades, but only after three years of internecine struggle. The Civil War began as an attempted military coup from Franco's Moroccan base, but continued as a terrible series of raids, reprisals and revolutionary actions, even within the Republican coalition; while the decisive struggle pitted Nationalists against Republicans, within the latter camp communists sometimes killed anarchists, anarchists killed communists and communists killed each other. The intervention of Nazi Germany and Fascist Italy on one side, of the Soviet Union and an international corps of leftist volunteers on the other, stepped up the combat's deadliness. But by 1939 the superior military organization and supplies of the Nationalists had beaten down their enemies. For the next three decades Franco's Falange ruled Spain without serious threats to its hegemony.

In both Spain and Portugal, furthermore, the aging dictators of the 1960s made constitutional arrangements that eased the transition to limited representative government – a monarchy in Spain, a republic in Portugal – without more than minor attempts at revolution. Salazar died in 1970, Franco in 1975, without major succession crises. Nevertheless, in 1974 a Portuguese junior officers' *coup d'état*, fed by dissatisfaction with the state's enervating military commitment in Portugal's African colonies, generated a large popular mobilization against Marcello Caetano's successor regime. Portugal hovered at the edge of a revolutionary situation for two years, then drifted into the routine chaos of parliamentary politics.

In Spain, the Carrero Blanco regime of 1969 to 1973 attempted to rein in the working-class mobilization of previous years as well as the increasingly active Basque separatist movement (ETA). The ETA assassination of Carrero Blanco ended that phase, introducing three years of governmental vacillation in the midst of which Franco died. Franco's designated heir, king Juan Carlos, rode out a vast wave of worker action by steering the country quickly toward referenda and elections to determine the new regime's character. In 1981, a group of military officers, miming the country's normal politics of half a century earlier, failed in an attempted coup. Thus both Portugal and Spain saw last gasps of military intervention before settling into their versions of parliamentary politics.

In Iberia, the track from communal, patron–client and dynastic to class-coalition and national revolutions ran a bit askew. In the name of ancient rights, national revolutions insisting on venerable privileges and treaties rather than general rights to independence were already beginning in Aragon during the sixteenth century and succeeding in Portugal and Catalonia during the seventeenth. Into the 1870s, on the other hand, Portugal and Spain continued to produce dynastic revolutions in the company of class-coalition revolutions heavily involving the military. The Iberian timetable of revolutions corresponded precisely to the process by which states formed in that part of Europe. To recapitulate the obvious, the Iberian kingdoms of the sixteenth and seventeenth centuries remained segmented states sustained by rising, then declining overseas incomes, limited domestically by well-entrenched noble, municipal and provincial privilege, and repeatedly engaged in efforts to enhance their revenues, dynastic prospects and international positions through the tightening of central control. Their revolutions of the time embodied resistance of various segments of their polities to those efforts.

During the eighteenth century centripetal and centrifugal parties lived in uneasy equilibrium, but armed resistance to the French invasion and occupation after 1800 gave the military autonomous power they had not previously possessed. During the nineteenth century, and well into the twentieth, alliances of military officers with bourgeois fragments and/or dynastic claimants (now sometimes taking on a nationalist tinge in Catalonia) dominated revolutionary situations. With time, dynastic blocs weakened as class coalitions strengthened, but the military remained incessant participants. Their installation of authoritarian regimes after 1930, however, eventually integrated both Spain and Portugal more firmly into the world capitalist economy, a process which in turn generated substantial working classes and expanding bourgeoisies. As aging dictators relaxed central controls, bourgeois–worker coalitions formed and became substantial political presences. At the deaths of Franco and Salazar, their heirs had no choice but to deal not only with bourgeois–worker coalitions, but also with the remainders of the authoritarian regime and with their armed forces; their negotiations with the three created the politics of the 1980s.

Spain and Portugal, then, followed revolutionary paths diverging markedly from those of the Low Countries, not to mention from standard models of great revolutions. Perhaps the most dramatic divergence appeared in the rapid shift from relatively rare attacks on the state in the name of violated privilege to incessant intervention of the professional armed forces in the state's operation, often in alliance with one civilian contender or another. The creation of a professional, domestically recruited standing army after 1790 and the great consolidation of the state under French influence undoubtedly contributed to that shift. Yet some features of their experience are familiar from other parts of Europe, notably the increasing centrality of bourgeois–worker coalitions to liberal revolutions from the 1830s onward. As the states and economies of Iberia came to resemble those elsewhere in Europe, so did their revolutionary situations.

The Balkans and Hungary

Revolution followed yet another itinerary in the Balkans and Hungary, one that corresponded to the region's interstitial position. The Balkans served for centuries as the western terminus of great invasions and migrations from the Eurasian steppe and as a transit point for trade between Europe and Asia. Substantial mountains stood at the region's Adriatic and Mediterranean slopes, the Carpathian range arched to the north-east, while between the mountain masses the Danube and its tributaries flowed to the Black Sea through two plains punctuated by the Transylvanian Alps. The region's population consisted largely of small peasants, herdsmen, fishermen and warriors, although in the great plains landlords were able to assemble large estates and drive peasants into servitude.

For centuries before 1492 the Balkans enjoyed importance as a crossroads of Eurasian trade. Active commerce made it possible for principalities to prosper by taxing the flow of goods instead of drawing all their income from the local population. However, as the Ottomans began to conquer and to monopolize the trade and as Indian Ocean traffic began to diminish the importance of caravans, that strategy became less feasible; the region's states became weaker, and their nobles drew more and more of their income from exploitation of peasants. The Balkans' population, topography and interstitial location inhibited its integration into any single political unit, even more so its unification into a single coherent entity – although at various times Bulgarians, Serbians, Hungarians and Turks all made efforts to dominate the whole peninsula. Turks came closest. Even under the Ottomans, however, leaders of lineages, chiefs of bands and large landlords enjoyed great autonomy, at the expense of incessant, murderous competition with each other. The region's nobles and churchmen commonly elected their kings – often one king per faction – and would-be kings had to fight for their crowns.

Balkan kings usually took their thrones in the shadows of great powers. For most of the last millennium, the Balkans have lived at the edge of competing Empires – Mongol, Tatar, Byzantine, Russian, Polish-Lithuanian, Habsburg, Ottoman. Whenever one of them has expanded far, its local rivals and victims have found powerful allies among its rivals to check that one's conquests. Nominal Balkan rulers also faced serious local competitors: the nobles who prized their own freedom to exploit the peasantry, sometimes aspired to royal power themselves, usually played a part in selecting kings, and often served as profit-taking tax collectors for the imperial power. The Ottoman Empire graded its extraction as a rough function of distance from Constantinople and the insecurity of its military control, demanding no more than regular tribute at the peripheries of its conquests, installing systems of indirect rule (including variants of tax-farming) in more heavily penetrated regions, and organizing relatively direct extraction by agents of the state near the centre. Most Ottoman-held areas of the Balkans fell into the first two categories.

How far out a locality stood on the continuum affected the relative support of Ottoman armies and officials for princes or nobles; on the whole, tribute strengthened princes while tax-farming bypassed princes and strengthened nobles. As these factors shifted over time, the tendencies of princes to lead rebellions against the Ottomans and of nobles to lead rebellions against princes shifted as well. Those whom the Ottoman regime favoured, in general, supported the regime. One type of imperial control or another has prevailed in the region over almost the entire period since 1492. With the Soviet bloc shattered, NATO disintegrating and Muslim powers bashing each other, today is the first time in hundreds of years that the Balkans have lain vulnerable to only one empire, an exotic variety: the European Community.

As of 1492, the Ottomans were expanding energetically. They had taken Constantinople in 1453, Bosnia in 1462, Albania in 1467, the Crimea in 1474 and were threatening Hungary; by 1526, they were to occupy Buda. They were battling Venice for control of Dalmatia, Albania and the Morea. At their peak in the mid-sixteenth century, the Ottomans ruled almost all of the Balkan peninsula, including significant parts of what is now Hungary. In fact, Ottoman expansion and contraction set the major rhythms of Balkan revolutions between 1492 and 1992. Only after World War I did the region's inhabitants cease to live in strong connection with whatever power based itself in Constantinople.

The prevalence of conquest and territorial competition in the Balkans blurred the line between war and revolution more than elsewhere in Europe. Furthermore, the customary small-scale warfare of mountaineers and steppe nomads meant that some regions wavered at the edge of revolutionary situations – strongly contested state sovereignty – for decades at a time. Multiple religious divisions (Muslim, Roman Catholic, Greek Orthodox, Bulgarian Orthodox, Serbian Orthodox, Calvinist, Lutheran, Unitarian and more) grew up with new empires, then outlived them; as a consequence, religious and political frontiers became matters of contention longer and more bitterly than in any other large region of Europe. Would-be conquerors repeatedly found local claimants to state power with whom they could ally themselves. In a certain light, the Balkans have experienced revolution almost continuously for 500 years.

The Balkans of the last five centuries differed most obviously from the Low Countries in being much less commercialized and urbanized. They differed most emphatically from the Iberian peninsula in having fewer great landlords and autonomous cities but even greater and more shifting fragmentation of sovereignty. Those differences profoundly affected the pattern of revolution in the Balkans. There, communal and dynastic revolutions often fused, since when peasants rose against their lords, rival nobles were so regularly available to take their side. The sixteenth-century expansion of the Ottoman Empire, its station-keeping of the seventeenth century and its contraction from the eighteenth to the twentieth century entailed revolutions in which communal, dynastic, patron–client, military, national and even class-coalition forms merged.

Table 3.4 lays out the essential chronology of relatively large and long revolutionary situations in the Balkans and Hungary. The chronology presents only the high waves of a continuously stormy sea. It includes, for example, the major Albanian rebellions of 1910 and 1912, but omits the smaller insurrections of Albanians in 1900, 1905, 1906, 1907 and 1909. It shows us three main kinds of events: (1) succession wars of the sixteenth century; (2) peasant rebellions from the early sixteenth to the early twentieth century; and (3) resistance of local and regional populations to external control, from the Croatian rebellion of 1570 to the Croatian–Serbian war of 1992.

Hungary's succession struggle of 1526–8 illuminates the contingency of rule in that fractionated region. Ottoman forces inflicted a stunning defeat on massed Hungarian armies at Mohacs in 1526. King Louis of Hungary, a member of the Habsburg clan, died fleeing from the battlefield. Soon a majority of the nobility elected as their king Janos Zapolyai, a wealthy landlord and military leader. But a minority, including the widowed queen, opted for Habsburg archduke Ferdinand. Open warfare broke out between the supporters of the rival kings. In the short run, Ferdinand drove out Zapolyai, but in the longer run Ferdinand fought a losing battle against the Ottomans while Zapolyai (encouraged, indeed recognized, temporarily by the Ottomans) governed significant parts of the country. Under these circumstances, it is unsurprising that neither Zapolyai nor Ferdinand won. The Ottomans, *tertius gaudens*, did. By 1541, Ottoman forces had conquered Buda. Although Transylvania (with Zapolyai's infant son its first prince) remained as a semi-independent buffer state, the Ottoman Empire now covered almost all of the Balkan peninsula.

For the next two centuries, dynastic struggles often rent the empire's centre, but affected the Balkans only indirectly. In Constantinople and its hinterland, Janissary troops and civilian rulers competed for control between the 1560s and the nineteenth-century dissolution of the Janissaries; leaving incessant regional struggles aside, major rebellions involving Janissaries occurred in 1566, 1622, 1803–4, 1807 and 1826. In the Balkans, those battles served chiefly as opportunities for the assertion of local rights against the weakened centre. The French Revolution had few direct repercussions in the region, the Napoleonic Empire more: in 1809, France acquired from Austria what it called the Illyrian Provinces (Dalmatia, Istria, Carinthia, Carniola and territory on the right bank of the Sava). It rebuffed the bid of Serbian nationalists for aid against their Ottoman overlords. Napoleon's conquests demonstrated the vulnerability of states that had previously seemed overwhelming and ratified the principle of nationality as a basis of independent state formation. The acceleration of independence movements from 1803 onward marked a dramatic change from the eighteenth-century politics of provincial rebellion.

Numerically, struggles with current or would-be imperial powers dominated the region's events over the five centuries after 1492. The history of Balkan revolutions consists largely of the changing forms and participants in what (from the perspective of twentieth-century nation-state mythology) would be called wars of national liberation. Even the bourgeois-liberal revolutions of 1848–9 in the Habsburg Empire involved a very strong element of national liberation. Following Evan Luard's teleological terminology, I have called most of these revolutionary situations 'independence wars', with the understanding that before 1815 they generally ended with a suzerain, new or old, still in place. In 1803, for example, the pasha of Janina seized central and southern Albania

Table 3.4 *Revolutionary situations in the Balkans and Hungary, 1492–1992*

1509–12	Ottoman succession wars	1862	Military coup in Greece, king deposed
1514	Hungarian peasants' uprising	1862	Independence war in Bosnia
1515	Styrian peasants' uprising	1862	Independence war in Serbia
1526–8	Hungarian succession war	1866–8	Revolt in Crete
1566	Janissary revolt in Constantinople and Belgrade	1875–8	Insurrections in Bosnia, Herzegovina, Bulgaria
1570–3	Rebellion in Croatia	1878	Independence wars in Bosnia, Herzegovina, Thessaly during Russo-Turkish war
1572–4	Rebellion in Moldavia		
1594–8	Rebellions in Wallachia-Moldavia-Transylvania	1878	Independence war in Crete
1604	Hungarian resistance to Habsburg Counter-Reformation	1885	Pro-Bulgarian revolution in Eastern Roumelia
1605–6	Protestant rebellion in Hungary and Transylvania	1888	Peasant insurrection in Romania
		1896–8	Independence war in Crete, Greek and British intervention
1607–8	Haiduk rebellion in Transylvania	1902–3	Independence war in Macedonia
1618	Protestant rebellion in Bohemia	1905	Independence war in Crete
1622	Janissary *coup d'état* in Constantinople	1907	Peasant insurrection in Moldavia
1655	Seimeni revolt in Wallachia	1908–9	Young Turks' revolution in Ottoman Empire, including insurrection in Macedonia
1670–82	Intermittent rebellions in Hungary		
1683–99	Repeated wartime rebellions in Wallachia, Moldavia and adjacent areas	1909	Independence war in Romania
1703–11	Independence war of Hungarians vs. Habsburgs	1910	Albanian insurrection
1730–1	Rebellion in Turkey	1912	Independence war in Albania during Balkan war

1770	Greek rebellion against Ottomans
1784–5	Peasant rebellion in Transylvania
1803	Rebellion in Greece
1803–22	Rebellion and civil war in Albania
1803–4	Bulgarian rebellion in alliance with Janissaries
1804–17	Serbian independence wars (formal settlement only in 1830)
1807	Janissary revolution in Adrianople and Constantinople
1821–4	Independence wars in Moldavia, Wallachia
1821–5	Independence war in Crete
1821–31	Independence war in Greece
1826	Janissary rebellion in Constantinople; dissolution of Janissaries
1830–5	Independence war in Albania
1831–6	Independence war in Bosnia
1843	Pro-constitutional uprising in Greece
1848	Independence war in Moldavia
1848–9	Revolution in Hungary, Bohemia, Moravia, Transylvania, Wallachia
1852–9	Independence wars in Montenegro
1861	Revolt in Herzegovina, supported by Montenegro
1918–19	Bloodless revolution in Hungary, ending in foreign military intervention
1923	Overthrow of Stamboliski in Bulgaria
1935	Venezelist rising in Greece
1938	Revolt in Crete
1943–5	Anti-fascist resistance in Yugoslavia, elsewhere
1944–9	Greek civil war, Soviet takeovers in Eastern Europe
1955–6	Enosis struggle in Cyprus, with British intervention
1956	Attempted revolution ended by Soviet intervention in Hungary
1963–4	Civil war in Cyprus
1968	Regime liberalization terminated by Soviet intervention in Czechoslovakia
1974	Turko-Cypriot war, including guerrilla warfare in Cyprus
1989–91	Overturning of communist regimes in Albania, Bulgaria, Hungary, Romania and Yugoslavia
1991–	Civil war in Croatia, Bosnia-Herzegovina

for himself, then sought to add Greek territory to his new kingdom; the Ottoman sultan's armies did not capture and execute the pasha, thereby neatly ending the rebellion, until 1822.

During the nineteenth century, as the capacity of the Ottoman Empire diminished visibly, independence wars (frequently aided and abetted by other European powers) exploded throughout the Ottoman Balkans. The Russo-Turkish war of 1877–8 coupled with insurrections in Bosnia, Herzegovina, Thessaly and Crete; Bulgarians joined with Russian forces against the Turks, and thereby achieved independence under Russian tutelage at the end of the war. Romania, Montenegro and Serbia also gained recognition of their contingent independence. But at the same time Austro-Hungarian troops occupied the former Ottoman territories of Bosnia and Herzegovina. By 1908, the Austro-Hungarian Empire was annexing those two territories, thus frustrating the ambitions of Serbia to expand and of Croatia (then a subdivision of Hungary) to join in an independent federation of southern Slavs, literally a Yugoslavia. As the Ottomans receded, Russia, Hungary and Austria competed for Balkan hegemony. True independence remained illusory.

In the Balkans, peasant rebellions did not differ from anti-imperial actions so much as it might seem, since the Ottoman Empire commonly assigned rights of tax collection to warriors and landlords, who were the chief targets of such rebellions. The great Hungarian peasant revolt of 1514 was not anti-imperial, for Hungary was then still a relatively independent state; the Ottomans would take another dozen years to occupy most of its territory. But where noble magnates practically constituted the state and were using their power to drive the peasantry into greater and greater subjection, the revolt certainly had an important anti-state component. When archbishop Bakocz called for a crusade against the Ottomans and received thousands of peasant volunteers, he lacked nobles to lead them, and turned to professional Ottoman-fighter Gyorgy Dozsa.

As the army moved south and gained strength, however, its members began to accuse their lords of treachery, attacking noble castles to underline their point. It took an army to put them down. 'Dozsa and his followers,' reports Janos Bak,

were taken prisoner and, around July 25 1514, horribly executed. Dozsa, accused of wanting to be king, was 'enthroned' on a stake, and his companions, starved for days, forced to bite into his burning flesh. The quartered body of the peasant leader was exhibited on the gates of towns across the Plain. (Bak, in Sugar 1990)

Any enemy of Hungarian nobles became *ipso facto* an enemy of the state. Impaling, quartering and displaying mutilated bodies had long served rulers of South-eastern Europe as broadcasts of their power. In response to this rebellion, or using it as a pretext, nobles moved quickly to impose even deeper servitude on the peasantry by law. That servitude, one of the most onerous in Europe, lasted more than two centuries.

The Wallachian peasant revolt of 1655 took on greater importance than usual for three reasons. First, it coincided with a major financial and political crisis in the Ottoman regime, which could not find the means to support its large military establishment; the sultan had Grand Vizier Ibshir Pasha executed that year after his failure to restore order. Second, the rebellion brought together mercenaries (the Seimeni) whom the empire was trying to disband and peasants who murdered and robbed the region's tax-collecting boyars. Third, the Wallachian governor called on foreign (Transylvanian) troops to help him break the rebels. Thus by ricochet peasant rebellion against landlords took on national and international implications.

The Moldavian peasant revolt of 1907, to take a third example, concentrated more exclusively on questions of land. It began with demands for redistribution of the properties of large landlords and Jewish estate managers, and grew to a huge encampment of peasants around the city of Iassi. In the course of consolidating, peasant forces sacked landlords' houses, occupied land and created their own military units. It took the army and the reserves, 120,000 strong, to disperse them, at the cost of close to 10,000 rebels dead (Berend & Ránki 1977: 56). But by then Romania had become a more or less independent power squeezed between a still hearty Austro-Hungarian Empire and a receding Ottoman Empire. For a while, peasant rebellions did not immediately bring into play coalitions between outside powers and would-be rulers.

With the collapse of the Austro-Hungarian and Ottoman Empires, the end of World War I brought multiple revolutions to the Balkans: the independence wars of Bohemia, Moravia and Slovakia that eventuated in the formation of Czechoslovakia, the bloodless revolution in Hungary that ended in bloody Allied military intervention, the equally bloodless revolution in Bulgaria that ended (but only in 1923) with the violent overthrow of Stambolis- ki. Between then and World War II, only Greece lived through revolutionary situations. As Axis forces advanced and (especially) as they withdrew during World War II, resistance movements in Greece and Yugoslavia brought their countries to the edge of revolution; the multiple resistance forces then allied variously with British liberators to engage a full civil war in Greece that only calmed in 1949.

Whether the various changes of government then occurring within the Soviet zone of occupation count as revolutions remains open to debate. The struggle over Greek Cypriots' proposals of union between Cyprus and Greece (1955–9), which led to active British military intervention, certainly qualifies as civil war. The renewal of hostilities in 1963–4 and then in 1974 again drew Cyprus into civil war. The Soviet interventions in Hungary (1956) and Czechoslovakia (1968) terminated revolutionary situations precipitated by the local regimes' efforts at liberalization in those satellite countries. National and anti-imperial revolutions, then, continued to flourish in the Balkans. 1989, however, brought their culmination.

The Balkan anti-communist revolutions of 1989 proved that the region's states had consolidated significantly under Soviet in- fluence. The least consolidated were no doubt those least directly influenced by the Soviets: Yugoslavia, Greece and Turkey. With the decline of the Soviet menace, the inspiration of Soviet disin- tegration and the enticement of closer ties to the vibrant economy of Western Europe, Yugoslavia fell into fragments in a process initiated by resistance of ethnic Albanians to tighter central (that is, Serbian) control.

By 1991, Serbs and Croats had lunged into civil war, and the former provinces were seeking international recognition as inde- pendent states; as a consequence, ethnic minorities within those proto-states were mobilizing as well, forming alliances with co- ethnics in neighbouring proto-states. In Greece the parliamentary wrangling and cries of corruption that resulted from a complicated interplay of patron–client chains brought down Andreas Papan- dreou, but nothing like civil war broke out. In Turkey (long at odds with Greece over the partition of Cyprus into Greek and

Turkish sectors), ethnic Turkish refugees from Bulgaria weighed down an already burdened economy, the country served as a staging area for the American attack on Iraq, and the subsequent displacement of Iraqi Kurds gave the state new difficulties with its own Kurdish minority. Again, endemic struggles fell far short of civil war.

Things went otherwise in Hungary, Bulgaria, Albania and Romania. In Hungary, intense manoeuvring among critics and office-holders led the Hungarian Socialist Workers Party to dissolve itself and a reorganized government to declare itself the Hungarian (no longer People's) Republic, yet all this occurred without an open break in the polity. In Bulgaria, long-time communist ruler Todor Zhivkov left office in a bloodless Soviet-approved coup, a wild variety of state oppositions entered public view, and the communists began disestablishing themselves, but again no fully revolutionary situation developed. Indeed, 1989's closest approach to a Bulgarian revolutionary break came before Zhivkov's fall, in confrontations with Muslims who were resisting forced assimilation into Bulgarian nationality, then in the departure of some 320,000 Muslims for Turkey. In Albania, the palaeocommunist regime held on through the storms of 1989, but did not survive subsequent economic crisis and bleeding of refugees to Italy. Yet no open revolutionary situation formed there either.

Among these four collapses of communist regimes, Romania's was the most revolutionary in process, if not in outcome. Although mild signs of opposition to Ceausescu's authoritarian rule appeared earlier in 1989, the real crisis began with the resistance of an ethnic Hungarian Lutheran pastor, Laszlo Tokes, to government attempts at silencing his advocacy of ethnic and religious rights. When security forces fired on demonstrators against Tokes' removal, they drew the line between regime and opposition more sharply than ever. On Ceausescu's return from a trip to Iran a few days later, his calling of a Bucharest rally to display support for the regime gave an opportunity to opponents; instead of cheering, crowds shouted against Ceausescu. After a day of milling and manoeuvring, the bulk of the army joined the demonstrators as a National Salvation Front seized power, the dictator and his wife fled, other regime opponents captured, tried and executed them, and Ceausescu's security police gave up an attempt to restore their own order. Most likely hundreds died during one stage or another of the fighting. Romania's struggles had the face of popular revolution, but also harked back to the long Balkan tradition of independence wars.

Comparisons, Connections, Conclusions

The revolutionary histories of the Low Countries, the Iberian peninsula and the Balkans did not unfold in perfect independence of one another. Branches of the Habsburg dynasty figured importantly in all three regions. Napoleon's conquests reorganized states in the Low Countries, Iberia and Dalmatia, while accelerating demands for independence within the European territories of the Ottoman Empire. The Dutch and Belgian reforms of 1847–8, the Spanish and Portuguese liberal *coups d'état* of the mid-nineteenth century and the revolutions of 1848–9 in Habsburg territory all rested on bourgeois-led mobilizations against chartered privilege, drawing on a common vocabulary of popular sovereignty, citizens' rights and parliamentarism. All three felt the profound transformations of the European state system between 1492 and 1992: the consolidation of political power into centralized, differentiated, clearly bounded, but well-connected states, the creation of mass standing armies drawn from the civilian population, the increase of state capacity to tax, conscript, educate, adjudicate and regulate.

Nevertheless, each of the three regions followed a characteristically different revolutionary trajectory as a function of two principal factors: (1) the changing balance of coercion and capital within the region; (2) the region's changing geopolitical and geo-economic position. In the Low Countries, we witness the politics of a deeply capitalist land neighbouring powers that were far more capable of drawing warriors from their own soil. There, the changing relations of burghers to landlords, workers, farmers and rulers defined the possibilities of revolution during a full five centuries. Neither pure peasant revolts nor pure dynastic struggles ever occurred along the transition from communal/dynastic/patron–client to national/class-coalition revolutions. Yet adjacent states frequently invaded and intervened; Napoleon's fateful battle of Waterloo, after all, took place not in France but in the southern Netherlands.

In Iberia, the possibilities of revolution long resulted from encounters of opposites: the noble-ridden countryside with privileged municipalities and with coastal regions heavily involved in world trade and imperial adventure, the perquisites of empire with the fragmentation of sovereignty, the pride of royalty with the state's financial incapacity, the weight of bureaucracy with the autonomy of military magnates. In Iberia communal revolutionaries early took on a national edge, while dynastic competition stayed on to couple with both national and class-coalition revolutions.

In the Balkans and Hungary, expansion and contraction of empires based elsewhere set the intricate rhythms of revolutions. While dynastic struggles at the centres of encroaching empires repeatedly spilled over into local revolutionary situations, for several centuries dynastic revolutions only occurred in the presence of communal – especially peasant – revolutions. Communal revolutionary situations frequently appeared on their own when imperial power faltered. More distinctively, national revolutions appeared early and often, while until recently class coalitions rarely created revolutionary situations without a strong element of nationalism. The fact that the major landholders in Ottoman regions were generally Muslims, and generally withdrew from the region with independence, promoted that strong junction of nationalism with class coalitions.

Differences among revolutionary experiences in the Low Countries, Iberia and the Balkans immediately strike the eye. The most stunning difference sets off the Low Countries from the other two regions: revolutionary situations continued to erupt in Iberia and the Balkans up to the recent past, while almost ceasing in the Low Countries with the end of the independence war against Spain. Once firmly in control of the exiguous state, the Low Countries' burghers went about their commercial business without killing each other in struggles for political priority. With the partial exception of the revolution for Belgian independence in 1830–3, with its distinct tone of nationalism, the few subsequent revolutionary situations in the Low Countries pitted bourgeois-led class coalitions against aristocratic and/or royal central power. In Iberia and the Balkans, meanwhile, revolutionary situations opened up all the more frequently after 1800, with military seizures of power especially prominent in Iberia and independence movements salient in the Balkans.

If in all three regions national and class-coalition revolutions displaced revolutions based on dynasties and constituted communities, from 1492 onward bourgeois–landlord–artisan class coalitions loomed larger in the Netherlands than any simple chronological scheme would allow, while Iberia often fused dynastic and class-coalition bases for revolution and the Balkans produced Europe's largest, longest cluster of national revolutions. Thus the scheme (communal + patron–client + dynastic) → (military) → (national + class-coalition) helps in sorting out the gross chonology and revolutionary situations throughout Europe, but requires modification according to a region's combinations of state formation and capitalist transformation.

What modification? Most obviously the general correspondence between revolutionary and non-revolutionary politics in regions that varied from coercion-intensive to capital-intensive. Landlords, their private armies and the peasants they exploited long occupied pivotal positions in revolutionary processes where coercion prevailed, while bourgeois and urban artisans figured much more prominently in capital-intensive areas. The military means of rebellion varied according to essentially the same pattern: burgher militias crucial in the Low Countries, professional soldiers prominent in Iberia, private armies and guerrilleros prevalent in the Balkans. As a result, when class coalitions had long taken over revolutionary situations in the Low Countries, military revolutions continued to prosper in Iberia, and national revolutions broke out repeatedly in the Balkans.

The three regions' histories reveal the affinity of revolution and war. Almost every violent transfer of state power during the 500 years under review occurred during war, as an act of war or as a consequence of war. The Revolt of the Netherlands began in resistance to war-driven taxes and ended within a series of international wars. The Thirty Years War facilitated the great rebellions of 1640 in Portugal and Catalonia. Note the multiple revolutionary situations initiated by the Napoleonic Wars between 1803 and 1815 or the Russo-Turkish war in 1878. As Russia and the Ottoman Empire fought their titanic nineteenth-century battle, territories of the Ottoman Balkans began to break away or even to join the wars on their own. War and revolution not only stimulated each other, but also merged.

The correspondence between war and revolution was imperfect. Although military interventions secured the outcomes, for example, the Belgian Revolution of 1830 and the Austrian Empire's revolutions of 1848–9 did not stem directly from international war. Nor did each war produce its own revolution: the Low Countries suffered invasion after invasion between 1477 and 1945, but only a minority of the invasions produced more than fleeting divisions of the polity, and only a half-dozen of them initiated transfers of power. In nineteenth-century Iberia, the relation of revolution to war was strong but indirect. The build-up of military forces during the Napoleonic Wars and the collapse of Iberian Empires during and after those wars left substantial, autonomous armies with greatly reduced international military obligations; they turned their energies to the seizure of state power. Spain and Portugal scarcely participated in international conflicts between 1815 and 1898, but generated numerous forcible transfers of power, often with armed intervention by neighbouring powers. The necessary condition for revolution was not war, but failure of the state's military capacity. Nevertheless, that failure happened most often as a consequence of war.

How much does this way of understanding the relationship between revolution and the transformation of states illuminate the revolutionary histories of regions we have not yet explored? Do the great revolutions of England, France and Russia, in particular, look different through this lens? The next three chapters will take an unconventional look at revolutions in the British Isles, France and Russia. In each case, we will survey the entire period since 1492. But the analysis will magnify one century in each area: 1600–1700 for the British Isles, 1750–1850 for France, the twentieth century for Russia. It will aim not at a new model of great revolutions but at refreshed understanding of relations between great revolutions and their political settings.

4

The British Isles

Britain Encounters Revolution

British history now provides a much-thumbed manual for the avoidance of revolution, yet how well the demonstration works depends entirely on the times and places we place under scrutiny. If we examine England and Wales alone, we must indeed search back to 1687 for the opening of a fully revolutionary situation. If we include Scotland, the date jumps forward to 1745. If we expand our inquiry to the whole British Empire, we discover anti-colonial rebellions into the 1950s. If we turn our gaze to Ireland, we see Ulster still aflame today. From 1492 to 1992, the British story of revolution passes by many other channels, but begins and ends in Ireland. Over 500 years, English rulers tried repeatedly to subjugate Ireland, at the cost of repeated revolutionary situations and at least one revolutionary outcome. Vis-à-vis London, Dublin never quite gave up its independence. Today, pungent Ulster still gives Westminster its strongest taste of revolution.

Defining the British Isles as consisting essentially of Ireland, Scotland, Wales, England and immediately adjacent islands, then using the word 'British' loosely to describe all their inhabitants, let us ask how the histories of the various states that occupied the territory impinged on its revolutions. Let us concentrate on the great seventeenth-century time of revolution, but place its series of upheavals in the longer run of British state formation. We will discover deep transformations in the character of British revolutions as British states changed shape and as Britain's position in the world of states altered.

Let us also defy teleologies that make present-day Ireland and Great Britain natural outcomes of long developmental processes. We will then encounter contingency in states and revolutions that could easily have turned out quite differently – right down to which distinct states might now exist. Within the range of capital and coercion, we will see variety, from the concentrated capital of London and its satellites to the heavy emphasis on coercion in Ireland and Highland Scotland. We will watch Britain's emergence as a great centre of world capitalism complementing its rise as a military and imperial power. In contrast to strongly capitalistic state formation in the Low Countries as well as to relatively coercive state formation in Iberia and the Balkans, we will notice the British states (especially England) steering a middle course in which capital and coercion sometimes battled, but eventually joined forces.

The density and pattern of urbanization gives evidence of Britain's changing position in the European economy. At the end of the fifteenth century, south-eastern England lay on the western edge of Europe's densest urban field, the one centred in Flanders; Scotland and Ireland stood quite outside it. By 1750, the London region constituted one of Europe's most important poles of urban concentration, while both southern Scotland and the vicinity of Dublin belonged firmly to London's field. Since then, other European centres have arisen to compete with London, but the British Isles as a whole have continued to belong to Europe's major urbanized lands. In 1500, British cities exceeding 5000 people included Bristol, Colchester, Coventry, Edinburgh, Exeter, King's Lynn, London, Newcastle, Norwich, Oxford, Shrewsbury, Yarmouth and York – a dozen places in England, one place in Scotland, none in Wales and none in Ireland. By 1750, the British Isles had at least forty-five such cities, including seven in Scotland and five in Ireland; London alone had 675,000 inhabitants (de Vries 1984: 270–1). By 1992, the United Kingdom's urban population ran to 95 per cent of the total, while that of Ireland had reached about 60 per cent. With that urbanization, both the relative importance of capital within British life and the connection of British capital to world capital increased enormously.

In 1492, three important states and dozens of semi-autonomous jurisdictions (such as the Channel Islands) cohabited the British Isles. Except at moments of royal succession, the English state had acquired substantial priority within its own territory, while the Scottish state's control of its hinterland remained uncertain, and Ireland's faced contestation every day. All of England lay under its king's writ, despite the considerable autonomy of such great northern lords as the Percies, and although the state (as compared, say, with the papal states or Burgundy) could demand relatively little of its subjects. In return, it did little for them either.

English troops had put down Wales' last rising, that of Owen Glendower, by 1409. The support against Richard III Welshmen gave to Henry Tudor after his landing in 1585 cemented ties between Wales and England. England was thenceforth able to treat Wales as a royal apanage. In international affairs, Ireland acted as a fractious colony with only furtive, intermittent foreign relations, Scotland held a distinct position as a minor European state, and England was a European presence to be reckoned with. By 1492, English ships were becoming a major maritime force in both commerce and war. In both regards, England maintained strong ties to Flanders, then the heart of Europe's textile trade. Long peripheral to European affairs, England was becoming a major power, a process that also drove Scottish leaders farther into European connections in search of counterweights to English predominance and occasionally tempted Irish warlords to connive with foreign rulers.

As a commercial power, the English state drew a major part of its tax revenue from customs rather than relying essentially on poll or property taxes. Rents from royal domains still supplied some 40 per cent of Henry VII's income, but as costs of war inflated, Tudor monarchs relied increasingly on taxation (Clay 1984: I, 251–2). Of the state's estimated 461,500 pounds of ordinary revenue in 1610, 31 per cent came from rents and feudal dues, 54 per cent from customs and only 15 per cent from other sources (Kennedy 1964: 8). Until the seventeenth-century Long Parliament and Civil War, the crown tapped these 'ordinary' revenues on its own authority, but turned to parliament for the extraordinary funds required by war.

War became much more expensive as England's involvement in continental politics expanded after 1580. As elsewhere in Europe, the increasing use of gunpowder, artillery, siege warfare, salaried infantrymen and fortifications that could withstand all of them inflated the costs of royal armies and greatly complicated military problems of supply; it stopped being feasible to have each small unit supply its own arms and infrastructure. Three results followed: (1) the crown gradually alienated its own property; (2) kings and queens turned increasingly to parliament for revenue from land taxes; and (3) parliament gained increasing control over all royal revenues. In the 1640s, parliament overcame a long anathema to impose excise taxes on food and drink. Over the next few centuries, English commercialization made customs and excise the major sources of state income. Their falling under parliament's control gave the Lords and the Commons ever-increasing leverage in public life.

By 1492 the House of Lords represented the nobility and the church, while the House of Commons brought together landholding gentry and substantial merchants. With parliament's financial support, Henry VII and the later Tudors were able to build up substantial state power while reducing great lords' private armies. They also virtually eliminated privately owned fortresses except near the Scottish frontier, while building up the fortified places controlled directly by the crown. Henry VIII withdrew the English church from Rome, seized its revenues and expropriated the monasteries, which both augmented his income and brought the clergy under state control. From Henry VII to Elizabeth I, the Tudors checked English magnates and expanded the state, a process that incited a large series of rebellions but eventually enlarged the government's powers.

Like the Dutch a half-century earlier, the seventeenth-century English found themselves engaging in fierce struggles at home just as they were becoming a dominant force abroad. With the reorganization of state finances and administration under Dutch influence, they built a most unusual state: more top-heavy than its Dutch rival, but compact, credit-worthy, efficient and still relying on rather autonomous gentry and clergy for much day-to-day administration at the local and regional levels. The combination of a strong queen or king who wielded considerable control over the armed forces, a parliament that exercised substantial oversight of state finances, an extensive network of royally sanctioned courts, a rapidly proletarianizing rural population, a disappearing peasantry, a proliferation of small-scale manufacturing, a prospering yeomanry and a collaboration between enterprising landlords and merchants made England a formidable state.

Scotland brought together landlords, cotters, herders and fisher-folk. The country remained independent despite contested English overlordship, extensive intermarriage of its royal families with those of England and numerous English military efforts to incorporate it. By 1492, the Stuart clan had established a claim to hereditary kingship in Scotland stronger than that exercised by any family in Poland, Russia or Hungary. As insurance against English threats, Scottish rulers had maintained intermittent alliances with France since 1295. Those alliances did not, however, keep the English at bay. In 1513, Scotland's king James IV died in battle with the English at Flodden Field. His successor James V died in 1542 after yet another English invasion.

Nevertheless, Scotland prospered at the margins of French and English influence, veering toward a French connection as Mary Queen of Scots became queen of France as well in 1559, then seeing Mary's son James become king of England in 1603. Protestant doctrines made great advances in Scotland from the 1520s onward. With English encouragement, the Scots set up a state Protestant church in 1560 as a check on their absent Catholic queen. Her French relatives and allies, distracted by their own wars of religion, could not stop the change. (Between 1637 and 1660, revolutionary Scotland disestablished that church. In 1690, the new king William of Orange was to help engineer deposition of the Scottish Episcopal Church in favour of bishopless Presbyterianism. The first Scottish national church was, however, very episcopal.) But not all of the British Isles turned Protestant: Ireland remained a recalcitrant colony, Catholic in all but the great lords settled there by England and the small Scots-English 'plantations' of the north.

Ireland, an essentially agrarian land, lacked a single sovereign of its own. Its regional warlords maintained considerable autonomy, meeting in a separate parliament at Dublin that English governors controlled only with difficulty. Outside the English Pale (four medieval counties around Dublin), most people spoke Gaelic, not English. The Catholic Church served as a great connector of Irish people. As of 1492, Ireland had actually become more Gaelic since the Anglo-Norman regime of two centuries earlier had faded. Foreign and domestic opponents of the current English ruler often found allies among Irish lords, who on the whole still gained their titles of nobility from the headship of warrior clans rather than from royal recognition of their services.

In 1487, for example, an assembly of Irish churchmen and nobles had crowned Lambert Simnel, the Yorkist pretender to the English crown, king of England. Simnel launched his abortive invasion of England from Ireland in the company of Irish men at arms. Again in the 1530s, Henry VIII's chief minister Thomas Cromwell generated a major revolt in Ireland by attempting to displace the Anglo-Irish magnate, the earl of Kildare, in favour of an English deputy more beholden to the crown. Even when Henry VIII assumed the title of Irish king in 1541 his power did not extend throughout the land. Seen from the west side of the Irish Sea, Irish revolutionary situations – at least up to 1691 – look less like rebellions within an established state than like mixtures of mass resistance to external conquest with bitter wars for local pre-eminence.

Despite their incessant interaction, then, England, Scotland and Ireland had substantially different experiences with state formation. Up to the eighteenth century, all three histories require rather distinct treatment. From then on we must still hold Ireland's revolutionary experience apart in order, precisely, to see its interdependence with the political histories of England, Wales and Scotland.

If wars with England formed the states of Scotland, Wales and Ireland, both those struggles and wars with the rest of the world shaped the English state. Table 4.1 lists the major wars British states engaged in outside the British Isles between 1492 and 1992. The incomplete catalogue documents three crucial facts: (1) the incessant involvement of England in military action between the late fifteenth century and the recent past; (2) the expansion of British wars outside of Europe after 1750, through the ages of colonization and decolonization; and (3) the nearly exclusive concentration of Irish and Scottish armies in wars within the British Isles. Outside of Britain, autonomous Scottish and Irish troops worked almost exclusively as mercenaries. From the sixteenth century to World War II, on the other hand, England ranked as one of the world's great military powers, a condition that entailed armed conflict throughout the world.

Except for massive contests over French territory during the Hundred Years War, until the mid-sixteenth century England played secondary roles in European continental conflicts. From no later than the destruction of the Spanish Armada (1588), however, every major European power including the Ottoman Empire had

Table 4.1 External wars of British states, 1492–1992

1489–92	French–English war	1839–40	Intervention in Egypt–Turkey war
1511–14	War of the Holy League	1839–42	Chinese wars
1512	War of Navarre	1839–52	Intervention in Argentine–Uruguayan war
1521–6	First war of Charles V	1843	Sind war
1526–9	Second war of Charles V	1845–6	Sikh war
1544–6	Ottoman war	1845–7	Maori war
1549–50	French–English war	1846–50	Intervention in Portuguese civil war
1556–9	Franco-Spanish war	1848–9	Sikh war
1562–4	First Huguenot war	1851–2	Basuto war
1568	English–Spanish Caribbean war	1852–3	Burmese war
1585–1604	War of the Armada	1854–6	Crimean War
1618–48	Thirty Years War	1856–7	Anglo-Persian war
1621	English war with Algiers	1856–60	Chinese wars
1624–5	English–Moroccan war	1857–9	Indian Mutiny
1635–7	English–Moroccan war	1863–5	Bhutan war
1650–4	Portuguese–English war	1863–9	Maori war
1652–5	Anglo-Dutch Naval War	1865	Ashanti war
1655–9	Anglo-Spanish War	1867–8	Ethiopian war
1655	English war with Tunis	1873–4	Ashanti war
1663–7	Anglo-Dutch Naval War (French intervention 1665–7)	1878–81	Afghan war
		1879–80	Zulu war
1670	English war with Algiers	1879–81	War in Transvaal
1672–9	Dutch War of Louis XIV	1880–3	Basuto war
1675–6	English war with Tripoli	1882	Egyptian war
1681–2	English war with Algiers	1882–5	Sudanese war
1688–97	War of the League of Augsburg	1885–6	War in Burma
1700–21	Second Northern War	1893–4	War with Matabele, Shonas
1701–14	War of the Spanish Succession	1894	War with Bunyoro
1718–20	War of the Quadruple Alliance	1896–9	War with Matabele, Shonas

1726–9	British–Spanish war	1896–1900	War with Ashantis
1740–48	War of the Austrian Succession	1897	War in western Nigeria
1753–63	Seven Years War and its North American antecedents	1897–9	War with Ugandans, Sudanese
		1899–1902	Boer War
1757	Bengal war	1899–1904	Somali war
1776–83	Mahrattas war	1900–1	Intervention in China's Boxer Rebellion
1776–83	War of the American Revolution	1903	War in northern Nigeria
1781–4		1904	War in Tibet
1789–92	Mysore wars	1906	Zulu war
1798–9		1913–20	Somali war
1792–1802	French Revolutionary Wars	1914–18	World War I
1802–4	Mahrattas war	1918–21	Russian Civil War
1803–15	Napoleonic Wars	1919	Afghan war
1806–12	Russo-Turkish war	1920–2	Intervention in Greek–Turkish war
1812–14	War of 1812	1921–2	Moplah war
1814–16	Gurkha war	1939–45	World War II
1816	Algiers war	1945–9	Palestine war
1817–18	Mahrattas war	1945–9	Indonesian war
1821–9	Greek independence war	1946–54	Indochinese war
1823–6	Burmese war	1947–66	Malayan independence war
1824–6	Ashanti war	1949–53	Korean war
1825–30	War with Tasmanians	1952–4	Kenyan civil war
1827	Navarino Bay	1953–7	Sinai War
1828–34	Intervention in Portuguese civil war	1955–9	Cypriot war
1830–3	Intervention in Belgian independence war	1963–4	Intervention in Cyprus civil war
1833–40	Intervention in Spanish civil war	1963–6	Intervention in Indonesian–Malaysian war
1838–42	British–Afghan war	1963–7	Intervention in South Arabia
		1982	Malvinas/Falklands war with Argentina

to reckon with English arms. Starting in the early seventeenth century we find English fleets battling North African corsairs and European rivals in the Mediterranean while competing with Portugal, Spain and Holland in the Caribbean, the Atlantic and the Pacific. Furthermore, despite setbacks such as the independence of thirteen rich American colonies in 1783, the British incessantly extended their overseas territories well into the twentieth century. If in temperate zones it coupled armed conquest with extensive colonization, in temperate and tropical zones alike Britain held its empire by force of arms.

War became more frequent. If we break down the number of new wars begun by century, the distribution looks like this:

1492–1591	11	1792–1891	44
1592–1691	14	1892–1991	31
1692–1791	11		

For sheer frequency of new wars, the nineteenth century tops the list; for deadliness, the twentieth century, where two world wars outshadowed in their destruction any military actions British states had previously undertaken. The enormous acceleration in wars after 1790 occurred especially outside of Europe, in pursuit of empire. Only after World War II, furthermore, did wars of withdrawal from empire begin to predominate.

For centuries, European states have gained power over their subject populations chiefly in times of war; Britain is no exception. From the Glorious Revolution of 1687–9 onward, the conduct of incessant war in Europe, in areas of colonial expansion and on the seas expanded the British state's power. The establishment of a stable union with Scotland (1707), although it incited wars with Stuart claimants to the Scottish throne in 1715 and 1745, enhanced the state's domestic scope while increasing its commercial presence in Europe. Wars with American colonists, with revolutionary France and with Napoleon again fortified the state, as king and parliament collaborated in creating an extractive, efficient fiscal system. The army withdrew from domestic conflicts, concentrating increasingly on conquest and control of rebellious colonies, including an Ireland that now (1800–1) nominally belonged to a United Kingdom.

During the eighteenth and nineteenth centuries, British capital concentrated, the country industrialized, agriculture completed its proletarianization, cities swelled and population grew at an unprecedented pace despite substantial emigration from England and Ireland. In the course of fierce combats that stemmed from the conjunction of an increasingly demanding state with the growth of a capitalist world, the British built a great apparatus of state intervention. As compared with other European states, parliamentary institutions and voluntary civic commissions played an exceptionally large part in public life. Even in the twentieth century, however, wartime mobilization continued to be the principal circumstance in which the British state expanded and took on new activities (Cronin 1991: 2–4).

In Europe as a whole, the line between wars and revolutionary situations only became clear as states established clear priority within their territories, acquiring well-marked frontiers and strong central organizations. The generalization certainly applies to British experience. Early conflicts in the catalogue of major revolutionary situations (see table 4.2) therefore often straddle the boundary between war and revolution. By this count, civil wars and rebellions shook Scotland fifteen times between 1496 and 1745. English armies almost always took part.

When did armed struggle between Scottish and English forces become properly revolutionary? Obviously when we can treat England, Scotland and Wales as a single polity. But when was that? From the half-accepted fifteenth-century English claim to Scottish overlordship? In 1603, when a Scots king ascended the English throne? In 1657–9, during Cromwell's close, if abortive, union of the two countries? In 1707, when England formed a British parliament by incorporating the Scottish assembly into its own? Wherever precisely we place the transition, it is clear that the subordination of Scotland to English-British hegemony took place through lethal combat, remaining uncertain at least until 1746.

The case is even more dramatic for Ireland. English rulers certainly tried to dominate Ireland; they experimented constantly with carrots and sticks, especially sticks. Ireland became the major proving ground for forms of surveillance and repression, including the famed nineteenth-century police, that later found their way into Great Britain (Broeker 1970; Clark & Donnelly 1983; Fitzpatrick 1985; Palmer 1988). Until the early eighteenth century, Irish warlords fought each other almost continuously. In addition, major armed struggles between British and Irish forces broke out more than fifteen times between 1493 and 1969, with plenty of lethal skirmishing and raiding in between. They have not ceased

Table 4.2 *Revolutionary situations in the British Isles, 1492–1992*

Date	Event	Date	Event
1493–6	Irish rebellion on behalf of Perkin Warbeck	1595	Rebellion of Catholic lords, Scotland
1496–7	English–Scottish succession war	1595–1603	Rebellion of Hugh O'Neill in Ireland, Spanish intervention
1497	Rebellion of Cornwall	1608	Irish revolt of Sir Cahir O'Doherty
1504	War between English allies and their Irish opponents in Ireland	1639–40	Scottish rebellion: the Bishops' Wars
1513–15	English–Scottish succession war, with French intervention	1641	Rising in Ulster
1522–3	English–Scottish war	1642–7	Civil War in England, Ireland, Scotland
1532–4	English–Scottish war	1648–51	Second Civil War in England, Ireland, Scotland
1534–6	Irish rebellion of Silken Thomas	1655	Penruddock rising in Salisbury
1536–7	Pilgrimage of Grace	1660	Monk's coup, Restoration of James II
1540–3	Pacification in Ireland	1666	Revolt of Scottish Covenanters
1542–50	Succession war with Scotland	1679	Rebellion of Scottish Covenanters
1549–50	Kett's Rebellion, Cornish Rebellion	1685	Monmouth and Argyll rebellions
1553–4	Wyatt's Rebellion	1687–92	Glorious Revolution in England, Scotland, Ireland, with intervention by France
1559–60	English–Scottish succession war, intervention by France	1715–16	Jacobite rebellion in Scotland
1559–67	Succession struggle over earldom of Tyrone, Ireland; rebellion of Shane O'Neill	1745–6	Scottish rising
1565–7	Religious struggles in Scotland	1798–1803	Insurrections of United Irishmen, with French intervention
1568–73	First Desmond rebellion in Ireland	1916	Easter Rebellion in Ireland
1569	Rebellion of Catholic lords of the North	1919–23	Civil war in Ireland, Irish independence
1579–80	Second Desmond rebellion, rebellion in Leinster, intervention by Pope, Spain	1969–	Intermittent guerrilla warfare in Northern Ireland

today. In 1987, one side or the other in Northern Ireland killed ninety-three people. Another ninety-three political murders occurred in 1988, sixty-two in 1989.

Anglo-Norman warriors prevailed in some parts of Ireland from the eleventh century. Starting in the 1550s, English regimes deliberately established colonies of their own people – actually more Scots than English – in Ireland. They also systematically dispossessed Catholic landlords, especially after Cromwell's invasion of royalist Ireland in 1649 and William's invasion of newly royalist Ireland in 1690. As a consequence, Catholics owned 59 per cent of Irish land in 1641, 22 per cent in 1688, 14 per cent in 1703 and a mere 5 per cent in 1778 (Moody & Martin 1987: 201, 220). Despite the declaration of a United Kingdom in 1800 and the integration of the Irish parliament into the British in 1801, Ireland as a whole never behaved as a docile segment of a larger state; almost all of the time, someone somewhere in Ireland was actively challenging British sovereignty. Irishmen also battled each other for control of the Irish state, however subordinate it was to England, repeatedly between 1504 and the present.

Within England and Wales, revolution followed a very different history. During the Tudor and Stuart consolidations of power, England produced major rebellions: the Cornish revolt (1497), the Pilgrimage of Grace (1536–7), rebellions of the South-west and East Anglia (1549–50), Wyatt's Rebellion (1553–4), a revolt of northern Catholic lords (1569), two Civil Wars (1642–7 and 1648–51), the Monmouth rebellion (1685) and the Glorious Revolution (1687–9). Then, save faint echoes of Scottish and Irish rebellions, silence: no more fully revolutionary situations, with visibly fragmented state sovereignty, in England or Wales.

The people of England and Wales did not then retreat into decorous or whimpering compliance with authority. Eighteenth-century English and Welsh crowds gained fame for their unruliness, revolutionary cabals thrived during the earlier years of the French Revolution, agrarian rebellions in the old style persisted to the 'Swing' and 'Rebecca' revolts of the 1830s, rural conflicts recast themselves in later nineteenth-century claim-making of agricultural labourers, and Welsh miners continued to rage against employers until their coalfields started to run out in the 1920s.

Conflict did not subside, but it disarmed. Within England and Wales, the state's enormous predominance with respect to armed force restrained attempts to seize power while hard-fought bargains created means of strenuous claim-making short of revolution. Bargains included expansion of the franchise, relaxation of religious restrictions on office-holding, freeing of association and assembly and routinization of public meetings, marches, petition campaigns and demonstrations as forms of political claim-making. Even the vast mobilizations over Catholic Emancipation, parliamentary reform and Chartism between 1823 and 1848 occurred with much talk of revolution but little violence and no serious attempts to seize state power by force.

Struggles for Control

Sixteenth-century English, Scots and Irish struggled over serious stakes: who was to rule their lands, and how. Between 1492 and 1603, three overlapping sorts of revolutionary situations appeared in the British Isles: (1) succession struggles in England, Ireland or Scotland; (2) direct resistance to English rulers' claims for greater power and revenue; and (3) attempts to hold off royally initiated religious changes. Dynastic revolutionary situations, communal revolutionary situations and combinations of the two prevailed. Despite the strenuous resistance of Irish and Scots to English hegemony and the strong involvement of peasants and artisans in some rebellions, it would be hard to label any of the sixteenth-century revolutionary situations as national or class-coalition. As leading actors, succession struggles cast magnates and their clienteles. In resistance to new claims, communities of interest such as municipalities and guilds took prominent parts, while in religious conflicts communities of identity – Catholics, Calvinists, anabaptists and so on – led the way. Both the actions and the actors, to be sure, overlapped. Religious reform, for example, generally enhanced royal control over the personnel, wealth and policies of state churches. Those who resisted religious innovation were therefore defending both substantial rights and religious identities.

Many other sorts of armed struggles occurred during those turbulent times. Opposition to enclosure of commons or manorial waste, drainage of fens and cutting of forests all attacked the livelihoods of local people who hunted, gathered, fished or even farmed on land to which they had no more than customary claims.

They animated the vast majority of England's village-level revolts between 1492 and the seventeenth-century revolutions (Manning 1988; see also Charlesworth 1983: 9–16). In times of shortage and high prices, forcible seizures of grain also occurred from time to time, especially in London's hinterland and western textile regions, but they were almost always unarmed (Charlesworth 1983: 68–74).

These events fell short of revolutionary situations because they rarely occurred simultaneously, because the participants lacked substantial armed force and because at no time did rebels exercise sustained control over some segment of the state or gain other people's acquiescence in that control. Questions of enclosure, rack-renting and other rural abuses certainly arose during the period's great rebellions, but the occasions for clear splits in the polity consisted of enlarged royal claims, succession struggles and religious innovations.

Five factors account for those occasions' exceptional revolutionary potential. First, they inevitably touched large areas of the country rather than the scattered localities usually involved in struggles over rural property. Second, they all bore directly on the state. Third, they frequently engaged salient and widely shared identities as well as the rights or privileges attached to them. Fourth, they were likely to align some magnates, including lords who possessed their own military forces, with segments of the populace against the country's rulers. Finally, they were likely to affect many parts of the country simultaneously, a condition that greatly facilitated the coalescence of local into national rebellions.

Between 1492 and 1603, most major successions in Ireland, Scotland or England generated significant bids for power on the part of magnates whose future influence was at stake. Here is a case in point: the accession of Mary Tudor as English queen in 1553, at the death of sixteen-year-old Edward VI, stimulated a series of struggles. During Edward's six-year reign, under the influence of Protector Somerset, the English state church had moved significantly toward Protestant creed and practice. But Mary had grown up Catholic, and remained unmarried; hence great lords and churchmen recognized their considerable interest in both the person and the marital plans of the new sovereign. Anticipating the difficulty as his death approached, Edward had designated Lady Jane Grey, a Protestant cousin, his successor. The duke of Northumberland soon married his son to Lady Jane; at Edward's death, Northumberland proclaimed Lady Jane queen, but recruited too small a following to sustain the claim. He lost his head for the effort. Mary contracted a marriage with Philip, heir to Charles V of Spain, who was unmistakably Catholic.

At that point, a group of nobles proposed to match Mary instead with Protestant Edward Courtenay, a descendant of Edward IV, organizing a military conspiracy on behalf of their programme. Most of the conspiracy soon fell apart. Nevertheless, abortive insurrections formed in the West and the Midlands before Sir Thomas Wyatt of Kent raised 3000 armed men, seized some of the queen's ships as they awaited the arrival of Mary's husband-to-be Philip, and threatened London. The queen's forces held up against Wyatt's assault. Her courts then had Wyatt and almost a hundred of his co-conspirators executed; Lady Jane Grey and her husband also lost their lives. Only at that point did Mary establish her effective claim to the crown; she soon married Philip, joined Spain in war against France and began the burning of Protestant churchmen at the stake. Protestant conspirators had rightly anticipated what was at issue in her accession and marriage.

Britain's sovereigns most often made dramatic new demands on their subjects, thus generating revolutionary resistance, in pursuit of military strength. New taxes lay at the centre of their efforts. Rulers often preferred taxes to direct military assistance; the money allowed them to rent professional soldiers who would do what they were told as long as they received their pay, and when paid off would even depart. Private and regional armies, not to mention county militias, set their own terms for participation in military efforts, remaining on hand and under arms afterwards as potential threats to royal power.

In 1497, for example, Henry VII demanded large 'subsidies' in lieu of direct military support for his campaign against Scotland, where the Yorkist pretender Perkin Warbeck had gathered a following. A band of some 15,000 men marched from Cornwall to London in order to voice their objections against cash subsidies for the king. After a brief battle, royal forces won the day. Henry had the principal leaders ostentatiously executed and levied fines of 14,699 pounds against Cornish participants in the rebellion (Fletcher 1968: 16). From the royal perspective, one advantage of a checked insurrection over covert resistance was that fines and escheated revenues came to the crown. It also established publicly the right and capacity of the crown to collect the taxes it required.

In contrast to the Netherlands or, especially, various German states, British sixteenth-century religious struggles rarely pitted a population committed to new religious forms against a crown determined to preserve the old. On the contrary, English rulers generally led a reluctant people away from well-established beliefs and practices in the name of a renewed state church. In Ireland, English innovations encountered solidly Catholic resistance. In Scotland, it is true, Calvinism gained a large popular base before becoming the state church's creed. But concerted rebellions occurred overwhelmingly in the sixteenth-century British Isles not on behalf of new beliefs, but when the state sought to install new forms of religion that impinged directly on entrenched rights and identities. Only with the seventeenth-century Stuart accession did the situation reverse; then a powerful parliamentary group, not to mention much of Scotland, advanced austere Protestantism against the 'popery' of their kings. Religious divisions and their politics became more complicated because Ireland, a major source of soldiers, remained predominantly Roman Catholic.

Sixteenth-century religious innovations came from a state that was marking off its independence from the papacy, adapting to changes in Protestant thinking and asserting greater control over ecclesiastical assets and apparatus. Revolutionary situations therefore arose when important segments of the population openly refused to accept innovations, denying the state's authority to impose them. Similar divisions between state religious policy and popular practice, fortified by strong regional leadership from gentry and bourgeoisie, appeared in the Pilgrimage of Grace (1536–7), Scottish religious struggles (1565–7), the rebellion of northern Catholic lords (1569), the rebellion of Scottish Catholic lords (1595) and almost every Irish revolutionary situation from the 1530s to the 1600s. The period's religious rebellions more often drew on the entire population of a community or a region than did succession struggles or resistance to taxation. The spectacular Pilgrimage of Grace no doubt recruited the broadest cross-section of the population, aligning as it did whole communities of the North, including some gentlemen, against Henry VIII's dissolution of monasteries and then more generally against the king's seizure of the old church.

The great rebellions of 1549 combined elements of all three types – succession struggles, new royal demands and religious innovations – with agrarian issues that by themselves would not have generated large-scale revolutionary situations. At Henry VIII's death in 1547, ten-year-old Edward VI became king, with the duke of Somerset as Protector and effective head of state. That situation in itself created something of a succession crisis, especially since Somerset soon set about instituting Protestant-tinged religious reforms and attacking rivals who had gained substantial power under Henry VIII.

In East Anglia, local agrarian issues, including enclosures, incited extensive petitioning, discussion and action in the multiple encampments that paralysed much of the region. While rebels controlled Norwich and other large sections of East Anglia, they sought to correct those agrarian wrongs. Yet it was the strong connection with the 1547 attainder of the duke of Norfolk, major conservative property-holder in East Anglia, that provided an opportunity for a diverse coalition of anti-conservative yeomen and notables to form (MacCulloch 1979: 53–9). In that light, the cluster of risings takes on the profile of a succession crisis.

In the South-west, the burning question was the imposition of the English-language Book of Common Prayer in place of the Latin missal. In the course of the Prayer Book Rebellion, armed rebels held dozens of towns in Cornwall and Devon, besieging Exeter itself (if unsuccessfully) for over a month. The rebels' demands began as follows:

1   We will have all the general councils and holy decrees of our forefathers observed, kept and performed, and who-soever shall gainsay them, we hold as heretics.
2   We will have the laws of our sovereign lord King Henry VIII concerning the six articles to be used again as in his time they were.
3   We will have the sacrament hung over the high altar, and thus be worshipped as it was wont to be, and they which do not thereunto consent, we will have them die like heretics against the holy Catholic faith.
4   We will have the Mass in Latin as it was before, and celebrated by the priest without any man or woman communicating with him. (Cornwall 1977: 115)

In short, they sought abrogation of the crown's recent religious reforms – not a return to Roman Catholicism, but a restoration of the rituals and practices Henry VIII had retained from the Roman church.

Between 1492 and 1603, in short, succession struggles, rebellions against royal exactions and resistance to religious innovations directly reflected the ways in which Tudor rulers were reshaping their state. They by no means represented the only issues about which ordinary inhabitants of England, Wales, Scotland and Ireland were inclined to fight. Enclosures, rack-renting, ecclesiastical tithes and similar practices repeatedly aroused rural conflicts and rebellions, but at a much smaller scale than the state, and without any effort to seize or supplant the state apparatus. Revolutionary situations stemmed from those issues and divisions that had national scope. Transformations of the state strongly affected what those issues and divisions would be.

Conditions favouring revolutionary situations therefore differed significantly in sixteenth-century Ireland, Scotland and England. In Ireland, English overlords were merely trying to maintain their hold in a hostile environment, protect their national enclaves and make the country pay for its English-imposed military establishment. Meanwhile, Irish leaders formed alliances and battled each other in order to increase their advantages within the country. In Scotland, the English made repeated unsuccessful efforts to establish direct control over the state and to check the recurrent Scottish threat to their own Tudor dynasty, while the king and great lords of Scotland sought to defend their stake against English encroachment. In England and Wales, English rulers were actually extending their control over church and state apparatus, checking the autonomies and private armies of great lords, but still facing the menace of overturn or reversal at each succession.

By Elizabeth I's death in 1603, the British had created a substantial state in England and Wales, if not in Scotland or Ireland. That state lived, however, under great financial pressure. Rapid population growth was generating important price rises, which meant that fixed revenues bought less and less each year. At the same time, the English were actually involving themselves more extensively in war at home and abroad. The hiring of mercenaries constituted by far the crown's greatest cost, and they were getting more expensive. To cope with her financial needs, Elizabeth had mortgaged crown lands and ransacked the kingdom for bits and pieces of income, yet by the end of her reign England owed 60,000 pounds to the United Provinces and was having the greatest difficulty paying for its wars in Ireland and the Netherlands (Dietz 1932: 86–99). James I inherited a state under great fiscal stress.

Eleven Revolutionary Decades

Directly or indirectly, fiscal pressure contributed to the long seventeenth century's many revolutionary situations. In Ireland, the century began with rebellion. As Great Britain warred with Spain in 1597, Hugh O'Neill, earl of Tyrone, had joined Ulster lords in their struggle to oust the English. Despite Spanish intervention on the rebels' side, however, the English quelled the rebellion by 1603. Then English plantations on Irish soil began in earnest. Only five years later, in 1608, Sir Cahir O'Doherty led his own Irish rebellion, the last until the Ulster rising of 1641, in which Protestant Old English made common cause with their Catholic neighbours against intervention from London. Irish battles of 1642–7 and 1648–51 interlaced with the English Civil Wars, during which Charles I, tottering on the throne, enlisted the support of Irish renegades. After Charles' death in 1649, Irish leaders continued to battle against English rule, only to be checked bloodily by Cromwell's invading force.

At the invasion of England by Protestant William of Orange (1687), Catholic Ireland again rose in arms. In 1689, deposed James II landed in Ireland and joined with Catholic forces to besiege Londonderry. Irish people called the subsequent battles the War of the Two Kings: Rí Séamus and Rí Liam. The rival English kings met at the Battle of the Boyne (1690), after which James fled to France. His Irish supporters fought on with French assistance until 1692. From that pacification, however, no major revolutionary situation formed in Ireland for over a century.

As for revolutionary outcomes, a great deal depends on the time scale we adopt. If we allow a substantial transfer of power over a state that lasts a month or more to qualify as revolutionary, then we must no doubt certify as revolutionary in outcome the lost rebellion of Hugh O'Neill (1595–1603), since it led to the flight of many Irish Catholic lords from Ireland and the substantial seizure of Irish lands by Englishmen. Similarly, the massive transfers of land that followed Cromwell's reconquest of Ireland in 1649 constituted another deep shift of power over the state, the institution of a Protestant ruling class. The Restoration of Charles II mitigated the Cromwellian revolution, but by no means overturned it. Further confiscations that followed William of Orange's succession to the English throne simply consolidated the Protestant revolutions English overlords had engineered earlier in the century.

In Scotland, revolutionary situations appeared in 1639–40, 1642–7, 1648–51, 1666, 1679, 1685, 1687–92 and 1715–16. From 1637, Scots stood close to rebellion against the English attempt to impose Episcopalian conformity, forming their own Scottish Kirk without bishops. Only in 1639, however, did they raise armed force and seize a major outpost of civil power, Edinburgh Castle; the first confrontation with Charles ended without a battle, but the Second Bishops' War (1640) led to British defeat at Scottish hands, Scottish occupation of northern England and royal commitment to pay for the occupying force – a commitment that led to Charles' recalling of England's parliament after eleven years of personal rule. After the pacification of 1641, Charles fled to Scotland, aligned himself with the losing faction in a struggle for Scottish power, and thus abandoned Scotland to Presbyterians.

As civil war generalized in the British Isles, Scots generally supported the parliamentary cause, invading England again in 1644 and splintering into civil war themselves in 1645. By 1647, nevertheless, Scottish forces had shifted to alignment with Charles, who had allied himself with parliamentary Presbyterians against the army. Cromwell defeated an invading Scottish army at Preston Pans (1648), but many Scots moved to support Charles II after his father's beheading in 1649. Charles Jr. landed in Scotland (1650), where his supporters proclaimed him king and led a force back into England. The English did not stamp out Scottish resistance until 1651. The next Scottish rebellion came in 1666, when Presbyterians lashed out futilely against Episcopalian predominance; they tried again in 1679. In 1685, the duke of Argyll failed in an effort to raise armed support against English rule and episcopacy, but William's invasion of England in 1687 gave Presbyterians another chance.

Intermittently over the next five years Scots fought Scots and English, with the most common alignment being (Highlanders + Episcopalians + Stuart supporters) against (Lowlanders

+ Presbyterians + supporters of William). In 1708 James Edward
(the Old Pretender) made an ineffectual landing in Scotland, then
retreated hastily. During the Jacobite rising of 1715 which followed the accession of Hanoverian George I, James Edward tried
again, but lost without a major battle. The second Jacobite rising of
1745–6, during which James Edward's son Charles (the Young
Pretender) invaded England on his behalf, marked the last major
armed bid of Scots against English hegemony.

As compared with revolutionary situations, revolutionary outcomes did not flourish in seventeenth-century Scotland. Scots
came closest with the abolition of the Episcopal Church and its
hierarchy in the Second Bishops' War; Presbyterians gained official power they had already exercised informally. We might
equally place Cromwell's subordination of the Scottish state to the
English (1652–60) at the margin of revolutionary outcome. On the
line would also fall Charles II's restoration of episcopacy in 1660
and the return of Presbyterian hegemony in 1692. But nothing like
Catholic Ireland's massive subjection to English Protestant landlords occurred in Scotland.

In England and Wales, major revolutionary situations appeared
in 1642–7, 1648–51, 1655, 1660, 1685 and 1687–9. Two took the
classic form of succession struggles: the 1655 rising in which
Colonel John Penruddock sought to organize military support for
Charles II and the 1685 attempt to place Charles II's illegitimate
but Protestant son, the duke of Monmouth, in line for the crown
ahead of the Catholic James. All the others divided the population
deeply. All but the risings of 1655 and 1685 yielded revolutionary
outcomes – substantial transfers of power over the state. Their
cumulative effect, furthermore, left a lasting mark on British social
life: forming a compact, financially effective state, durably
establishing an Anglican ascendancy, containing royal power,
placing a parliamentary coalition of landlords and merchants in
substantial control of national affairs, leaving to landlords and
parsons the regulation of local business, promoting the proletarianization and industrialization of the country as a whole, advancing
the conditions for agrarian and then industrial capitalism.

That deep impact constitutes the principal claim of 1642–92 to
contain one or two great revolutions. The *précis* for Ireland and
Scotland have already forecast most of these features, for good
reason: Irish, Scottish and English crises interlocked. In 1642,

parliament capped seventeen years of struggle with Charles I by refusing to finance troops for the pacification of Ireland and Scotland unless he formally conceded major powers to parliament. At Charles' rejection of the demands, parliament's raising of its own army, and Charles' mobilization of his army at Nottingham, a revolutionary split in the polity had occurred. It was not to close temporarily until 1647, when Charles had become the army's prisoner but the rift between (largely independent) army and (substantially Presbyterian) parliament had not itself broken open. By the next year, the army had expelled Presbyterians from parliament, which left three intersecting wars to rage: Scotland vs. England, Presbyterians vs. independents and royalists vs. the army. The king's execution at the orders of an army tribunal (1649) simply sealed the divisions, which endured to Cromwell's military victories of 1651. At this point the revolutionaries emulated their predecessors by going to war against the Dutch until 1655. In 1655, Colonel John Penruddock led a small rebellion at Salisbury against Cromwell's arbitrary rule, gaining nothing by it but his own execution.

In 1660, after seventeen months of struggle between parliament and army had followed Cromwell's death, General Monk brought an army from Scotland and seized power to re-establish parliament, which after new elections invited Charles II in as king. More wars with Holland ensued. We have already watched the struggles of 1687–92 from Ireland and Scotland: at the birth of a son, quite likely to be raised Catholic, to Charles' openly Catholic successor James II, his opponents invited Protestant William of Orange to displace the king. As grandson of Charles I and husband of princess Mary, Protestant daughter of James II, William had substantial claims to royal authority in England. William landed, yet another civil war began, James fled and, in close collaboration with London's merchants, William and Mary established a new regime. By the end of 1689, parliament and the new rulers exercised effective control over England and Wales. The subjugation of Ireland and Scotland took another three years. For all the conflicts in Ireland and Scotland, from that point England and Wales never again saw a serious revolutionary situation – a real division of control over the state with armed force on both sides.

It is, of course, perverse to separate the histories of Ireland, Scotland, England and Wales as my account has; the tracing of revolutionary situations between 1603 and 1716 makes their interdependence all the more obvious. But that is the point: international wars, colonial rebellions, civil wars and revolutions continuously overlapped and reinforced each other. To single out the English Revolutions of 1642–51 and 1687–9 from the continuous flow of contention is to distort their character fundamentally.

Why did these revolutionary events occur? Although the thought makes historians wince, most historical explanation concerns what did *not* happen as much as what *did* happen. It consists of surveying what else was possible in a given time and place, in order to say why it did not happen. The 'why' refers to causes and effects, to choices and consequences, to processes that made one condition more likely than another. To explain the multiple British revolutionary situations and outcomes of the seventeenth century – here defined oddly but usefully as 1603–1716 – necessarily breaks into several tasks: specifying which events are to be explained; stating what else could plausibly have happened when those events occurred; explaining why those non-events did not occur; tracing the major effects of the events that did occur. Even in the extremely mentalistic form of history that reduces great social changes to the decisions of a few powerful individuals, the same logic applies: identify the crucial decisions; enumerate other decisions the actors could, in principle, have made; say what ruled out those other decisions; follow the decisions' consequences.

In the case of the revolutionary British seventeenth century, historians are competing in each regard: what is to be explained, what else could have happened, why those things did not happen, what resulted (see, e.g., Braddick 1991; Clark 1986; Hirst 1986; Richardson 1977; Russell 1982, 1990, 1991; Stone 1972; Underdown 1985). For us, the first part is fairly easy: we must explain the extraordinary series of revolutionary situations that formed and ended in the British Isles between 1603 and 1716.

Hypothetical Revolutions

What else could have happened is more difficult, but not impossible. In 1640, after eleven years of rule without parliament and several efforts to impose episcopal religious forms on the Scots,

Charles I's minister the earl of Strafford led an army against Scotland only to lose Newcastle-upon-Tyne and permit Scottish occupation of English territory. Meanwhile Charles was trying to get a newly assembled parliament to grant him funds for a larger Scottish expedition. Speaking of that crisis, G. E. Aylmer speculates:

> Strafford might have done what some of his enemies feared or alleged that he meant to do: namely to have some of the Country leaders in both Houses arrested and charged with treason, for having incited the Scots to rebel, even for having encouraged them to invade England, and for seditious correspondence with the French government . . . Alternatively, failing this kind of bold, perhaps admittedly reckless, preemptive blow, the King could at once have offered generous concessions, have played for the support of the Lords, and – as in 1629 – have given the Commons enough rope with which to hang themselves. (Aylmer 1986: 16)

Aylmer's type of speculation certainly requires intimate knowledge of the era's politics. The problem here, however, is not to ruminate about alternatives at the rim of each revolutionary situation but to state more generally what paths states and revolutions might have followed through that fateful seventeenth century. Considering the histories of other European states in the same period, we might map the range of alternative paths the British Isles could have followed into four possible paths: Dutch, Balkan, Iberian and French. The Dutch and Balkan paths are implausible, for reasons that are in themselves instructive. The Iberian and French paths are at least conceivable; examining why they did not happen helps explain how Britain followed the course that it did.

The Dutch course would have entailed devolution of the previously centralizing monarchy into a composite federation of municipalities and other jurisdictions enjoying autonomy within their own territories but retaining the capacity to act together in international affairs. The Balkan trajectory would have meant splintering into landlord-centred patron–client clusters, each maintaining a military establishment, some acquiring recognition as independent states, but all recurrently subject to invasion and tribute-taking of adjacent or indigenous empires. If the British

Isles had all resembled London and its hinterland, the Dutch path could have occurred. But the presence of Ireland and Scotland, not to mention the less commercialized sections of England and Wales, made such an outcome inconceivable. Conversely, the central influence of London and other important trading cities in the British Isles ruled out anything resembling the Balkan path of state formation and revolution. British landlords themselves had already allied and intermarried with the country's great merchants. Given the configurations of coercion and capital in seventeenth-century Britain, we need take seriously only those possibilities in the range of the Iberian and French paths – not precise repetitions of one or the other, but reorderings of state and revolution corresponding approximately to their recastings of coercion and capital.

The Iberian path would have produced a division of British territory into three distinct states, each sustained by a separate set of external relations and dynastic continuities. Ireland, Scotland and England-Wales would have maintained the individuality of Spain and Portugal, perhaps with their own rebellious equivalents of the Basque country and Catalonia. In terms of events, the seventeenth century would have seen both Irish and Scottish lords succeeding in one of their many rebellions and establishing a unified monarchy within their own territory, most likely with external support from France or Spain. (Sweden, then still a major military power, would have been another possible ally.) In terms of conditions, we would have to imagine a greater capacity of the English parliament to impose its will on Stuart kings as well as parliamentary willingness to let Ireland and Scotland go their separate ways. Oliver Cromwell did not display that willingness; on behalf of parliament, he led conquering expeditions to both lands.

The French path would have led in a quite different direction. By the seventeenth century, French wars (both domestic and international) had formed a relatively powerful central monarchy exercising considerable military, judicial and financial control over a large, contiguous, composite territory and population through the mediation of warlords, regional assemblies, ecclesiastical establishments and big-city municipalities that maintained great autonomy within their own domains. Seventeenth-century France as a whole lived under very indirect rule. The century's wars, however, moved France one notch closer to direct rule.

In the Fronde of 1648–53, shifting alliances of urban power-holders and great warlords opposed royal demands for greater subordination and financial support in connection with the enormous expenses of wars against Habsburg power – the Holy Roman Empire and Spain. With the vast rebellion bloodily subdued, Cardinal Mazarin acted vigorously for fourteen-year-old Louis XIV and Louis's mother. Peace with the Emperor (if not with Spain) aiding, he reduced the crown's demands for major war taxes, invented a series of fiscal expedients including the accelerated sale of offices, co-opted great nobles into the king's service and established regular royal agents in the provinces in place of the extraordinary commissioners, or intendants, dispatched by his predecessor Richelieu when emergency sounded, and whose removal had been one of the sovereign courts' strongest demands as the Fronde began.

The regularization of intendants was crucial; those provincial representatives of the crown enjoyed great discretion within their own jurisdictions, but ultimately depended on royal favour for their survival. Although they worked closely with established parlements, courts, bishops, municipalities and military governors when they could, their administration contained and diminished the enormous autonomies those power-holders had previously enjoyed. As a consequence, village communities, local landlords, parish priests and merchants all looked increasingly to royal administration rather than to regional power-holders as the effective government.

What form could a British version of French experience have taken? The French path would have required a resumption of the Tudor subordination of parliament, great warlords and outlying regions of the British Isles, including Scotland and Ireland, to royal rule. It would somehow have bypassed and/or co-opted the old regional magnates to draw local dignitaries into the royal web. We must imagine a Charles I checking the resistance of great merchants and landlords to the expansion of his autonomous military power, using that augmented power to dispossess or co-opt major warlords in England, Scotland and Ireland, and striking bargains with both parliament and regional power-holders that maintained (or even augmented) their honours and privileges while diminishing their power to block royal military action, international relations or dynastic policy.

Such a scenario was not utterly implausible. Many elements of the French scenario actually happened episodically in seventeenth- and eighteenth-century Britain: Charles I did, for example, succeed in ruling and financing his rule without parliament from 1629 to 1640, did in his last desperate years fashion alliances with parliamentary Presbyterians, and did retain many supporters among great lords in England, Wales and Scotland. As late as the end of November 1648 – two months before his execu- tion – Charles was negotiating successfully (if not necessarily in good faith) with parliament to retain his office at the cost of conceding broad guarantees for individual liberties. Only Colonel Pride's famous purge of 6 December annulled parliament's favour- able vote to that effect.

Britain did not, obviously, emulate France. Take the king's calling of what became the Long Parliament in 1640. At that point, a Scottish army occupied an important section of northern Eng- land and, like Mongols in Muscovy, had negotiated a tribute of 50,000 pounds as its price for not advancing farther into England. Many Englishmen, including something like half of parliament, sympathized with the Scottish opposition to the king's push for episcopal supremacy (Russell 1991: 164–70). The king now found himself in exactly the fix he had been trying to avoid for fifteen years: out of cash, in debt to many peers, absolutely dependent on parliament's tax power for payment of his debts and further prosecution of the war, no longer capable of dismissing parliament if it became recalcitrant.

Parliament did become recalcitrant. What is more, many of the king's most zealous opponents came to define the issue as a clash of identities: true religion (their Calvinism) against popery (the king's advocacy of ecclesiastical hierarchy and its attendant ceremony). That clash of identities had a material side, since the restoration of an Episcopal church carried with it the threat that those who had taken over church properties during a century of expropriation would lose their stake. Although France experienced several civil wars during the sixteenth and seventeenth centuries, no French king ever put himself in so vulnerable a relation to his lords and financiers as did Charles I of Britain.

What form, then, did the British path actually take? Later Tudor and early Stuart monarchs moved away from the organization of military force by direct levies toward the use of borrowing against taxation to buy it on the market. But they never secured enough control over revenues to assure maintenance of their military forces from one year to the next; during the Scottish wars of 1639–40, Charles I faced the recurrent prospect of watching an unpaid army and then (after Scottish forces occupied northern England) two unpaid armies disintegrate or mutiny. Meanwhile, rebels could typically call on direct unpaid levies of their supporters.

King Charles confronted a formidable foe. London merchants and financiers simply would not tolerate his attempt to extend royal prerogative into their domain, which they regarded as an unforgivable breach of basic rights: as Linda Popovsky remarks,

> It was the extraordinary conflict that developed between the crown and important members of the London merchant community during Charles's reign which ultimately impelled the Commons in 1629 to take what its leaders conceived to be the principled step of refusing the king's demand for passage of the tonnage and poundage bill and to denounce all who paid the unsanctioned duties as 'Capitall Enemies to the Kingdome and the Liberties of the Subject'. (Popovsky 1990: 45–6)

Faced with parliamentary resistance to his demands for financial support, Charles I dismissed parliament in 1629 and made peace with Spain and France in 1630. Nevertheless, he continued to build up the navy, pursued naval operations in the Mediterranean and sought to finance military efforts by means of an application of wartime levies on ports – Ship Money – to the whole kingdom in peacetime. At the same time he renewed his efforts to install episcopal authority in Scotland.

By 1642, Charles was facing armed opposition in England, Scotland and Ireland. He replied to vulnerability, furthermore, by extending his demands. Result: resistance that further exposed royal weakness, greater opposition, eventually open civil war. From that point on, four revolutionary situations flowed into each other: Scotland vs. England, Ireland vs. England, royalists vs. supporters of parliament, Presbyterians vs. independents. Within England, the largest cleavage separated those who were involved in London's commercial network from everyone else. Armed struggle or the threat of armed force decided the issue of each revolutionary situation. The creation of an unprecedented New Model Army in 1645, indeed, not only established the principal instrument of Oliver Cromwell's power, but rapidly turned the tide from an indecisive standoff with royal forces to decisive victories in England, Scotland, even Ireland.

Great Britain's position astride both coercion and capital underlay these struggles, but it also conditioned their outcomes. No one could rule seventeenth-century Britain who did not both enlist London's commercial might and rein in great warriors elsewhere within the isles. Even the mighty Cromwell did not quite manage that stretch. Cromwell's revolutionary regime lasted about a decade, then (after Cromwell's death) succumbed to its own internal divisions. Checking rebellion in Scotland and Ireland while warring first against the Dutch and then against the Spanish put great stress on that regime. Although it was more successful in raising customs and excise revenues, its large military efforts faced it with some of the same fiscal problems as Charles I had; by 1651, it too was selling off crown and clerical lands. Returning Stuart kings had even fewer reserves of their own as leverage against parliament and against London's merchants than their unhappy predecessors had enjoyed.

Proximate conditions for revolutionary situations include the appearance of contenders making mutually exclusive claims to state power, popular support for those competing claims and incapacity or unwillingness of rulers to suppress the competition. By this standard, various parts of the British Isles remained in or near revolutionary situations most of the time between 1639 and 1692. Why? In general, three circumstances promote revolutionary situations: (1) increasing discrepancies between what rulers demand of their best-organized subjects and their own capacity to compel compliance; (2) attacks on major identities and their perquisites within the subject population; (3) diminution of rulers' power in the presence of well-organized competitors. In seventeenth-century Britain, all three circumstances combined to create revolutionary situations.

Each time English rulers prepared for war – whether against continental powers or against rivals in Scotland and Ireland – they demanded far more from parliament than they could possibly compel. Much of the time they doubled the risk by decreeing religious conformity that attacked the identities and privileges of major power-holders in England, Scotland or Ireland. Each time their fiscal and religious demands misfired, moreover, their rivals took hope at the prospect of checking or reversing them, while their ostensible supporters gained incentives for defection from the royal cause.

Revolutionary outcomes result from convergence of a revolutionary situation with visible weakening of rulers' power. Revolutionary outcomes in seventeenth-century England, Wales, Scotland and Ireland certainly conformed to that formula: in England and Wales, failed royal attempts to seize fiscal and religious control led to enhancement of parliamentary power; the state grew stronger, the crown's relative position within it weaker. In Scotland, revolutionary outcomes chiefly affected the relative positions of Presbyterians and Episcopalians, which is to say roughly Scottish autonomists and anglophiles; when kings faltered, Presbyterians gained. Irish autonomies, in contrast, declined dramatically during the revolutionary century. They declined as a direct consequence of failed rebellions followed by fierce English retaliation. We must reverse the mirror in order to understand that the weakening of Irish warlords opened the way for what were essentially revolutions from above . . . or from outside. English commercial vigour contained Irish military zeal.

With the Glorious Revolution and the Hanoverian succession emerged a monarchy that could wield great power abroad and considerable power at home on condition – and only on condition – of engineering strong parliamentary support. After 1716, Hanoverian kings became past masters at creating patronage among lords, churchmen and gentry that would assure support for such costly adventures as the Seven Years War. At the same time, a significant segment of lords and merchants (the distinction was diminishing) developed an interest in British imperial expansion. The imperial reach of chartered companies, port-city merchants, ship owners and the royal navy augmented the demand for an effective central state. By the end of the eighteenth century Great Britain was collecting the equivalent of about 25 per cent of its national commodity output as taxes, as compared with 15 per cent in France (P. K. O'Brien 1988, 1989).

The great growth of state strength effectively excluded ordinary people of England, Wales and Scotland (not to mention almost all of the Irish) from power at the national level. Only the further expansion of the state during the Revolutionary and Napoleonic Wars changed that fact; then the state's enormous fiscal and military demands on its citizenry generated concerted popular opposition. Such leaders as Pitt checked the opposition by means of massive repression for radicals and workers, on the one hand, and considerable concessions to bourgeois-led movements such as anti-slavery, on the other. Both the repression and the concessions, however, trapped the state into collaboration in the creation of a public arena in which (on condition of using respectable means) ordinary citizens could voice their positions on major issues of national politics. By the 1820s, the consequent opening of the polity was facilitating large popular mobilizations, sometimes successful, around the rights of religious minorities, parliamentary representation, legalization of workers' mutual-aid societies and the organization of work.

Iberian, French and British paths shared a number of properties. In all of them, expenses of war – first of all, the massive Thirty Years War – consumed financial reserves on which monarchs had previously relied and drove them into confrontations with the capitalist institutions that alone could supply the credit and tax revenue required to support seventeenth-century military forces. In all of them, rapid population growth drove up prices to make the costs of state activity all the more burdensome. In all of them, the crown faced two-sided opposition: from bourgeois who resisted royal interference in their international commerce but insisted on veto power when it came to financial transactions; from great lords who protected their immunities, autonomies and privileges against the central state's expansion. In Iberia, France and Britain, monarchs could gain chiefly from playing the one opposition against the other. But that was by no means always possible, especially where the two oppositions met and sometimes allied in a national assembly.

Why, then, did the British path win out over the Iberian path, the French path and other hypothetical alternatives in their vicinity? In his *Behemoth*, completed around 1668, Thomas Hobbes gave an important clue:

B. But how could the King find money to pay such an army as was necessary for him against the Parliament?
A. Neither the King nor Parliament had much money at that time in their own hands, but were fain to rely upon the

benevolence of those that took their parts. Wherein (I confess) the Parliament had a mighty great advantage. Those that helped the King in that kind were only lords and gentlemen, which, not approving the proceedings of the Parliament, were willing to undertake the payment, every one, of a certain number of horse; which cannot be thought any great assistance, the persons that paid them being so few. For other moneys that the King then had, I have not heard of any, but what he borrowed upon jewels in the Low Countries. Whereas the Parliament had a very plentiful contribution, not only from London, but generally from their faction in all other places of England, upon certain propositions (published by the Lords and Commons in June 1642, at what time they had newly voted that the King intended to make war upon them) for bringing in of money or plate to maintain horse and horsemen, and to buy arms for the preservation of the public peace, and for the defence of the King and both Houses of Parliament; for the repayment of which money and plate, they were to have the public faith. (Hobbes 1990: 112–13)

In short, the access of parliament to London's commercial network, both internal and external, gave it crucial advantages in a world where military force had begun to depend on financial solidity. To that limited extent the seventeenth-century upheavals rightly gained the reputation of bourgeois revolutions.

Revolution's Dulled Edge

Except for the landings of Stuart pretenders in 1715 and 1745, neither Scotland, England nor Wales experienced a serious revolutionary situation after 1691. The revolution-renewed state endured many stresses after then, including the impact of war on a far larger scale than seventeenth-century statesmen ever conceived. But the creation of formidable military and imperial machines, the system of indirect rule through gentry and clergymen that prevailed into the nineteenth century, the increasing strength of a parliament based on the fusion of landed and commercial power, and the co-optation of a Scottish ruling class that was increasingly drawn into the same capitalist networks as England's all worked to reduce the likelihood that a viable alternative to the existing government would form. From that point on, Scottish, Welsh and English challengers to state power and policy frequently appeared, but they bid chiefly for the protection or establishment of rights within the existing system. Hence the enormous eighteenth-century importance of 'rights of freeborn Englishmen'. Even the vociferous movement of support for the French Revolution of 1789 led by such figures as Thomas Paine, Richard Price and Joseph Priestley called chiefly for popular sovereignty as the granting of rights already inherent in the British system but unfortunately stifled by eighteenth-century corruption. After 1691, revolutionary challenges did not come from England, Wales or Scotland, but from Ireland.

The most serious threat to the state's continuity after 1691 formed, indeed, in Ireland. Pacified Ireland continued as a colony, its government split between a parliament limited to Protestants and an administration imposed by Westminster. Although British governors came to tolerate Catholic religious observance, from the Glorious Revolution British law excluded Catholics from public office. In 1782–3, as an indirect consequence of British losses in North America, the Irish parliament received expanded power and autonomy. Then in 1800–1 the British moved instead to incorporate Irish Protestants directly into the British parliament, a measure that made the political inequality between Irish Catholics and Protestants all the more acute. Protestant lords held the great bulk of the land, while, except in Ulster, those who worked it were overwhelmingly Catholic. Meanwhile, Irishmen continued as warriors, now supplying great numbers of mercenaries to continental armies, including the French armies against which the British warred repeatedly between 1688 and 1815.

Under pressure of its American wars, the British government overcame its repugnance to arming Catholic Irishmen in the 1770s. In compensation the Catholic Relief Act of 1778 granted a few concessions to Catholics, including the right of Catholic soldiers to swear allegiance to the crown without abjuring their faith. Proposals to extend those concessions in Scotland and England incited major struggles in Great Britain, including London's Gordon Riots of 1780. At the same time, armed Protestant Volunteers who formed to protect the home front while Irish soldiers were fighting in America became a significant force in Irish national politics.

Two forms of local conflict intersected. On one side, tenants fought landlords and their agents in one of Europe's most enduring agrarian struggles; both Protestants and Catholics formed groups to resist rack-renting and dispossession. They took such names as Whiteboys and Hearts of Oak. On the other, Catholic raiders (more often based in towns and among agrarian middlemen) repeatedly attacked local symbols, instruments and representatives of British rule. During the 1790s, a much more centralized force, the United Irishmen, organized in Belfast, Dublin and elsewhere. At first the United Irishmen agitated openly for parliamentary reform, an agitation that contributed to the extension of Catholic rights in 1792. Catholics finally gained the franchise in Ireland after a century of exclusion. Under the leadership of Wolfe Tone, however, they moved toward insurrection and collaboration with Britain's French enemy.

In 1796, a French invasion force failed to reach Ireland and junction with the United Irishmen. Duly warned, the British sent new military forces in for ferocious repression of the United Irishmen. In May 1798, the United Irishmen engaged in a series of desperate but poorly coordinated regional rebellions; some 30,000 soldiers and civilians died as a direct consequence of military action. The rebellions had collapsed before French expeditions arrived in August and September. British forces captured the French ship on which Wolfe Tone was serving, tried him, convicted him, but lost their opportunity for an exemplary execution when he killed himself in November 1798. An attempt by Robert Emmet to stage a sequel in 1803 dissolved in little more than a Dublin street demonstration and Emmet's execution. If it fell far short of shaking British power in Ireland or Great Britain, the United Irishmen's insurrection of 1798 constituted the most serious revolutionary threat faced by the eighteenth- or nineteenth-century state. It led directly to Pitt's successful effort to form a co-optative United Kingdom in 1800-1.

Ireland returned to bifurcated politics: great campaigns for Catholic Emancipation, then for varying degrees of independence, at a national and international scale, guerrilla warfare against landlords and dignitaries at a local and regional scale. Although both had large followings, neither approached the edge of revolution during the nineteenth century. An 1848 attempt at insurrection by activists of Young Ireland ended in dismal failure, but left a network of revolutionaries who ten years later organized the Fenians in both Ireland and the United States. The Fenian rising of 1867 again fell far short of serious threat to established authority.

Occasionally the two forks crossed, as in the Land War of 1879–82, when demonstrations, boycotts and protective actions formed against evictions and rent rises at the same time as raiders attacked the properties of landlords. Both had their effects, one in moving parliament toward weakening of the Protestant establishment and the redistribution of property, the other in defining Ireland as ungovernable at a distance.

By 1914, Ulster's Unionists and southern Ireland's anti-British militants were arming, drilling and threatening one another. During World War I, Irish nationalists took advantage of Britain's distraction and of Irish opposition to the prospect of military conscription by taking arms and declaring a republic, only to suffer massive repression. That repression, however, drew the line between England and Ireland more clearly than ever before, facilitating the post-war mobilization of Sinn Féin – long present as a critical minority – as the Irish national party. Sinn Féin committed itself openly to independence. By 1919, Britain and Ireland were again at war, this time in the deadly interplay of guerrilla warfare and reprisals. By 1921, they had negotiated a treaty that gave dominion status to an Irish Free State, from which the voters of Northern Ireland quickly opted out.

Within Northern Ireland, guerrilla warfare resumed, continuing intermittently to the present. In the South, defenders of the treaty with Great Britain fought advocates of a republic in an open civil war lasting until 1923. Between 1937 and 1949 the Irish Free State occupied an ambiguous position at the edge of the British Empire, remaining neutral during World War II. In 1949 the Irish parliament (Dáil) declared its state a republic and thereby severed its uncertain ties to the Commonwealth. The separation occurred with great emotion, but without an open revolutionary situation.

The United Kingdom, however, still claimed control of six counties in Northern Ireland. Starting in 1968, civil rights marches on behalf of the Catholic minority led to violent confrontations with police and Protestant counter-demonstrators, until the British government sent in troops the following year. Although the struggle has waxed and waned, every year since then has seen guerrilla warfare among British troops, Protestant activists, segments of the Irish Republican Army and other armed forces on all sides. British authorities have tried many combinations of repression, conciliation and subvention, but none has ended the state of civil war. Given the continued existence of villages and neighbourhoods in which British authority does not effectively run, we can reasonably consider the entire period from 1969 to 1992 a continuous revolutionary situation in Northern Ireland.

In squinting retrospect, the history of relations between Ireland and England looks like one long nationalist revolution. Unquestionably some Irish people were struggling against English control at almost every point between 1492 and 1992. Nevertheless, we should notice the profound change in the organization of Irish revolutions over the 500 years. During the sixteenth and seventeenth centuries, the effective units of collective action in Ireland consisted largely of patron–client chains led by warlords. No one of them ever established clear priority over the rest; utter independence from England would therefore have posed a fearsome question: who shall rule here? From the top, Irish struggles and rebellions fall clearly into the category of dynastic revolutionary situations.

As the English gained power and systematically displaced Catholic landlords, dynastic revolutionary situations joined with communal revolutionary situations in which local populations defended their Catholic identities against outsiders. Only during the nineteenth century, as class-coalition and national revolutions were generalizing elsewhere in Europe, do we see a popularization of the Irish cause at a national level. Such organizers of mass associations as Daniel O'Connell forwarded that popularization, as the formal incorporation of Ireland into the United Kingdom dramatized its stakes. To the extent that it united Catholics of diverse classes against Protestant landlords, the revolutionary mobilization partook of class-coalition politics as well. But on the whole national solidarities – the claim that a homogeneous, oppressed people deserved their own independent state – prevailed. Changes in the actual character of the Irish and British states caused the evolution from dynastic and communal to national revolutions.

What of the British Isles as a whole? We might schematize the political histories of the three principal British states in rough phases, shown in table 4.3. The scheme is a drastic simplification, but it serves to contrast the partial merger of England, Wales and

Table 4.3 Political histories of the three British states, 1492–1992

Years	England and Wales	Scotland	Ireland
1492–1603	aggressive, turbulent state expansion	struggle with England, modest state expansion	fragmented territory of conquest
1603–1714	revolutionary struggle and consolidation	consolidation, struggle, incorporation in Britain	resistant but increasingly settled and controlled colony
1714–1815	expanding, war-making, conquering state	weakening resistance, increasing incorporation	negotiation, guerrilla warfare, partial incorporation in Britain
1815–1914	consolidation of capitalist, imperial state	state expansion, contained conflict	guerrilla warfare, economic turmoil, semi-colonial position
1914–1945	capitalist empire dominated by war	centralization and extension of state	guerrilla warfare to independence wars, state consolidation, contained struggle
1945–1992	disintegrating empire, capitalist welfare state, political stalemate	modest devolution, economic decay, contained conflict	state expansion in South, guerrilla warfare in North

Scotland with the perpetual distinctness of Ireland; the mild nationalist movements of the 1960s and thereafter in Scotland and Wales did little to change the contrast.

These transformations of British states and their military power deeply altered the character of revolutionary situations and outcomes between 1492 and 1992. Except in Ireland, the overwhelming increase in the military strength of the state vis-à-vis its citizens after 1689 contained any possibility that an effective revolutionary coalition could form; struggle continued, but within the channels set by relative consensus among the ruling classes. The growing prominence of parliament similarly channelled popular politics into efforts to influence national legislation rather than to attack holders of power. The bargains struck with ordinary people in the course of the state's military expansion between 1750 and 1900 – rights of association, expansion of suffrage, beginnings of welfare legislation – created some elements of democracy and a popular stake in the system. As a result, serious revolutionary situations disappeared from England, Wales and Scotland as they recurred, and continue to recur, in Ireland.

5

France and Other Frances

Bretons vs. Frenchmen

In July 1488, the army that duke Francis II of Brittany assembled to defend his sovereign state against French assault included 6400 Bretons, but it also numbered 3500 Spaniards, 800 Germans and 400 Englishmen. They faced a well-armed French force of 15,000 men: French, Swiss and Neapolitan. It was not the first time, by any means, that 'Breton' and 'French' forces had met in pitched battle, but it was one of the last. The Breton side left 6000 dead on the field, the French 1500. With that battle and Francis II's death not long afterward, the French crown acquired almost definitive control over its small seafaring neighbour after centuries of struggle.

France's king Charles VIII, to be sure, did not read the combat of 1488 as a war between sovereign states. During the thirteenth and fourteenth centuries, Breton dukes had repeatedly recognized their feudal subordination to France. For a century or more, litigants in Breton courts had been appealing cases to the parlement of Paris, a connection that supplemented the French king's claim to suzerainty in Brittany. When Brittany's duke declared his own parlement sovereign in 1485, the French crown instituted proceedings that led its Chamber of Peers to convict Francis II *in absentia* of high treason (1488). That conviction justified the French assault on Brittany. Vigour in vindictiveness is a notable attribute of conquering kings.

It was a time of muscle-flexing for France. For forty years French kings Charles VII, Louis XI and Charles VIII had been stitching back together a realm badly rent by the Hundred Years War. Anjou, Bar, Maine and Provence had recently come under the crown's direct control. In the 1490s not only Brittany, but also Burgundy, Naples and Milan were entering its grasp. Spain's Ferdinand and Isabella, Maximilian of Habsburg (soon to be Holy Roman Emperor) and king Henry VII of England all strove to contain French expansion; they had all aided the Breton cause, but had been unable to stem French arms so close to home. One condition of the 1488 Treaty of Sablé between Brittany and France was the expulsion of all foreign troops from Brittany, another the French king's veto over prospective husbands for twelve-year-old heiress Anne de Bretagne.

Soon after Anne's coronation in 1489, Brittany broke into a triangular war among her supporters, French forces and a coalition of great Breton lords who had their own claims to control Anne's marriage and succession; Habsburg and Tudor armies again intervened, now ostensibly on Anne's behalf. Yet the French prevailed one more time, this time for good. After a dizzying series of realignments, negotiations and intimidations, Anne married France's king Charles VIII in 1491. (Just to be sure, at Charles' death in 1498, his uncle and successor Louis XII also married Anne de Bretagne, for which manoeuvre he had to secure a scandalous annulment of his previous marriage to Jeanne, daughter of Louis XI.) Charles bought off Spain with the cession of Roussillon and Cerdagne while purchasing peace with the Empire and England as well. Soon he took advantage of his solidified position in a great invasion of Italy. French kings were deeply involved in their ultimately unsuccessful Italian conquests over the next forty years.

Question: Were the Breton struggles of 1488–91 revolutionary? *Answer*: As usual, it all depends what you mean by revolution. This time it turns out to depend especially on whether we regard the Brittany of that time as part of France – precisely what the participants were fighting about! To the extent that we think of France in 1488 as a unitary state including Brittany and of the supporters of Brittany's duke Francis II as its disloyal subjects, we define the Breton situation as revolutionary. By the *de facto* subjugation of Brittany to the French throne (finally made *de jure* by the union treaty of 1532), we might even characterize the outcome of 1491 as revolutionary. To the extent that we consider Brittany and France to have been two distinct sovereign states, however, we move toward a picture of 1488–91 as a set of international wars paralleled by civil war within Brittany, ending in conquest of one state by the other.

These ultimately arbitrary definitional decisions matter less than the political circumstances they bring to light. Late fifteenth-century France did not consist of a neatly bounded territory governed by a well-seated central administration, but of composite lands variously and often contingently attached to the French monarch and his allies. Brittany, for example, existed as a distinct duchy until 1536. Its own semi-independent Estates flourished into the Revolution of 1789, while its parlement did not establish a regular relationship with other French courts until 1553.

Like all large European states of its time, the French state ruled through broadly autonomous intermediaries, maintained a great variety of compacts with different classes and regions and demanded relatively little but tribute of its nominal subjects. In those days, revolutionary situations arose principally when the crown sought major increases in powers or revenues, when it sought to impose an alien identity on a subject population, or when rival claimants to sovereignty activated their claims. As the struggle between France and Brittany illustrates, the three circumstances often overlapped.

Over the long run, France experienced far fewer revolutionary situations than Iberia or the Balkans and somewhat fewer than the British Isles. French kings eventually managed to weld a large space into a single centralized state, something that never happened in Iberia, the Balkans or the British Isles. In pursuit of war-making capacity, the French crown and its agents pressed the population for money, supplies and manpower. Through intense effort and struggle, the French state stomped out regional autonomies and particularities. In the zone that would become the France of our day, as a result, there were fewer states at risk to revolution – just one, most of the time – hence fewer chances of revolutionary situations, through most of the last 500 years than existed in other comparable areas of Europe.

During the sixteenth and seventeenth centuries, nevertheless, France passed through many revolutionary situations, including major tax-induced regional rebellions, repeated Catholic–Protestant wars and the Fronde. During the eighteenth and nineteenth centuries, France went to the brink of revolution far less often, but crossed the edge spectacularly when it did: 1789–99, 1830, 1848–51 and 1870–1 marked some of Europe's most important revolutionary crises. Thereafter, classes and parties struggled bitterly, but no fully revolutionary situation occurred again in metropolitan France except during the closing months of World War II. To decide how revolutionary those months were, furthermore, we must resolve a thorny question: how much popular following Vichy and Nazi authorities retained in 1944. Sidestepping questions of fundamental loyalty, it seems that the balance of acquiescence shifted rapidly in 1944, therefore that multiple power, the essence of a revolutionary situation, only appeared in passing.

If we were to move armed struggles in French colonies and overseas territories from the inventory of external wars to the catalogue of revolutionary situations, to be sure, the balance would change drastically: the 1958 coup sprang from a *pied noir* seizure of power in Algeria, and to this day French troops remain active in tumultuous former colonies such as Chad. Within its home territory, nevertheless, the French state has not faced a sustained revolutionary situation since the nineteenth century. Even such bitter struggles as the separation of church and state (peaking in 1905) and the sit-down strikes of 1936 took place without quite splitting the state in two. The *coup d'état* that brought de Gaulle to power in 1958 occurred without an open split in control over the metropolitan state; in an orderly transfer under severe threat of insurrection, the National Assembly grudgingly granted de Gaulle his extraordinary powers. By 1880 a previously revolutionary state had consolidated its power to a degree matched by few other European countries.

The shift from frequent to rare revolutionary situations occurred in a state that was performing as a world power through most of the period, playing a central part in European wars, building a formidable empire, trading and intervening in most corners of the earth. The catalogue of external wars (see table 5.1) says as much, beginning as it does with general European conflicts, extending to the Americas and Africa, eventually reaching to China, Indochina and the Middle East. France's reliance on substantial land armies rather than the navies in which the Dutch and the British long specialized formed a large, durable bureaucracy and a fearsome military presence within the country.

Table 5.1 French external wars, 1492–1992

1489–92	War with England, Spain, Empire	1803–15	Napoleonic Wars
1495–6	Italian expedition	1821–9	Intervention in Greek revolt
1499–1504	War of the Holy League	1830	Conquest in Algeria
1508–10	War of the League of Cambrai	1830–3	Intervention in Belgian revolution
1511–13	War of the Holy League	1833	War vs. Annam
1515–16	Italian wars	1838–9	Mexican intervention
1521–5	Italian wars	1839–47	Conquest in Algeria
1528–9	War vs. Empire	1839–52	Intervention in Argentine–Uruguayan war
1542–4	European war	1844	War vs. Morocco
1542–3	Intervention in Swedish civil war	1854–6	Crimean War
1549–50	War with England	1856–60	War in China
1552–5	War with Empire	1857–61	Conquest in Senegal
1555	War with Portugal in Brazil	1859	Lombard war
1556–9	European war	1860	Intervention in Syrian war
1559–60	Intervention in Scottish civil war	1861–7	Mexican expedition
1565	War with Spain in Florida	1870–1	Franco-Prussian War
1566–7	War with Portugal in Brazil	1873–4	Tonkin war
1566–8	Intervention in Spanish–Dutch war	1881–2	Conquest in Tunisia
1572–1609	Intervention in Spanish–Dutch war	1881–5	Conquest in Senegal
1582–3	War with Spain in Azores	1882–5	Tonkin war
1588	War with Savoy	1883–5	Conquest in Madagascar
1590–8	War with Savoy	1890–2	Conquest in Senegal
1594–8	War with Spain	1890–4	War vs. Soudan
1600–1	War with Savoy	1892–4	Conquest in Dahomey
1609	War vs. Tunis	1893	War vs. Siam
1619	War vs. Algeria	1893–5	Tuareg war
1624–6	War of Valtellina		
1628–31	War with Empire, Spain		

1629	War vs. Morocco	1894–5	Conquest in Madagascar
1635–48	Thirty Years War	1896–7	Conquest in Upper Volta, Niger
1635–59	War with Spain	1900–1	Conquest in Chad
1644–69	Intervention in Venetian–Turkish war	1900–1	Intervention in China's Boxer Rebellion
1647–8	Intervention in Spanish–Neapolitan war	1900–11	Conquest in Central Africa
1663–4	Intervention in Turkish–Austrian war	1907–11	Conquest in Morocco
1665–7	English war	1912–17	War vs. Morocco
1666	War vs. Tunis	1914–18	World War I
1667–8	War of Devolution	1917–21	Intervention in Russian Revolution
1670–2	War vs. Tunis	1919–20	Intervention in Russo-Polish war
1672–9	Dutch war	1919–26	Rif war
1682–3	War vs. Algiers	1920	Syrian war
1683	Iroquois war	1920–2	Intervention in Greek–Turkish war
1683–4	Spanish war	1925–6	Syrian war
1687–9	Iroquois war	1930–1	War in Vietnam
1688–9	War vs. Algiers	1939–45	World War II
1688–97	War of the League of Augsburg	1940–1	Thai war
1689–91	Intervention in Ireland	1945	Syrian war
1701–14	War of the Spanish Succession	1946–54	Indochinese war
1710–11	War vs. Portugal in Brazil	1947	Madagascar war
1718–20	Spanish war	1952–4	Tunisian war
1733–5	War of the Polish Succession	1953–6	Moroccan war
1740–8	War of the Austrian Succession	1954–62	Algerian war
1741	War vs. Tunis	1955–60	Cameroun war
1754–6	North American War	1956	War vs. Egypt
1756–63	Seven Years War	1957–8	War of Western Sahara
1778–83	War of American Independence	1962–92	Intervention in Chad
1792–1802	French Revolutionary Wars		

Meanwhile, France also became a major presence in the world of capital. The French economy's size and variety alone gave it importance, from the great commercial farms of the Paris basin to the polyvalent crafts of the Alps and the seafaring of Marseille, Bordeaux and St. Malo. Although in terms of industrial production Britain and Germany eventually surpassed France, for three of our five centuries the French economy was arguably Europe's pace-maker; even during the nineteenth and twentieth centuries French production remained formidable. Consider, for example, the estimates of gross national product shown in table 5.2 (Bairoch 1976: 281; the figures are equivalents of 1960 US dollars). By this measure only Russia, with its immensely larger population (in 1830, some 62 million to France's 32 million) had a richer economy than France's in 1830, only Russia, Germany and the United Kingdom in 1913. The French economy, in short, was losing ground to those of Germany and the United Kingdom, but was still growing.

France accounted for roughly 15 per cent of Europe's gross product in 1830 and 11 per cent in 1913. Very slow nineteenth-

Table 5.2   Estimates of gross national product in Europe, 1830–1913

Country	1830	1860	1913	Average annual rate of growth (%), 1830–1913
Austria-Hungary	7210	11,380	26,050	1.6
Belgium	1098	2882	6794	2.2
Bulgaria	?	616	1260	1.4*
France	8582	16,800	27,401	1.4
Germany	7235	16,697	49,760	2.4
Greece	?	365	1540	2.8*
Netherlands	913	1823	4660	2.0
Portugal	860	1175	1800	0.9
Romania	?	950	2450	1.8*
Russia	10,550	22,920	52,420	2.0
Serbia	?	345	725	1.4*
Spain	3600	5300	7450	0.9
United Kingdom	8245	19,628	44,074	2.0
Europe	58,152	114,966	256,845	1.8

*1860–1913

Table 5.3   Estimates of gross national product per capita in Europe, 1830–1913

Country	1830	1860	1913
France	264	437	689
Germany	245	354	743
Russia	170	178	326
United Kingdom	346	558	965
Europe	240	310	534

century population growth diminished France's relative economic bulk; in per capita terms (table 5.3, still equivalents of 1960 US dollars), however, France continued to contend, standing 10 per cent above the European average in 1830, 40 per cent above in 1860 and 30 per cent above in 1913 (Bairoch 1976: 286).

The distribution of cities tells a similar story. As of 1492, France as a whole was a much more urbanized and commercialized region than the British Isles, Iberia or the Balkans, although only its north-eastern corner shared the intense urban-commercial life of the Low Countries. At that time, Paris (about 100,000 inhabitants) and Lyon (50,000) disputed commercial dominance within the region, despite Paris' greater size; the connection of Lyon with Italian finance and trade gave it special prominence. Other French cities of 10,000 or more inhabitants then included Arras, Bordeaux, Dijon, Marseille, Nantes, Rennes, Rouen and Toulouse. In neighbouring Lorraine (then independent of France), Metz and Strasbourg also passed the threshold of 10,000.

By 1800, Paris dominated the French urban hierarchy much more definitively, with Bordeaux, Caen, Lyon, Marseille, Metz, Montpellier, Nantes, Nîmes, Orléans, Reims, Rouen, Strasbourg, Toulon and Toulouse – quite a similar list to 1492 – all topping 30,000 people. We might think of the 1492 hierarchy as the intersection of three urban networks, one representing the commercial activity of Mediterranean and Atlantic, a second tied to the commerce of Flanders, south-eastern England and northern Germany, a third summing up administrative ties to the French crown. Between the late fifteenth century and the Revolution of 1789, the monarchy moved considerably toward the nationalization of the networks into just two: a top-down administrative version and a bottom-up commercial version, the second weighted toward the north-east but reaching throughout the kingdom.

Eventually, the French monarchy imposed relatively uniform top-down relations on most of its territory. By the eighteenth century, the largest political distinction separated those provinces that retained Estates with the power to negotiate payments of direct taxes (*pays d'Etats* such as Languedoc, Burgundy and Brittany) from those *pays d'Elections* whose autonomous governments had given way to royal courts. But that distinction only sharpened under Louis XIV's centralizing rule. Between the 1490s and the 1650s, the crown faced repeated challenges – challenges so severe that, well into the seventeenth century, France could easily have devolved into a composite empire of multiple languages, divided religion and tribute-taking warlords instead of the relatively unitary state it became.

Dynastic revolutionary situations, communal revolutionary situations and their intersections then prevailed. During the sixteenth and seventeenth centuries, major revolutionary situations arose in France chiefly when popular rebellion converged with the manoeuvres of great lords against royal pre-eminence. Eventually Louis XIV, in the Fronde's aftermath, smashed or co-opted the power of autonomous nobles, including their capacity to field private armies. But before the heydays of Mazarin and Colbert, the monarchy encountered armed resistance over and over again. Resistance took two great interlocking forms: Protestant rejection of the Roman Catholic Church's authority, mass reaction to war-driven taxation. Although class coalitions formed repeatedly on a local scale, regional and national revolutionary situations typically combined dynastic and communal features.

Protestants against Catholics

During the sixteenth and seventeenth centuries, organized Protestants provided the greatest single threat to a strong, centralized monarchy. The Protestant Reformation shook established authorities wherever it took hold in Europe, if only because ruling dynasties had long relied on the Roman Catholic Church as an ally in government, as a locus of sinecures for their unmilitary members and as a source of revenues for war and royal

Table 5.4 *Revolutionary situations in French states, 1492–1992*

1548	Pitaud insurrection in Guyenne	1648–53	The Fronde
1562–3	First war of religion	1655–7	Tardanizat rebellion (Guyenne)
1567–8	Second war of religion	1658	Sabotiers rebellion (Sologne)
1568–9	Third war of religion	1661–2	Bénauge rebellion (Guyenne)
1572–3	Fourth war of religion	1662	Lustucru rebellion (Boulonnais)
1574–6	Fifth war of religion	1663	Audijos rebellion (Gascony)
1577	Sixth war of religion	1663–72	Angelets guerrilla warfare (Roussillon)
1578–9	Seventh war of religion	1675	Papier Timbré, Bonnets Rouges (or
1579–80	Eighth war of religion		Torrében) rebellions (Brittany)
1585–98	Ninth war of religion	1702–6	Camisard rebellions of Cévennes,
1594–5	Croquant rebellions in South-west		Languedoc
1614–15	Civil war in Brittany	1768–9	Corsican rebellion
1617	War of Mother and Son	1789–99	French Revolutions and
1619–20	War of Mother and Son		counter-revolutions
1621–2	Huguenot wars	1815	Hundred Days
1625	Huguenot wars	1830	July Revolution
1627–30	Huguenot wars (English intervention)	1848	French Revolution
1629–30	Croquant uprising	1851	Louis Napoleon *coup d'état*, insurrection
1635–6	Croquant uprising	1870	State collapse, occupation, republican
1637–41	Croquant uprising		revolutions
1639	Norman rebellion	1870–1	Multiple Communes
1643–4	Revolt of South-west	1944–5	Resistance and Liberation

administration. In mapping the Reformation, we must distinguish between the geography of initial popular response and the geography of final religious resolution; the map of Protestantism flickered, after all, from about 1525 to 1650. France proved quite hospitable to the second wave of reform, especially that identified with Jean Calvin, but eventually returned overwhelmingly to Catholicism. The French story contrasted sharply with that of Germany, where large regions converted massively to the statist Lutheran version of Protestant organization and remained there.

Protestants gained their strongest bases in Germany for three related reasons. First, amid Germany's fragmented sovereignty the Pope had retained more autonomous power than elsewhere in Europe except for his own domains in Italy; that made him an obvious target without giving him the secular power to defend himself. Second, German regional princes often lacked the capacity to enforce religious conformity in the face of determined coalitions between reforming merchants and artisans. Third, many municipalities and petty rulers seized on Protestantism as a means of marking their distance from a Catholic Holy Roman Empire – not to mention as an occasion for appropriating church properties and revenues. Thus the electors of Saxony protected Martin Luther (whom the Pope and many Catholics would have been delighted to burn) from papal and imperial prosecution throughout his lifetime.

Not that converts to Lutheran, Calvinist or Zwinglian beliefs behaved as mere political opportunists. The Protestant Reformation articulated a long-germinating popular dissatisfaction with corrupt church officials while introducing new rigour into popular belief and practice. In the German Peasants' War of 1524–6, thousands of ordinary people (to Martin Luther's distress and condemnation) laid down their lives on behalf of Thomas Müntzer's millenarian doctrines. With respect to the final success of institutional Protestantism, nevertheless, the big differences from region to region of Europe lay less in the popular appeal of Protestant beliefs than in the options of local, regional and national authorities among crushing, tolerating or promoting the promulgation of one Protestant creed or another.

In the era's segmented states, it mattered greatly whether intermediate authorities belonged to the same religion as their nominal rulers. Patrons who were religious dissidents had greater reasons to defend their own communities against royal interference, greater claims on the loyalty of their own subjects and greater opportunities to appeal for aid from co-religionists outside the realm. In France, tradesmen and artisans provided the mass base for Calvinism, and at a local level converts to Protestantism often fought bitterly with churchmen and municipal oligarchs. Where Protestants won their local battles, they commonly seized church property to sell it off or convert it to public uses, paying public debts in the process. But at a national scale, open Protestant–Catholic struggles consisted chiefly of efforts by a Catholic crown to suppress the autonomies of Protestant grandees and municipalities. During the century after 1560, they competed and interleaved with war-inspired taxation as the most common origins of France's revolutionary situations.

Luther had relatively little following in France; his doctrine of salvation by faith within an authoritarian church respectful of existing civil powers had less appeal than the more separatist and populist Zwinglian and Calvinist programmes, with their extensive lay participation and collective discipline. It also helped that Calvin himself was a French exile and that the bulk of his early disciples spoke French. Within France, Protestantism made footholds chiefly in cities where aristocratic governors tolerated or even promoted the Protestant cause (Knecht 1989: 8). Its strength peaked somewhere around 1560; a census done in 1561 for admiral Coligny, the great Protestant leader, listed 2150 Protestant congregations in France as a whole. Then the concerted armed struggles began. Protestants dwindled in numbers as their political strength declined.

A typical dynastic succession crisis precipitated the wars of religion that tore France apart between 1562 and 1598, just as the resolution of that long dynastic crisis brought them to an end. When king Henry II suffered fatal wounds in a 1559 tournament, Catherine de Medici came to power as mentor of her fifteen-year-old son Francis II. With guidance from the Guise family, Catherine intensified persecution of Protestants, who had entertained hope of better treatment under the new regime. Protestant factions then schemed repeatedly to place one of the Protestant princes of the blood, Anthony or Louis of the Bourbon family, on the throne. When Francis II died in 1560, his ten-year-old brother Charles IX succeeded him, and Catherine de Medici formally took office as regent in place of Anthony, who was by then much compromised in his dealings to regain his lost kingdom of Navarre from Spain. That step gave the then Protestant Bourbons yet another grievance against the ruling Catholic Valois.

At that point, Catherine moved toward greater toleration of Protestants, who nevertheless demanded more than she offered. Over the next two years, popular struggles between local groups of Catholics and Protestants became ever bloodier as manoeuvring for national power intensified between the Bourbons and the Guises. In a condition of interregnum, open warfare began. The first French war of religion (1562–3) pitted royal forces against municipalities – notably Rouen and Lyon – taken over by Protestant activists. It ended with the edict of Amboise, which granted significant political and religious rights to Protestants. The first war set the pattern for subsequent hostilities: military campaigns for a season or two; manoeuvring of Protestant and Catholic grandees around the war's outcome and access to royal power; a truce, treaty and edict that few participants thought would last.

The second war (1567–8) illustrated the intertwining of domestic religious divisions, dynastic conflict and international politics. In 1564 and 1565, Catherine de Medici had taken the court on a grand tour that included (in April 1565) talks in Bayonne with Spain's duke of Alba. Catherine failed to negotiate marriages between the French royal family and those of Spain and the Holy Roman Empire, while Alba tried vainly to get Catherine to take a stronger anti-Protestant stand, not least against the Calvinist rebels of the Low Countries. That same year, Spanish forces destroyed a French expedition to Florida. While the court was on its long journey, members of the Guise, Montmorency and Bourbon families (the three great rivals of the Valois for royal power in France) moved troops in and out of Paris as they vied for control of the capital.

In 1567, the duke of Alba marched troops down the so-called Spanish Road along France's eastern border on the way to strike at the rebellious Netherlands, a military move the French took as a threat. Although for a moment it looked as though French Protestant and Catholic nobles might unite against the Spanish, Huguenot forces were soon organizing to capture the court and inciting armed seizures of major towns. The prince of Condé led a military assault on royal armies that considerably advanced the territory controlled by Protestants. Nevertheless Condé, his troops dwindling, accepted a return to the same conditions that had issued from the previous war.

Other Protestant–Catholic wars succeeded in 1568–9, 1572–3, 1574–6, 1577, 1578–9, 1579–80 and 1585–98, punctuated by treaties, assassinations, rebellions, plots and massacres. Most notable of the latter was the series of attacks on Protestants beginning on St. Bartholomew's day, 1572; perhaps 13,000 Protestants, starting with admiral Coligny, died in bloodbaths throughout the land. Later wars increasingly involved great lords who aspired to shares, or even monopolies, of royal power. At the same time, Protestants repeatedly complicated the issue by lending aid to the Low Countries' Protestant rebels, who were locked in combat with very Catholic Spain. By 1584, under Guise leadership, a formidable Catholic military League had formed within France to combat the more disjointed Protestant forces. Massive civil wars only ceased when Protestant Henry of Navarre inherited the throne, converted back to Catholicism, gradually coaxed assent to his rule from the major factions and parlements, and staked out a guaranteed place for Protestants in the French polity. Protestants gained control of fortresses and walled cities of their own. The Edict of Nantes (1598) cemented the *modus vivendi*.

It lasted no longer than most watered cement. Henry IV dealt gingerly with his former co-believers up to his assassination in 1610, but his successors Louis XIII and Louis XIV spent much of their royal energy reducing Protestant advantages. Louis XIII first beat down bids for power by his own mother (Marie de Medici), Richelieu and their allies, who included a number of Protestant magnates. After that, Louis (now guided by Richelieu) repeatedly attacked Protestant strongholds. Louis XIII even besieged La Rochelle, which drew on English support to withstand royal armies in 1627 and 1628. Smaller-scale struggles with Protestant lords and municipalities continued for twenty years.

Once past the terrible shock of the Fronde, Louis XIV began the slow strangulation of Protestant power, with the revocation of the Edict of Nantes (1685) greatly tightening his hold. By then, he had weakened autonomous Protestant municipalities and dissolved the private armies of great Protestant lords – indeed of any lords at all. Even mighty Louis XIV, however, faced the fierce Protestant rebellion of the Camisards, rural and small-town Protestants of the

Cévennes and Vivarais (1702–6); only scorched-earth tactics plus judicious bargaining by royal agents finally checked them. Although bitter Protestant–Catholic struggles resurfaced in southern France during the 1790s, repression and co-optation of Camisards squelched forever the threat of Protestant rebellion in France.

War, Taxes and Revolutionary Situations

The sixteenth century brought France rapid population growth, rising prices, declining real wages and increasing rents, thereby benefiting landlords and causing difficulty for anyone who lived on wages, fixed income or rented means of production. Under these conditions, the rentier church and nobility prospered, peasants and workers suffered, and the state's revenues – increasingly dependent on fixed taxes rather than fluctuating rents – became more and more inadequate for royal war-making. As a consequence, the crown borrowed heavily while pressing for new taxes and better collection of the old. When taxed unjustly or beyond their capacities, ordinary people resisted. Between 1514 and 1551, serious tax rebellions took place in the cities of Agen, Bordeaux, La Rochelle, St. Maixent, Sarlat, Niort, Saintes, Périgueux, St. Foy, Duras and the regions of Comminges, Guyenne, Dauphiné, Auvergne, Velay and Agenais (Heller 1991: 42–4). Only the Pitaud insurrection of 1548 in Guyenne appears in our catalogue of revolutionary situations because only in that case did the rebels hold substantial instruments of state power (including the city of Bordeaux itself) for more than a month (Le Roy Ladurie & Morineau 1977: 825–35). But even the sub-revolutionary rebellions cost thousands of lives. They stemmed from essentially the same processes as the more deeply revolutionary situations.

Amid the many peasant and urban revolts of the 1590s, for example, that of the Croquants swept much of south-western France in 1594, then formed again in Périgord during 1595. For thirty years the peasants of that region had suffered not only the routine depredations of war – rape, pillage, arson and devastation of their farms – but also taxation and rent-gouging from both sides of Protestant–Catholic struggles. During the wars they had acquired arms. In time-honoured order they assembled by parish, wrote down their grievances, elected officers and marched out to attack their oppressors. They formed armies of thousands that concentrated on taking cities and attacking the properties of exploitative nobles. The king's commissioner Boissize essentially co-opted the rebellion of 1594 by joining royal troops to local Croquant bands in the successful siege of an exploiter's castle, then persuading the irregulars to go home. Similarly, the Périgord rebellion of 1595 ended in a negotiated settlement and disarmament of peasant bands.

Even more so than military campaigns fought by retainers of great landlords, sixteenth-century peasant revolts took on a seasonal rhythm, since planting and harvesting depleted the manpower available for fighting. As a result, leaders of peasant bands had to strike fast and get results. That they often did: the rebellions of 1594 and 1595 put an end to the collection of taxes by agents of the local armies and caused the monarchy to abandon its hope of collecting back taxes (Bercé 1974: 290–1).

Peasant and urban rebellions had not ended, not by a long shot. The French monarchy reduced its external military efforts during the seventeenth-century's first three decades: small-scale war with Savoy over the marquisate of Saluzzo, attempts to check North African maritime marauders, manoeuvres to block Spanish access to Germany and the Low Countries through the mountain passes between Italy and Switzerland, renewed invasions of Spanish possessions in Italy, which brought Louis XIII and Richelieu into the fringes of the Thirty Years War. In 1634 they seized Lorraine. All this happened while civil wars rent the country; in 1627, for example, English forces invaded the Ile de Ré and sent a fleet to aid the Protestants who were holding nearby La Rochelle against royal assault.

The real acceleration in war-making occurred after 1635, when France became a major belligerent in the Thirty Years War. The shift toward greater international involvement generated a rapid rise in taxation: by one rough estimate the equivalent of two days' wages per capita per year toward 1620, around four days' wages in 1630, from eight to twelve days' wages in the 1640s (Tilly 1986: 134–5). Increased taxation did not in itself ordinarily generate rebellion, although it certainly incited tax evasion. Collective resistance occurred chiefly when authorities imposed new taxes in violation of old agreements and when some local figure visibly profited from the new tax. Sextupling the per capita tax burden, as happened between 1620 and the 1640s, nevertheless guaranteed that both would happen widely. The king's agents imposed forced sale of high-priced salt (the *gabelle*) on regions that had previously bought it off, removed municipal exemptions from poll taxes, collected excise on new commodities, seized cherished goods or imprisoned local officials for non-payment, while the impost repaid loans a tax-farmer or office-holder had made to the crown.

In these circumstances, local people often banded together to resist the payment and to attack its collectors. When multiple localities coalesced, or connected through shared leaders, regional rebellions resulted. When they joined forces with major rivals to the crown, they edged over into civil wars. Revived Croquant rebellions of 1629–30, 1635–6 and 1637–41 in the South-west illustrated the process of geographic aggregation perfectly, as in both cities and villages indignant local assemblies denounced the salt tax, participants went out to attack collectors, their houses or their offices, and groups from multiple localities joined into armies to march on a centre of tax collection. In May 1637, an army of 60 well-ordered peasant companies, led by nobles and a few commoners, gathered outside Bergerac and occupied the city for twenty days in the name of the Communes of Périgord. Although the peasant bands remained masters of the region for that time, royal troops managed to disperse them in June at a cost of some 2000 deaths on the two sides (Bercé 1974: 426–30).

From the early 1620s to the early 1650s, in almost every year an armed insurrection, or several, broke out somewhere in France. For the most part, their pattern resembled that of the Croquants, that of urban Protestants pressed by the crown, or the two together; royal threats or demands incited collective resistance, assemblies formulated grievances, local people attacked nearby agents or beneficiaries of royal policy, brokers or patrons connected local rebellions, armies formed of (sometimes reluctant) local volunteers, the armies seized control of strategic centres, the crown dispatched troops and plenipotentiaries, then some combination of battle, negotiation, flight and pacification ensued. The pacification was ostentatiously brutal where the crown had a clear advantage and not too many dignitaries were compromised, but more like routine bargaining over taxation where the crown's control remained uncertain.

Civil War and Repression

The Fronde (1648–53) formed during yet another succession crisis. Louis XIII died in 1643, when his heir Louis XIV was five years old. Louis XIII's widow Anne of Austria and cardinal Mazarin took over the government while continuing the war with Spain and combating another large cluster of insurrections in the South-west. At the same time they pressed the country for new taxes to sustain their vast military effort. The Fronde itself compounded the basic seventeenth-century forms of regional rebellion with a titanic, shifting struggle among magnates and the crown for dynastic power. The events were complicated enough:

1648 After a national meeting of high judicial bodies demanded restrictions on royal fiscal policy including recall of provincial intendants, peasants gathered in Paris to demand tax reductions, and an insurrection broke out in Pau. Mazarin first arrested leaders of the parlementary demands, then released them and granted the demands under pressure from a Parisian uprising.

1649 Ordering exile of the high courts, Mazarin and the royal family fled Paris, but the parlement of Paris took control of the city. Wide movements of support for the parlements appeared in Paris and elsewhere, but the prince of Condé's blockade of the capital forced concessions, including the royal family's return.

1650 Condé and his allies tried to remove Mazarin, for which the queen mother had them imprisoned. Condé's provincial supporters then organized widespread resistance, which doubled with popular movements in Bordeaux and elsewhere, but royal forces beat them down. Paris rentiers began vociferously demanding payment of their annuities.

1651 Princes and parlements successfully demanded Mazarin's departure, which brought Condé's liberation. Despite defections among the crown's opponents, popular struggles with royal troops continued, and Condé left to organize provincial forces. At the end of the year, Mazarin returned with troops of his own.

1652 Condé marched on Paris and captured the city as a popular insurrection (the Ormée) seized control of Bordeaux. Nevertheless, Paris divided between supporters and opponents of Mazarin, with the latter forcing his second exile. In another turn, Condé met increasing resistance and finally left France, which freed the king and the queen mother to return and begin repression of Frondeurs.

1653   Mazarin returned to Paris, the Ormée gave up control of Bordeaux and retaliation against erstwhile insurgents continued.

Almost continuously for five years, control over the French state split at least in two. The Fronde constituted a deeply revolutionary situation. The outcome of 1653, however, was only weakly revolutionary: a whole set of great lords and municipal oligarchs who had previously enjoyed formidable power and autonomy found themselves circumscribed by the state as never before. The Fronde had something in common with contemporaneous revolutions of the Low Countries and the Balkans, since in all three cases established actors in the existing state structure extended their normal jockeying for power and privilege into open defiance of the crown – always, to be sure, in the name of defending the monarch against evil or inept advisors. The chief difference is that in France the central power ended up much stronger than before.

The repression of Frondeurs and the subsequent reconstitution of royal authority had a profound effect on later opportunities for revolution. Between the Fronde's end in 1653 and the struggles immediately preceding the Revolution of 1789, the only more or less revolutionary situations to form in France were the religious struggles we have already surveyed and a series of regional rebellions centring on new taxes or the abolition of fiscal privileges: the Tardanizats, Sabotiers, Bénauge, Lustucru, Audijos, Angelets, Papier Timbré, Bonnets Rouges and Torrében rebellions (see table 5.4 for dates and places, Tilly 1986: 145–59 for summaries). Although the degree of antagonism to local nobles and bourgeois varied considerably among these rebellions, in general they resembled the earlier Croquants in raising whole communities against war-inspired royal demands for new payments. They differed from their predecessors, however, in attracting no patronage from great lords, in having great difficulty finding even petty nobles to lead their armed force. Nobles had deserted popular rebellion. Dynastic revolutions disappeared after their last great flaring in the Fronde. They left a purer form of communal revolutionary situation – now with almost no prospect of revolutionary outcome – in the smoke.

How did that happen? In essence, the crown quelled its greatest potential enemies and co-opted the rest. The razing of fortified castles, the disbanding of private armies, the abolition of urban militias, the prosecution of duelling, the building of a Versailles where great lords felt obliged to gather away from Paris, the very creation of a more professionalized standing army subordinated to royal administration the potential bearers of arms against the crown. The regularization of intendants in all major provinces (whether *pays d'Etat* or *pays d'Election*) diminished the autonomy of the military governors who had served so regularly as patrons and plotters before the Fronde. In fact, the solidification of regional administration under Mazarin and Colbert brought France as a whole one notch closer to direct rule; from the late seventeenth century to the Revolution, even village elites dealt regularly with royal officials such as the Sub-delegates who extended the intendant's surveillance into the *pays* within an intendant's Generality.

A Consolidating State

Given the Revolution's ghostly presence at the end of the eighteenth century, it is hard to escape teleology in thinking about the period between the Fronde and the 1780s. The state's spectacular collapse in 1789 tempts any historian to inspect its foundation for cracks in 1700 or 1750. Yet looking forward from those dates up to any point short of the 1780s we see little but continued expansion of the economy and the state. Eighteenth-century France had a large, relatively rich population and a broadly commercialized economy. Even after its substantial colonial losses – Quebec not least among them – in the Seven Years War, it played a major part in the slave trade and drew sustenance from the sugar of its Caribbean possessions. France's textiles were circling the world as its armies and navies conquered both in Europe and overseas.

Of the 134 years between the Fronde's end and the struggles of 1787 that led directly into the Revolution, France was at war somewhere during 86 – two years out of three. During thirteen decades it fought bilateral wars with Spain, England, the Dutch Republic and Portugal as well as the more general War of Devolution, War of the League of Augsburg, War of the Spanish Succession, War of the Polish Succession, Seven Years War and

War of American Independence. On the whole, the state emerged from those wars with enhanced fiscal and administrative powers.

If we were looking for revolution-inducing troubles in 1750, we would have to stare hardest at the way the state raised money. Repeatedly, the crown gained new revenues for its war-making by locating a rich individual or group, pressing the individual or group to pay handsomely for a royal privilege, then committing itself to enforce the privilege. Often the privilege was a long-enjoyed perquisite that the crown deliberately revoked or threatened; for example, nobles paid to have their nobility reconfirmed, or municipalities bought off the creation of new offices whose jurisdictions rivalled their own.

Tax-farming fit the pattern, since the royal coffers received substantial advances from those who contracted to collect a new tax, but royal troops often had to defend the tax-farmer from indignant citizens. So did the sale of offices, which brought in considerable cash fast and gave rich men an interest in the state, but also required the state to assure payment of the office-holders while guaranteeing their monopolies of remunerative judicial or administrative activities. So did the chartering, for a fee, of guild and municipal privileges, since the guild or municipality typically borrowed to pay the fee, pressed its monopolies harder to pay the debts thereby incurred and looked to royal forces for defence of those monopolies. Each time the state raised money in one of these ways, furthermore, it created another walled-off pool of privilege that would be harder to drain for new money in the future. It also meant that the state's principal creditors often held major semi-autonomous offices, had access to ample information about state finances and could therefore raise large obstacles to changes in state policy.

Since this manner of fund-raising put even customs and excise in the hands of powerful state clients, it set stringent limits to the state's ability to raise new money. That included money to pay back debt incurred during major wars. Royal attempts to liquidate the substantial debt incurred during the Seven Years War and, especially, the War of American Independence precipitated major struggles with France's great courts, especially its parlements, which were only prepared to collaborate in fiscal reorganization if they gained a greater say in financial policy. Those struggles led to multiple royal attempts to bypass the great courts: exiling the parlements, trying to rule by decree, creating the regional assemblies of 1787, finally calling the Estates General of 1789. The Estates General gave birth to the National Assembly. The very creation of the National Assembly issued a revolutionary challenge to the crown.

With the Seven Years War (1756–63), the parlement of Paris stepped up its opposition to royal taxation through its right to register or reject decrees. Louis XV and Louis XVI fought back by suspending or (more often) exiling the parlement and its provincial counterparts from their normal seats. France's spectacular colonial losses in the war, which included not only Quebec but also Senegal, St. Vincent, Dominica, Grenada and Tobago, discredited the state. In the war's aftermath, parlements were able to engineer expulsion of their long-time enemies, the Jesuits, from France. Yet the struggle continued; in 1771, for example, royal minister Maupeou and controller general Terray tried to reorganize finances by a series of actions including individual exile of *parlementaires*, abolition of their venal offices and supplanting of the Paris parlement by a half-dozen new jurisdictions that would lie directly under royal control. For four years the king's men gained ground, but Louis XV's death gave the parlements a chance to recoup. From 1776 to 1789 they constituted a great bulwark of opposition to royal policy. France's participation in the American rebels' victory over Britain in 1776–83, which brought St. Pierre, Miquelon, Senegal, Tobago and St. Lucia back under the French flag, did nothing to shake the opposition. On the contrary, the financial crisis it precipitated brought down the regime.

The national coalition had its ironies. Parlements that were sinkholes of aristocratic privilege and purchased royal office allied with peasants and bourgeois who railed against the expense, arbitrariness and corruption of government. What is more, the odd alliance eventually gained substantial support from the aristocracy and higher clergy, whose many privileges royal fiscal pressure was beginning to menace. Between 1787 and 1789 that coalition held France at the brink of a revolutionary situation. Whether we regard the situation as fully revolutionary depends on whether we regard its blocking of the state's power to impose new taxes as constituting dual sovereignty. Probably not.

Although the parlements never quite established their own alternative administration, they challenged royal power at every step, gaining wide popular support in the process. The crown riposted by establishing provincial assemblies and associated administrations (*commissions intermédiaires*) in *pays d'Election*, but those substitutes never commanded enough elite or popular consent to become effective vehicles for royal taxation or borrowing. The king's own supporters divided between partisans and enemies of the Swiss Protestant Necker, the supposed financial genius who had run up the debt during the American wars while making the public think him a master of sound management; Necker's chief contribution was actually to begin the difficult struggle against the great autonomy of France's financiers and for the creation of a government-controlled set of financial officials. The financiers and their allies forced Necker out. During the 1780s minister after minister attempted to organize royal finances and keep the government going as a growing party called for Necker's return to power. Meanwhile, the parlements checked every royal move toward a more effective fiscal system.

In May 1788 the government tried another coup against the parlements, arresting two leaders of resistance, declaring all parlements suspended and again creating courts to substitute for them. A general assembly of the clergy (themselves convoked to grant money to the crown) declared its solidarity with the parlements while the aristocracy (mindful of the threat to their own fiscal privileges) also generally aligned themselves with the opposition to royal policy. The parlement of Toulouse had the royal intendant arrested. Popular insurrections against royal officials formed in Brittany and Dauphiné; in Dauphiné nobles and municipalities went so far as to assemble the provincial Estates without royal convocation while mountaineers descended into Grenoble to protect the parlement from royal sequestration. During the autumn widespread blockages and seizures of grain reappeared for the first time in a dozen years.

In a setting of agitation through much of France, a formidable coalition called insistently for a national Estates General to settle the realm's problems. In August 1788, the king capitulated to that demand, dismissing two chief ministers in a row and recalling Necker the miracle-worker. The parlements returned to their capitals as every constituted political entity in France began preparing for elections to the Estates. Necker's accession to the Third Estate demand for double representation in the three-house

Estates General both assured substantial representation to France's regional bourgeoisie and initiated a split between commoners and aristocrats that eventually swung many of the latter, including the parlements, back to the king's side.

Revolutionary Processes

When, precisely, did a revolutionary situation open up – did an alternative coalition exercising state-like power come into existence? We could date the revolution from the assembly of the Estates General (5 May 1789), but only because of our retrospective knowledge of what the Estates would become. The Third Estate's designation of itself as the National Assembly (17 June) would be a stronger candidate, as would the joining of the other orders to the Third Estate (27 June). At the king's new dismissal of Necker (11 July), we see not only multiple popular demonstrations against the regime but also defection of royal troops, French Guards, to the opposition. By the time of the Bastille's fall (14 July), France's polity had unquestionably split in two. Sometime between 5 May and 14 July 1789, one of history's profound revolutionary situations began.

When did it end? The question is delicate, for it requires us both to decide whether the large emigration that began during the spring of 1789 located an effective segment of the French polity outside the national territory, and to gauge compliance with a succession of revolutionary governments. If we insist on a visible split between rival blocs, each exercising a semblance of state power within the country for a month or more at no less than a provincial level, then the calendar of revolutionary situations looks something like this:

May 1789–July 1789	Crown vs. Third Estate
June 1792–January 1793	Crown vs. revolutionary regime
March 1793–December 1793	Vendée rebellion; Mountain vs. Gironde, Federalists
August 1799–November 1799	Directory vs. royalists vs. Bonaparte

Within each of these periods, France experienced not one but a succession of revolutionary situations, as who ran the central apparatus shifted, coalitions among their opponents altered, the segments of state power controlled by the opposition changed and popular support for various contending factions fluctuated. In between these dates we see uneasy coalitions of rulers and recurrent rebellions, but no viable alternative coalition, hence no fully revolutionary situation. Since each of these clusters produced a substantial transfer of power, a strict application of our definitions leads to the conclusion that France went through four somewhat separate revolutions between 1789 and 1799. By a more relaxed standard, however, we might treat the entire time from the resurgence of parlementary opposition in 1787 to Napoleon's overthrow of the Directory in 1799 as one long revolutionary situation. The chronology compromises between the two by accepting the conventional interval of 1789 to 1799.

The outcomes of these struggles were multiply revolutionary. Recall where France began the revolutionary processes: like other European states, the French state of the eighteenth century only extended its direct top-down rule to the level of the region, the level of the *subdélégation*, the *élection*, the *sénéchaussée*, the *grenier à sel* and similar administrative units. At and below that level, the Old Regime state ruled indirectly, especially through the mediation of priests, nobles and urban oligarchies. During the eighteenth century, in search of funds for past, present and future military activity, state agents began pressing for various forms of direct rule that would bypass the privileges and resistance of the entrenched intermediaries.

In the Revolution, the state's new managers, battling the old intermediaries for control of revenues, loyalty and military power at the local and regional levels, improvised successive systems of direct rule in which capitalists, broadly defined, played the critical part. The creation of a new top-down administrative hierarchy drastically altered the relations between coercion and capital, inciting a new series of struggles for power within most French regions. Revolutionary attempts to institute direct rule and to displace old intermediaries incited widespread resistance, which took the form of open counter-revolution where the intermediaries had large followings and the national network of capitalists had only thin support.

Rule Transformed

What happened to France's system of rule during the revolutionary years? Before 1789 the French state, like almost all other states, ruled indirectly at the local level, relying especially on priests and nobles for mediation. From the end of the American war, the government's efforts to collect money to cover its war debts crystallized an anti-governmental coalition that initially included the parlements and other power-holders, but changed toward a more popular composition as the confrontation between the regime and its opponents sharpened. The state's visible vulnerability in 1788–9 encouraged any group that had a stifled claim or grievance against the state, its agents or its allies to articulate its demands and join others in calling for change. The rural revolts – Great Fear, grain seizures, tax rebellions, attacks on landlords and so on – of spring and summer 1789 occurred disproportionately in regions with large towns, commercialized agriculture, navigable waterways and many roads (Markoff 1985). Their geography reflected a composite but largely bourgeois-led settling of scores.

At the same time, those whose social survival depended most directly on the Old Regime state – nobles, office-holders and higher clergy are the obvious examples – generally aligned themselves with the king (Dawson 1972: ch. 8). Thus a revolutionary situation began to form: two distinct blocs both claimed power and both received support from some significant part of the population. With significant defections of military men from the crown and the formation of militias devoted to the popular cause, the opposition acquired force of its own. The popular bloc, connected and often led by members of the bourgeoisie, started to gain control over parts of the state apparatus.

The lawyers, officials and other bourgeois who seized the state apparatus in 1789–90 rapidly displaced the old intermediaries: landlords, seigneurial officials, venal office-holders, clergy and sometimes municipal oligarchies as well. At a local level, the so-called Municipal Revolution widely transferred power to enemies of the old rulers; patriot coalitions based in militias, clubs and revolutionary committees and linked to Parisian activists ousted the old municipalities. Even where the old power-holders managed to survive the Revolution's early turmoil, relations between each locality and the national capital altered abruptly. Village 'republics' of the Alps, for example, found their ancient liberties – including ostensibly free consent to taxes – crumbling as outsiders clamped them into the new administrative machine (Rosenberg 1988: 72–89). Then Parisian revolutionaries faced the problem of governing without intermediaries; they experimented with the committees and militias that had appeared in the mobilization of 1789, but found them hard to control from the centre. More or less simultaneously they recast the French map into a nested system of departments, districts, cantons and communes, while sending out *représentants en mission* to forward revolutionary reorganization. They installed direct rule.

Given the unequal spatial distribution of cities, merchants and capital, furthermore, the imposition of a uniform geographic grid altered the relations between cities' economic and political power, placing insignificant Mende and Niort at the same administrative level as mighty Lyon and Bordeaux. Within Old Regime France, cities whose commercial rank exceeded their administrative stature included, for example, Nîmes, Saint-Etienne, Roubaix and Castres; those occupying higher administrative than commercial rank included Tulle, Saint-Amand-en-Berry, Saint-Flour and Soissons (Lepetit 1988: 167–8).

The Revolution reordered that relationship. Among capitals of the eighty-six original *départements*, fifty-four were indisputably the dominant cities within their new jurisdictions, three won out through size over others that had higher administrative and fiscal ranks under the Old Regime, six maintained their administrative priority despite smaller size, twelve became capitals despite being neither the largest nor the highest-ranking of their regions and ten were too close to call (Lepetit 1988: 203–4). Larger cities that failed to win departmental capitals clustered disproportionately in northern France, with Atlantic and Mediterranean ports also having more than their share (Lepetit 1988: 208). The great discrepancies, however, did not appear on the local level, but as inequalities among the eighty-six capitals, now all nominally occupying identical administrative relations to the national capital.

As a result, the balance of forces in regional capitals shifted significantly. In the great commercial centres, where merchants, lawyers and professionals already clustered, departmental officials (who frequently came, in any case, from the same milieux) had no choice but to bargain with the locals. Where the National Assembly carved departments out of relatively uncommercialized rural regions, the Revolution's administrators overshadowed other residents of the new capitals, and could plausibly threaten to use force if they were recalcitrant. But in those regions, they lacked the bourgeois allies who elsewhere helped their confréres do the Revolution's work, and confronted old intermediaries who still commanded significant followings. In great mercantile centres, the political situation worked very differently. By and large, the Federalist movement, with its protests against Jacobin centralism and its demands for regional autonomy, took root in departmental capitals whose commercial positions greatly outpaced their administrative rank. Bordeaux, Marseille and Lyon are the obvious examples. In dealing with these alternative obstacles to direct rule, Parisian revolutionaries improvised three parallel, and sometimes conflicting, systems of rule: (1) the committees and militias; (2) a geographically defined hierarchy of elected officials and representatives; (3) roving commissioners from the central government. To collect information and gain support, all three relied extensively on the existing personal networks of lawyers, professionals and merchants.

Contrasts between the revolutionary experiences of Caen (a mercantile centre under the Old Regime) and Limoges (an administrative outpost of the monarchy) illustrate the point well:

> In Limoges, the central social conflict occurred within the political arena, disrupting and dividing the municipal administration of 1791–2. The bitter struggle between the Amis de la Paix and the Jacobin club embroiled the municipal council. The Jacobins not only prevailed as the dominant club in Limoges but gained control of the municipal council in 1792. In Caen, the fundamental conflict pitted wealthy bourgeois merchants against the nobility, a group in the process of being excluded from political participation. This conflict erupted most often on the edges of organized politics, with little real impact on them, and allowed the *haute-bourgeoisie* to remain virtually unchallenged in political office until after the federalist revolt. (Hanson 1989: 69)

As the system began to work, revolutionary leaders strove to routinize their control and contain independent action by local enthusiasts, who often resisted. Using both co-optation and repression, they gradually squeezed out the committees and militias. Mobilization for war put great pressure on the system, incited new resistance and increased the national leaders' incentives for a tight system of control. Starting in 1792, the central administration (which until then had survived in a form greatly resembling that of the Old Regime) underwent its own revolution: the staff expanded enormously, and a genuine hierarchical bureaucracy took shape. In the process, revolutionaries installed one of the first systems of direct rule ever to take shape in a large state.

That shift entailed changes in systems of taxation, justice, public works and much more. Consider policing. Outside of the Paris region, France's Old Regime state had almost no specialized police of its own; it dispatched the *Maréchaussée* to pursue tax evaders, vagabonds and other violators of royal will and occasionally authorized the army to quell rebellious subjects, but otherwise relied on local and regional authorities to deploy armed force against civilians. The revolutionaries changed things. With respect to ordinary people, they moved from reactive to proactive policing and information gathering: instead of simply waiting until a rebellion or collective violation of the law occurred, and then retaliating ferociously but selectively, they began to station agents whose job was to anticipate and prevent threatening popular collective action. During the Revolution's early years, Old Regime police forces generally dissolved as popular committees, National Guards and revolutionary tribunals took over their day-to-day activities. But with the Directory the state concentrated surveillance and apprehension in a single centralized organization. Fouché of Nantes became Minister of Police in the Year VII/1799, thenceforth running a ministry whose powers extended throughout France and its conquered territories. By the time of Fouché, France had become one of the world's most closely policed countries.

Going to war accelerated the move from indirect to direct rule. Almost any state that makes war finds that it cannot pay for the effort from its accumulated reserves and current revenues. Almost all war-making states borrow extensively, raise taxes and seize the means of combat – including men – from reluctant citizens who have other uses for their resources. Pre-revolutionary France followed these rules faithfully, to the point of accumulating debts that eventually forced the calling of the Estates General. Nor did the Revolution repeal the rules: once France declared war on Austria in 1792, the state's demands for revenues and manpower excited resistance just as fierce as the Old Regime's. In overcoming that resistance, revolutionaries built yet another set of centralized controls.

Resistance, Counter-revolution and Terror

Resistance and counter-revolutionary action followed directly from the process by which the new state established direct rule. Remember how much change revolutionaries introduced in a very short time. They eliminated all previous territorial jurisdictions, consolidated many old parishes into larger communes, abolished the tithe and feudal dues, dissolved corporations and their privileges, constructed a top-to-bottom administrative and electoral system, imposed expanded and standardized taxes through that system, seized the properties of emigrant nobles and of the Church, disbanded monastic orders, subjected clergy to the state and imposed upon them an oath to defend the new state church, conscripted young men at an unprecedented rate and displaced both nobles and priests from the automatic exercise of local leadership. All this occurred between 1789 and 1793.

Subsequent regimes added more ephemeral changes such as the revolutionary calendar and the cult of the Supreme Being, but the early Revolution's overhaul of the state endured into the nineteenth century, and set the pattern for many other European states. The greatest reversals concerned the throttling of local militias and revolutionary committees, the restoration or compensation of some confiscated properties and Napoleon's Concordat with the Catholic Church. All in all, these changes constituted a dramatic, rapid substitution of uniform, centralized, direct rule for a system of government mediated by local and regional notables. What is more, the new state hierarchy consisted largely of lawyers, physicians, notaries, merchants and other bourgeois.

Like their pre-revolutionary counterparts, these fundamental changes attacked many existing interests and opened opportunities to groups that had previously had little access to state-sanctioned power – especially the village and small-town bourgeoisie. As a result, they precipitated both resistance and struggles for power.

Artois (the department of Pas-de-Calais) underwent a moderate version of the transition (Jessenne 1987). In that region, large leaseholders dominated local politics, but only within limits set by their noble and ecclesiastical landlords. The Revolution, by sweeping away the privileges of those patrons, threatened the leaseholders' power. They survived the challenge, however, as a class, if not as a particular set of individuals: many office-holders lost their posts during the struggles of the early Revolution, especially when the community was already at odds with its lord. Yet their replacements came disproportionately from the same class of comfortable leaseholders. The struggle of wage-labourers and smallholders against the *coqs de village* that Georges Lefebvre discovered in the adjacent Nord was less intense, or less effective, in the Pas-de-Calais. Although the larger farmers, viewed with suspicion by national authorities, lost some of their grip on public office during the Terror and again under the Directory, they regained it later, and continued to rule their roosts through the middle of the nineteenth century. By that time, nobles and ecclesiastics had lost much of their capacity to contain local power-holders, but manufacturers, merchants and other capitalists had taken their places. The displacement of the old intermediaries opened the way to a new alliance between large farmers and bourgeoisie.

Under the lead of Paris, the transition to direct rule went relatively smoothly in Artois. Elsewhere, intense struggle accompanied the change. The career of Claude Javogues, agent of the Revolution in his native department of the Loire, reveals that struggle, and the political process that incited it (Lucas 1973). Javogues was a huge, violent, hard-drinking roustabout whose close kin were lawyers, notaries and merchants in Forez, a region not far to the west of Lyon. The family was in the ascendant in the eighteenth century, and in 1789 Claude himself was a well-connected thirty-year-old *avocat* at Montbrison. The Convention dispatched this raging bourgeois bull to the Loire in July 1793 and recalled him in February 1794. During those six months, Javogues relied heavily upon his existing connections, concentrated on repression of the Revolution's enemies, acted to a large degree on the theory that priests, nobles and rich landlords were the enemies, neglected and bungled administrative matters such as organization of food supplies, and left behind him a reputation for arbitrariness and cruelty.

Yet Javogues and his co-workers did, in fact, reorganize local life. In following his action in the Loire, we encounter clubs, surveillance committees, revolutionary armed forces, commissars, courts and *représentants en mission*. We see an almost unbelievable attempt to extend the direct administrative purview of the central government to everyday individual life. We recognize the importance of popular mobilization against the Revolution's enemies – real or imagined – as a force that displaced the old intermediaries. We therefore gain insight into the conflict between two objectives of the Terror: extirpation of the Revolution's opponents and forging of instruments to do the work of the Revolution. We discover again the great importance of control over food as an administrative challenge, as a point of political contention and as an incentive to popular action.

Contrary to the old image of a unitary people welcoming the arrival of long-awaited reform, local histories of the Revolution make clear that France's revolutionaries established their power through struggle, frequently over stubborn popular resistance. Most of the resistance, it is true, took the form of evasion, cheating and sabotage rather than outright rebellion. But people through most of France fought one feature or another of revolutionary direct rule. In the bustling port of Collioure, on the Mediterranean close to the Spanish border, popular collective action during the Revolution 'consciously or not, pursued the goal of preserving a certain cultural, economic, and institutional independence. In other words, popular action sought to challenge the French state's claims to intervene in local life in order to raise troops for international wars, to change religious organization, or to control trade across the Pyrenees' (McPhee 1988: 247).

Issues differed from region to region as a function of previous history, including the previous relations of capital and coercion. Where fault lines ran deep, resistance consolidated into counter-revolution: the formation of effective alternative authorities to those put in place by the Revolution. Counter-revolution occurred not where everyone opposed the Revolution, but where irreconcilable differences divided well-defined blocs of supporters and opponents on a large geographic scale.

France's South and West, through similar processes, produced the largest zones of sustained counter-revolution (Lebrun & Dupuy 1985; Lewis & Lucas 1983). The geography of official executions under the Terror provides a blurred but recognizable profile of counter-revolutionary activity. The departments having more than 200 executions included, in descending order: Loire Inférieure, Seine, Maine-et-Loire, Rhône, Vendée, Ille-et-Vilaine, Mayenne, Vaucluse, Bouches-du-Rhône, Pas-de-Calais, Var, Gironde and Sarthe (Greer 1935: 147). These departments accounted for 89 per cent of all official executions under the Terror. Except for the Seine and the Pas-de-Calais, they concentrated in the South, the South-west and, especially, the West. In the South and South-west, Languedoc, Provence, Gascony and the Lyonnais hosted military insurrections against the Revolution, insurrections whose geography corresponded closely to support for Federalism (Forrest 1975; Hood 1971, 1979; Lewis 1978; Lyons 1980; Scott 1973).

Federalist movements began in the spring of 1793, when the Jacobin expansion of the foreign war – including the declaration of war on Spain – incited resistance to taxation and conscription, which in turn led to a tightening of revolutionary surveillance and discipline. The autonomist movement peaked in commercial cities that had enjoyed extensive liberties under the Old Regime, notably Marseille, Bordeaux, Lyon and Caen. Sustained rural counter-revolution, on the other hand, broke out chiefly in regions whose revolutionary capitals had occupied relatively low ranks in the Old Regime's administrative, fiscal and demographic hierarchies, and whose bourgeois therefore had relatively weak influence in the surrounding regions (Lepetit 1988: 222). In those two kinds of cities and their hinterlands, France fell into bloody civil war.

In the West, guerrilla raids against republican strongholds and personnel unsettled Brittany, Maine and Normandy from 1791 to 1799, while open armed rebellion flared south of the Loire in parts of Brittany, Anjou and Poitou beginning in the autumn of 1792 and continuing intermittently until Napoleon pacified the region in 1799 (Bois 1981; Le Goff & Sutherland 1984; Martin 1987). The western counter-revolution reached its high point in the spring of 1793, when the Republic's call for troops precipitated armed resistance through much of the West. That phase saw massacres of 'patriots' and 'aristocrats' (as the proponents and opponents of the Revolution came to be called), invasion and temporary occupation of such major cities as Angers, and pitched battles between armies of Blues and Whites (as the armed elements of the two parties were known).

The West's counter-revolution grew directly from the efforts of revolutionary officials to install a particular kind of direct rule in the region: a rule that practically eliminated nobles and priests from their positions as partly autonomous intermediaries; that brought the state's demands for taxes, manpower and deference to the level of individual communities, neighbourhoods and households; that gave the region's bourgeois political power they had never before wielded. They consolidated their power through struggle. On 12 October 1790, at La Chapelle de Belle-Croix, Vendée, a number of people from neighbouring parishes arrived for Mass and Vespers armed with clubs.

> Seeing the local National Guard with their regular uniforms and arms, the strangers came up to them and said they had no right to wear the national uniform, that they were going to strip it from them, that they supported the cause of clergy and nobility and wanted to crush the bourgeois who, they said, were taking bread from priests and nobles.

They then attacked the Guards and the *Maréchaussée* of Palluau, who only fought them off with difficulty (Chassin 1892: II, 220).

In the mouths of Vendeans, to be sure, the word *bourgeois* conflated class and urban residence; nevertheless, the people of that counter-revolutionary region saw clearly enough that the two connected intimately. In seeking to extend the state's rule to every locality, and to dislodge all enemies of that rule, French revolutionaries started a process that did not cease for twenty-five years. In some ways, it has not yet ceased today.

For all its counter-revolutionary ferocity, the West conformed to France's general experience. Everywhere in France, bourgeois – not owners of large industrial establishments, for the most part, but merchants, lawyers, notaries and others who made their livings from the possession and manipulation of capital – were gaining strength during the eighteenth century. That they acquired landed property, that they collaborated with noble landlords, that the richer among them bought into nobility for the privileges, prestige and tax exemptions it afforded do not in the least gainsay the growing energy of that capital-manipulating class.

Throughout France, the mobilization of 1789 brought disproportionate numbers of bourgeois into political action. As the revolutionaries of Paris and their provincial allies displaced nobles and priests from their critical positions as agents of indirect rule, the existing networks of bourgeois served as alternate connections between the state and thousands of communities across the land. For a while, those connections rested on a vast popular mobilization through clubs, militias and committees. Gradually, however, revolutionary leaders contained or even suppressed their turbulent partners. With trial, error and struggle, the ruling bourgeoisie worked out a system of rule that reached directly into local communities, and passed chiefly through administrators who served under the scrutiny and budgetary control of their superiors.

This process of state expansion encountered three huge obstacles. First, as commonly happens at the outset of revolutionary situations, many people saw opportunities to forward their own interests and settle old scores open up in the crisis of 1789. They either managed to capitalize on the opportunity or found their hopes blocked by competition from other actors; both categories lacked incentives to support further revolutionary changes. Second, the immense effort of warring with most other European powers strained the state's capacity at least as gravely as had the wars of Old Regime kings. Third, in some regions the political bases of the newly empowered bourgeois were too fragile to support the work of cajoling, containing, inspiring, threatening, extracting and mobilizing that revolutionary agents carried on everywhere; resistance to demands for taxes, conscripts and compliance with moralizing legislation occurred widely in France, but where pre-existing rivalries placed a well-connected bloc in opposition to the revolutionary bourgeoisie, civil war frequently developed. In these senses, the revolutionary transition from indirect to direct rule embodied a bourgeois revolution and engendered a series of anti-bourgeois counter-revolutions.

Other Options

How else might the struggles of 1787 to 1799 have gone? Alternative paths opened up at least in 1787 (when, in principle, the crown could have prevailed over its opposition), 1789 (when a number of different reforming coalitions could have formed), 1791 (when the seizure of the church and preparations for war could have failed), 1793 (when multiple counter-revolutions almost gained the upper hand) and at each of the subsequent major *coups d'état*: 1794 (Thermidor), 1795 (Vendémiaire and the foundation of the Directory), 1797 (Fructidor), 1798 (Floréal) and 1799 (Prairial, then Brumaire). If the Federalists of 1793 had gained power, for example, they would still have faced a fierce foreign war, vengeful émigrés, an underground church, the great Vendée rebellion and an economic crisis, but they might well have compromised with some of these enemies while battling the rest and installing a significantly less centralized regime. We could no doubt speculate our way through a series of counterfactual revolutions, choice-point by choice-point.

More generally, we should take advantage of the histories we have already reviewed by considering the possibility of a Dutch path, an Iberian path, a Balkan path or a British path. Now we must look forward not from the 1600 that served as a reference point for my earlier speculations about alternatives to Britain's seventeenth-century revolutions but to 1750 or so, when the contest between parlements and crown grew acute in France. No doubt we can rule out the Balkan model immediately: as of 1750, Balkan states provided no plausible model for French development. They remained uncommercialized, fragmented in sovereignty, blessed or cursed with powerful landlords and subject to a tribute-taking empire. Dutch, Iberian and British paths, however, remained at least thinkable.

By that time, a Dutch path was unlikely in France, since the French crown had for a century simultaneously been sapping the autonomous military powers of great lords and municipalities in favour of a centralized administration while mortgaging its own fiscal power to office-holders, judicial institutions and those self-same municipalities. If France had fallen into semi-autonomous chunks (as seemed possible in 1789 and 1793), most likely a coalition of landlords, office-holders, churchmen and peasants would have blocked the masters of Bordeaux, Lyon and Marseille from gaining the sort of eminence their counterparts enjoyed in Amsterdam or Deventer. By 1793, nevertheless, the early Revolution's smashing of office-holders, great landlords and church opened the way to political arrangements more greatly resembling those of the Netherlands than would have been conceivable a decade earlier. Having made more room for mercantile capitalism by these measures, revolutionaries also opened space for

the characteristic decentralized government of mercantile capitalism. The irony is that French conquest of the Netherlands
eventually liquidated the Dutch model by imposing centralized
monarchy in place of the old centrifugal federation.

As for an Iberian path, by 1750 the Spanish and Portuguese
states had profited substantially from their colonies, had augmented their power vis-à-vis the Catholic Church by expelling the
Jesuits and gaining considerable control over national ecclesiastical
affairs, had installed more effective fiscal systems, and had thereby
centralized significantly. Spain remained a military and economic
power despite relative loss in both regards to France and England,
while Portugal had established strong, unequal commercial ties to
England. Still, in both countries, grandees, landlords and urban
patriciates enjoyed much greater autonomy than their French
cousins. Colonial revenues, furthermore, played much larger parts
in both states' finances than they did in French public finance. An
Iberian path would have moved France back toward the fragmented sovereignty of earlier centuries, but the greater commercialization of the French economy and the greater power of its
office-holders in 1750 would most likely have barred a transition
to Iberia's disputatious parochialism. Again, irony: French
conquest, plus the attendant loss of Latin American colonies,
enhanced Iberian state centralization, increased the autonomous
weight of the professional military, and thereby destroyed the
model that Iberia had offered in 1750.

What of a British path? We must take care to distinguish Great
Britain from Ireland. Fragmented and rebellious eighteenth-
century Ireland provided no model at all for France. Great Britain
(that is, England, Wales and Scotland) did. By 1750, Great Britain
was a looming commercial and military power with highly capitalized agricultural and industrial economies. Through parliament, a
coalition of landlords and bourgeois weighed heavily on the state,
in varying degrees of contest and collusion with a royal patron–
client network that drew on state power and offices for its
sustenance. Britain's continued commercialization, proletarianization and industrialization interacted with its expanding military
expenditure to enhance parliament's power while generating an
exceptionally vigorous popular politics at local and national scales.

In many respects, France *did* follow a British path, reaching
1850 with a relatively powerful national legislature, a contained

central authority, a strong bourgeois–landlord coalition, counter-vailing bourgeois–worker coalitions, a rapidly industrializing capitalist economy and vigorous popular politics. But France's successive revolutions made much of this possible. Without the revolutions – here is the point of these imagined alternatives – eighteenth-century France could have reached its nineteenth-century destination only through a close equivalent to revolution, some sort of state-led transformation that would have emptied the pockets of privilege the state's own policies had enlarged during the 150 years after 1600. Seen from the 1850s, something very like the revolutions of the 1790s begins to look indispensable.

Fifteen- to Twenty-year Regimes

The first revolutionary regime lasted only a decade, but it led to a series of regimes that lasted between fifteen and twenty years each: Napoleon's Consulate and Empire (1799–1814, with a respite in 1815), the Restoration (1815–30), the July Monarchy (1830–48) and the Second Empire (1852–70); only the Revolution of 1848 (which succumbed to Napoleon III's *coup d'état* in 1851) disrupted the rhythm before the Third Republic (1870–1940) utterly des-troyed it. Napoleon I's Concordat with the papacy (1801), his elevation to emperor (1804), his accelerated centralization of the state and his creation of a new nobility all transformed the state but each of them took place without a sharp division in the polity. Revolutions swirled around Napoleon in the Balkans, Spain and Latin America, including Haiti, but not in France itself. Not, that is, until 1814–15, when the advancing allies entered France, battled their way to Paris, forced Napoleon into abdication and exile, then saw him return from Elba (March–June 1815) to lead an assault against the occupying allies that ended with Wellington's defeat of Napoleon's forces at Waterloo. The subsequent allied occupation lasted until the French paid off their war reparations in 1818.

The July Revolution of 1830 resulted largely from king Charles X's attempt to stem by sudden repression the bourgeois working class republican mobilization of the later 1820s. His reactionary ordinances of July 1830 – dissolving the chamber of deputies, altering the electoral system and instituting tight controls over the press – amounted to a *coup d'état*. A Parisian insurrection mastered the city, seized the Hôtel de Ville and brought a provisional government to power. To head off a new republic, liberal deputies turned to Louis Philippe, duke of Orléans, who thus accepted investiture as a king made by revolution. Major worker–republican insurrections followed in Paris and Lyon, but the regime held on until 1848.

The July Monarchy fell in a way recalling the revolution that had brought it to power, but the bourgeois–worker republican coalition of 1848 was much broader and more demanding than eighteen years earlier. A Parisian uprising still played the decisive part in toppling the regime, as three days of street fighting in February sufficed to force Louis Philippe's abdication. Again, losing members of the national revolutionary coalition – notably skilled workers in Paris and other major cities – returned to the streets as the new government failed to meet its demands or to deal effectively with the agricultural and industrial depression that had already incited many local conflicts before the February uprising. The bloody June Days of 1848 pitted unemployed workers from the threatened National Workshops not only against the state but also against other unemployed workers recruited into the Parisian Mobile Guard. After the insurrection's failure, repression tightened dramatically. From Louis Napoleon's election as president in December 1848 to his *coup d'état* after an electoral setback in December 1851, the government gradually dismantled the national republican movement from the top down, but not far enough down to prevent another massive insurrection (this one not only in Paris but also through many French rural regions) against the 1851 coup.

Emulating his warrior-uncle, Louis Napoleon quickly made himself emperor (1852). He was soon undertaking the European wars his recent predecessors had avoided: the Crimean War with Russia (1854–6), war with Austria in Italy (1859) which led to the annexation of Savoy and Nice while facilitating Italy's unification under Piedmontese leadership and alienating Louis Napoleon's Catholic supporters by pitting him against the Pope, and, fatefully, war with Prussia (1870–1). Entered with confidence because of the French general staff's advance planning and mobilization, the war proved a quick, decisive defeat for France. As news of massive losses filtered back from the front, radical republicans organized autonomous Communes (unsuccessfully) in Marseille and (more successfully) in Lyon.

When the emperor himself surrendered with his troops at Sedan, radicals in Lyon and Marseille declared the founding of a republic, complete with Committees of Public Safety. In Paris, crowds invaded the National Assembly, precipitating a march to the Hôtel de Ville and yet another declaration of a revolutionary government there. The new government, dominated by Léon Gambetta, faced a siege of Paris by German armies. By January 1871, Paris had capitulated, but Gambetta and his government were organizing resistance from Tours. The ineffectual resistance collapsed when the provisional government accepted a peace treaty with Germany that ceded Alsace and some of Lorraine.

The Germans who occupied Paris in January disarmed the regular army, but not the National Guard, formed largely of workers and shopkeepers from Parisian neighbourhoods. By March, the National Guard had remobilized, created a central committee and prepared for resistance both to German occupiers and to the new government, now led by Adolphe Thiers and located in Versailles. The Parisians rebuffed Thiers' effort to reclaim cannon they had seized from army posts, then followed the example of Lyon and Marseille by organizing a Commune to govern the city and call for the decentralization of France as a whole into self-governing municipalities. Other short-lived Communes formed in Toulouse, Saint-Etienne, Narbonne and Le Creusot, as radicals attempted unsuccessfully to seize power in Nîmes, Limoges, Rouen and smaller towns. Parisian communards held the city until the week of 21 May, when troops from the Versailles government finally slaughtered them in the streets as they retreated from barricade to barricade. In reaction, monarchists gained support in the country as a whole. Nevertheless, they tolerated Thiers as a reluctantly republican president until German occupying forces left France in 1873, then elected Marshal Mac-Mahon president for seven years in presumed preparation for a Bourbon restoration.

The restoration aborted. In tense political manoeuvring that followed the German evacuation, republicans gained wide support in the chamber of deputies and the country at large while the monarchists dissipated their advantages. The improvised Third Republic lasted longer – seventy years – than any other regime since 1789. It weathered the populist challenge of general Boulanger (1886–9), violent encounters with syndicalists and anarchists, the travail of the Dreyfus Affair (1894–1906), multiple strike waves, struggles over separation of church and state (1901–5), World War I (1914–18) and the vast worker mobilization of the Popular Front (1936–9), only to succumb to another German invasion in 1940.

During the first few years of German occupation, France split by design into a north-eastern zone of direct German control and the area governed by the collaborationist Vichy regime. The small resistance of those first few years did not come close to constituting an alternative state, even an underground state, within France. Excepting the 1943 liberation of Corsica, not until Allied forces landed in Normandy (June 1944) did a quasi-revolutionary situation reappear in the country as a whole. August 1944 brought the peak, with insurrectionary strikes and seizures of city halls anticipating the arrival of Allied and Free French forces as Germans retreated.

Given the state's Napoleonic heritage, the importance of MacMahon in salvaging it after the revolutions of 1870–1, the presidency of Pétain at Vichy and the emergence of Charles de Gaulle as paramount leader when World War II ended, it is surprising that the military have played so small an autonomous part in French politics since the eighteenth century: a few small conspiracies against Napoleon, a threat from General Boulanger in the 1880s and nothing more of importance. The contrast with Spain and Portugal is dramatic. All the more surprising, therefore, is the approach to a military coup made by opponents to decolonization of Algeria in 1958. Committees of Public Safety took over Algiers and Ajaccio (Corsica) in May, as conspirators across the country readied for a militarily backed seizure of power in Paris. Before that happened, President Coty pre-empted the movement, inviting de Gaulle to form a new government with emergency powers.

With the endorsement of national referenda, de Gaulle proceeded to establish a Fifth, more presidential, Republic, to contain the movement for *Algérie française*, to decolonize French North Africa and to pursue an international politics of *Grandeur*. He held power for ten years, checking the vast movement of students and workers in May–June 1968, receiving massive endorsement in the referendum and election of June, but resigning after the defeat of another referendum on his proposed reorganization of regional administration in April 1969. Thus France's prime soldier-politician of the twentieth century left office without so much as a feint toward a military seizure of power.

The Long Run of Revolution

As happened in many other parts of Europe, France experienced repeated communal, patron–client and dynastic revolutionary situations during the sixteenth and seventeenth century, moved toward less frequent but more sweeping class-coalition revolutions in the eighteenth and nineteenth centuries, but eventually became less and less prone to fully revolutionary situations just as national-level political struggles became better organized. As compared with Iberia, the Balkans and (as we shall see) Russia, France endured remarkably free of military revolutions. Communal revolutionary situations – chiefly pitting Protestants against Catholics – tore France apart during the sixteenth and seventeenth centuries, but dissipated with the religious compromises of the eighteenth century; during the nineteenth and twentieth centuries, Protestant–Catholic enmities played no significant part in French national politics, while the issue of church–state relations repeatedly generated struggles falling short of revolution.

Between 1548 and 1793, state attempts to extract the means of armed force, especially money and men, from reluctant populations stirred major rebellions over and over again; then the regularization of taxation, its seating in elected legislatures and its incorporation into the programmes of major political parties all diminished its revolutionary potential as they increased its salience for public debate. Wine-growers' mobilizations and Poujadist movements notwithstanding, twentieth-century French citizens could hardly imagine the ferocity of the seventeenth-century's rebellions against tax collectors and their beneficiaries, rooted as those rebellions were in the defence of established rights and privileges. Even less could they understand the threat to the sixteenth- or seventeenth-century state that formed when great lords commanding private armies allied themselves with popular rebels. In between lay the utter emasculation of autonomous military powers.

With the exception of newly annexed areas such as Brittany and Corsica, national revolutionary situations hardly ever opened up in metropolitan France after 1492. Unlike the situation in the Balkans, the British Isles and even in Belgium, centralizing French kings soon turned away from any recognition of culturally distinct populations as holders of separate political rights. With the suppression of Protestants and, even more, the revolutionary imposition of Parisian norms on the country as a whole, the state effected a considerable cultural homogenization of its citizenry. Despite the partial constitution of regional populations such as Bretons, Occitans or Catalans as organized interest groups after World War II, the French state virtually liquidated national claimants to state power.

For national revolutions, we must turn to France's colonies, therefore chiefly to the nineteenth and twentieth centuries. The consolidation of state power in the metropole subordinated military forces to civilian rule, reduced the importance of dynastic claims and diminished the prospects for communal rebels of any kind, but made regimes more vulnerable to financial crises, military defeats and popular mobilizations at a national scale. The organizational changes in the state that occurred during and immediately after the greatest revolutions – notably 1585–98, 1648–53, 1789–99, and 1848–51 – profoundly altered subsequent political struggles. In these senses, the movement from segmented to consolidated state power, from indirect to direct rule, from parochial to national politics, from the state's relative detachment to its deep involvement in the national economy fundamentally transformed the incidence, process and impact of revolutions in France.

Remember the proximate conditions for revolutionary situations and outcomes:

Revolutionary Situation

1 The appearance of contenders, or coalitions of contenders, advancing exclusive competing claims to control of the state, or some segment of it.

2 Commitment to those claims by a significant segment of the citizenry.

3 Incapacity or unwillingness of rulers to suppress the alternative coalition and/or commitment to its claims.

Revolutionary Outcome

1 Defections of polity members.

2 Acquisition of armed force by revolutionary coalitions.

3 Neutralization or defection of the regime's armed force.

4 Control of the state apparatus by members of a revolutionary coalition.

The checklist is still tautologically true, a simple extension of the definitions for revolutionary situations and outcomes. Nevertheless, it helps considerably in pinpointing how changes in the French state and its position in the European system of states altered the prospects for revolution.

On the side of revolutionary situations, what contenders for power over the state could possibly arise and gain support obviously changed fundamentally from the early sixteenth century, when many magnates had plausible claims to a share of royal power or to state-like privileges within their own domains and when to declare a community Protestant was inevitably to assert new autonomies with respect to both secular and ecclesiastical authorities. In those days of private armies and municipal militias, furthermore, the crown frequently lacked the basic military means to put down armed challenges to its hegemony. The French state's consolidation after the Fronde and during the Revolution of 1789–99 shifted the state–civilian balance greatly and almost eliminated credible dynastic competitors for state power; Louis-Philippe and Napoleon III hardly resembled the warlord princes of Condé. Instead, the class coalitions promoted by representative and electoral politics became indispensable participants in the making and breaking of regimes. Under these conditions, ironically, foreign invaders gained even more influence over who was to rule in France.

That brings us to revolutionary outcomes. Defections of polity members remained important to effective transfers of power, but who those members were overturned completely between 1492 and 1992: from the king, his clients, powerful churchmen, landed magnates and a few rich urban oligarchies to organized representatives of a variety of classes and interests. The opportunities of revolutionary challengers to acquire their own armed force and neutralize or co-opt the state's armed force generally diminished with disarmament of the civilian population, but with a sharpening division of labour between police and army and the rebirth of militias in the form of National Guards, a sharp disruption in government operations such as the German invasion of 1870 offered armed civilians a temporary military advantage. The concentration of France's governing institutions in Paris, furthermore, made it increasingly possible to seize the whole country by capturing its capital city.

Other social changes clearly contributed to these alterations in the character of revolution: the eighteenth-century commercialization of agriculture, the growth of capital-intensive manufacturing, the nineteenth century's momentous urbanization, the political mobilization of agricultural and industrial workers, and so on through the staples of French social history. All these changes affected the identities, interests and organization of potential contenders for state power as well as influencing the state's day-to-day operations. Nevertheless, the incessant transformation of the French state played its own large part in when, where, how and with what effect revolutionary situations could open and close.

6

Russia and its Neighbours

Creating Russia

The portion of Europe occupied by the Soviet Union until the end of 1991 traces back approximately to the European lands of the Russian Empire at the closing of the Napoleonic Wars. Only the Crimean War, the civil war of 1917–21 and the German invasions of 1941–4 produced major disturbances in those frontiers. Yet if we search all the way back to 1492, we find no Russia there. Instead, in roughly the same territory, we find parts or all of the Teutonic Knights, the Republic of Pskov, the Principality of Moscow, the Principality of Riazan, the Khanate of the Golden Horde, the Khanate of the Crimea, the Khanate of Kazan, the Kingdom of Poland, plus a more vaguely bounded zone east of the Black Sea held stubbornly by Circassians.

In that region of Europe, the great imperial power was then the Jagellonian dynasty, which held Lithuania, Byelorussia, the Ukraine, Poland, Bohemia, Moravia and Hungary, but not Muscovy. Under two Ivans (the Great and the Terrible), it is true, a formidable Russian state began to take shape. Yet in between 1492 and the eighteenth century, not only an aggressive Lithuanian-Polish Empire but also a substantial Swedish monarchy and a mighty Ottoman Empire all reached for a while into the space the world would eventually come to think of as Russia. Up to the final partition of Poland in the 1790s, our cartography of what was to become 'Russian' must still reckon not only with a composite Russian Empire, but also with an Ottoman Empire and a Kingdom of Poland. Much more so than in France, the British Isles, the Low

Countries, the Balkans or Iberia, we are dealing with an initially small state that grew into a giant by gobbling up its neighbours.

Notice the temptations and dangers of teleology: it simplifies our story greatly to portray the European zone's transformation as a continuous, inevitable drive of Russia to fill an inviting empty space. Simplifies, and distorts. Given the advantageous economic and geopolitical position of actors on the western edge of the space in the fifteenth century, informed observers of the time could reasonably have expected that if the European economy prospered and adjacent states consolidated, one or two powers (no doubt Poland, Sweden or the Habsburgs) would move eastward and southward. That expectation would still have had to contend with the long viability of westward-moving empires from the steppe. Why couldn't yet another tidal wave of Mongols or Turks roll in from the east? To the south, furthermore, a proven land-grabber, the Ottoman Empire, strove repeatedly to expand its Eurasian holdings. Russia and the Ottomans battled for control of the lands above the Black Sea well into the nineteenth century. Russia had formidable competitors for the space it eventually claimed.

Only at the end of Ivan IV's reign (1533–84) did Muscovites begin the serious incorporation of Siberia and other territories between Russia and Japan. Despite frontiers that shifted continually according to the fortunes of war, Lithuania (which united with Poland in 1569) and Sweden continued to hold substantial parts of the Ukraine, White Russia and the Baltic region until eighteenth-century partitions of Poland rounded out a fairly stable north-west boundary for the Russian Empire. Nothing guaranteed that a single power would occupy the space between Finland and the Pacific. Nothing guaranteed that Muscovy, a secondary power in 1492, would be the principal agent of eastern and southern expansion. Even more so than in the British Isles or Iberia, the growth of a Russian Empire around a Muscovite nucleus represented only one of several ways state power could have regrouped in Europe between the Vistula and the Urals.

Yet it happened. Rulers from Ivan the Great to Ivan the Terrible concentrated their military efforts on pushing back Mongols and subjugating other Slavs. Russia had the distinction of ruthless, long-lived rulers. Ivan III (the Great) ruled from 1462 to 1505; in that European time of low life expectancy, child-kings and contested successions, a king who survived forty-three years already

had enormous advantages over his rivals. What is more, Ivan the
Great's successors, Basil III and Ivan IV (the Terrible), ruled
twenty-eight and thirty-seven years respectively. (Proof of longevity's importance appeared in the fierce faction-fighting among
nobles during Ivan IV's minority, from 1533 to 1547, at the
succession of Ivan's feckless son Fedor I in 1584, and in many a
later interregnum). Ivan III checked the Mongols, subdued the
great commercial state of Novgorod and established Muscovite
priority over other nearby Slav states. In another half-century,
a genuine Russian Empire had formed. By then it was pressing
the adjacent Livonian Knights, Polish-Lithuanian Empire and
Crimean Khanate. During the next two and a half centuries,
Russian expansion scarcely ceased.

That history of aggressive imperial expansion has immediate
implications for the analysis of revolution. Neighbouring powers
did not take kindly to Russian conquest; they fought tooth and
nail. When did their resistance become revolutionary? As the
forces of Muscovy and their Russian successors tried repeatedly to
subdue the Crimean (Krim) Tatars between the 1520s and the
1750s, for example, at what point did effective Tatar resistance to
Russian rule constitute a revolutionary situation? Well, the answer
runs, when the Empire had established effective control for some
time. But how should we gauge effective control? Given the
contingent, indirect rule the Russian Empire organized at its
periphery, the exact moment we choose must be arbitrary.

The conclusion – that whether resistance to empire is revolutionary comes down to a matter of definition – may seem to rob
revolution of its glory, or its horror. But it captures this book's
main point: the character, locus and outcome of revolutionary
situations varies systematically with the organization of states and
systems of states. Given the presence of a ruthlessly growing
empire, we should expect to find numerous cases in which an
adjacent people capitulated provisionally to the imperial power,
only to rebel again when the empire seemed vulnerable, when
imperial agents or collaborators made outrageous new demands,
when the now subject people acquired new means of action or new
allies. Those rebellions necessarily combined characteristics of
revolution with characteristics of anti-colonial war.

The multiple entities that in 1492 occupied the space eventually
to be called 'Russian' were the debris of empires, fragments that

remained after Scandinavians (Vikings in 'Varangian' integument) had ranged conquering through the territory from Baltic to Black Sea, and Mongols had burst in from the south-east. Various Mongol agglomerations exercised sovereignty over much of the space from the 1230s to the late fifteenth century, when Ivan the Great managed to shrug off their yoke. Mongol conquest worked best when it encountered established states drawing regular revenues from agrarian populations; Mongol overlords either battened on those states for tribute or swallowed them whole without much disturbing their internal organization. In either case, Mongol rule remained indirect and imperial, requiring symbolic subjection, regular tribute, irregular armed support, Mongol approval of new Slav rulers, loyalty to the khan vis-à-vis Mongol enemies and the occasional yielding of noble hostages, all in return for great autonomy within the territories of those princes who collaborated.

Indeed, Muscovy gained priority over its regional rivals in part by astute collaboration with agents of the Golden Horde. The final sacking of Moscow by Tatars in 1571 did not end Muscovite relations with the steppe people. Even after throwing off their overlords of the Golden Horde, Muscovites often co-operated with Mongol remnants, allying with Krim Tatars against Lithuania during the sixteenth century, enlisting Zunghar Mongols in the conquest of Siberia during the seventeenth, continuing to pay tribute to the Crimean branch until 1700. Relations between Russians and Tatars during the sixteenth and seventeenth centuries resembled those between European colonists and American Indians at the same time; after all, in the mid-eighteenth century the largest single item in the South Carolina colony's budget consisted of 'gifts' to Indians. On the American and Russian frontiers, ruthless men fought on both sides. Sixteenth-century English observer George Turberville likened Russians to Irishmen:

> Wilde Irish are as civil as the Russies in their kind,
> Hard choice which is the best of both, each bloody rude
>   and blind.

The difference, however, mattered. On their cramped island, Irish chieftains resisted an alien empire but also fought each other incessantly; in their vast space, one set of Russian princes won out over the rest, then built their own empire.

The Irish analogy disserves Russia in another important regard. Until recently, Ireland has remained peripheral to the main currents of European trade and communication. So long as the overland connection of Europe with East Asia prospered, the cities of Russia remained important points of Eurasian contact. Coming very late to the sea, Russians built almost all of their cities on the rivers that connected Eastern Europe's interiors, especially the Dnieper, the Volga, the Don, the Dvina and the Volkhov with their tributaries. As of the year 1000, Russia's urban system and commerce centred on Kiev, which may well have had 50,000 inhabitants; another mercantile city, Novgorod, held its own with some 20,000 (Rozman 1976: 45–6). The Mongol connection subsequently elevated Moscow to a central position it did not lose until the deliberate construction of St. Petersburg from 1703 onward. By 1500, with the Mongol grip slackening, Moscow, Vilna, Pskov, Novgorod, Smolensk and Bakhchiseraj (the latter in Tatar Crimea) all probably had 10,000 inhabitants or more (Chandler & Fox 1974: 27).

Even where they founded cities such as Bakhchiseraj, Mongol warriors commonly maintained their own tented encampments, ready to move out for the hunt or another war. Unlike the Mongols, Russians adopted an urban strategy of conquest, locating military forces, imperial agents, merchants and even landlords in cities as they extended their zone of control. The policy had three consequences. Firstly, agents of the state occupied favoured positions in most cities. Secondly, many nominal state employees, such as soldiers, also worked in agriculture, industry or services on their own account. Finally, predominant activities of cities changed when the imperial frontier shifted. As Muscovy expanded its perimeter, tsars built chains of fortress towns on the north-west and (especially) south-east frontiers, each chain being left behind as a string of connected mercantile and administrative headquarters when the zone of conquest moved on. Between 1636 and 1648, for example, Michael Romanov's regime was laying out most of the new towns in the *Belgorodskaia cherta*, a line eventually including twenty-nine fortified places that spanned the major routes of previous Mongol invasions. Soon those cities lay well behind the active frontier.

Starting in 1703, Peter the Great displaced the population centre to St. Petersburg by forcibly settling merchants, artisans, imperial officers and their servitors on the marshy land at the Neva's mouth, a site newly captured from Sweden. Peter, who had himself worked briefly incognito as a shipwright while visiting Holland

and England, conceived of St. Petersburg as a rather Netherlandish centre of shipbuilding and Baltic trade. He gave the city, after all, not a Russian but a Dutch name: Sankt Petersburg. By 1782, the new imperial seat had 297,000 residents to Moscow's 213,000 (Rozman 1976: 162, 183). A division of labour set in, with St. Petersburg the capital and principal port of entry from North-western Europe, Moscow the greatest centre for internal trade. Thus Russia built a huge, eccentric urban hierarchy focused on the Empire's north-western reaches but extending deep into Asia.

Russian, Polish-Lithuanian and Tatar States

For three centuries after 1500, Muscovy, then Russia, gained chevrons as one of Europe's most belligerent states, or series of states. First Muscovy conquered its immediate Slavic neighbours and fought off its Tatar overlords. Then Russia, still forming as a political entity, battled not only the mobile peoples to its east and south-east, but also formidable Swedish, Polish and Ottoman Empires to the north, west and south. Russia fought those powers head to head for centuries, and bore the scars. In the long run, the supplying, financing and administering of a large military organization has even more profound social effects than its sheer presence as a political force. As happened elsewhere in Europe, but in very different configurations, the deliberate creation of substantial military forces and the incessant conduct of war extruded civilian power structures that eventually contained the military and transformed the state's organization.

Nevertheless, geopolitics itself strongly influenced changes in Russian states. The 'law of opposite boundaries' followed the hallowed principle 'the enemy of my enemy is my friend'; regardless of other incompatibilities, powers located on opposite sides of a common foe often became allies. During the early centuries of imperial expansion, the game of alliances exposed Muscovy to unlikely influences: those of the Tatars and of German Protestants who both fought with Moscow against Catholic Poland.

In Ivan the Great's war of 1500–3 against Poland-Lithuania and the Livonian Knights, for example, Russians drew effectively on Tatar support. In the very process of freeing Russian territory from Mongol control, Ivan the Great and his successors borrowed many imperial devices from Mongol administration. Ivan himself adopted a very Mongolian device for indirect rule: installing 'service princes' of Novgorod and elsewhere who held their offices and the lands attached to them only so long as they served the tsar. Parallel to them, he created conditional land- and office-holders, *pomeshchiki*, who enjoyed estates, office, power and privilege for their own lifetimes alone, on condition of continued satisfactory imperial service.

For princes and *pomeshchiki*, service included the provision of armed force. At a time when Western European states were relying increasingly on the international market for mercenaries to staff their armies, Ivan was pioneering the creation of mass armies from imperial territory by a patrimonial system that reinforced the hierarchy and civilian service. From a scattering of caciques, citadels and clienteles (with the haphazard military forces that such arrangements always provided European monarchs) emerged a hierarchical, geographically ordered system of regiments and regional administrations strongly beholden to the ruler and his servitors.

As nobles became more subservient to their tsar, however, they also approached life-and-death control over their own peasants. Imperial legislation penetrated previously autonomous peasant communes, restricted mobility, increased the claims of landlords on their peasants' labour services and eventually erased the lines among free peasants, serfs and slaves. The erasure moved them all downward, not upward.

Not that the peasantry sank listlessly into the Russian mud. They fought all the way. On their own, peasants never created a revolutionary situation in Russia at a national scale. But peasant uprisings against oppressive landlords and tax-collectors recurred year after year. For *pomeshchik* estates alone, P. K. Alefirenko catalogues thirty-seven substantial uprisings (*vosstanie*) during the years 1730–60 (Alefirenko 1958: 136–53). When allied with Cossacks or dissident nobles, furthermore, peasants often supplied the shock troops of national rebellions just as they supplied the ranks of national armies. Nevertheless, they had a problem: for three centuries the state recurrently allied with landlords to put them down, farther down with each insurrection until the nineteenth century.

Similarly, from the establishment of a Moscow patriarchate in 1589, the orthodox church fell under the tsar's control and served his political interests, but only on condition of enormous room for manoeuvre within its own confines. Tsars organized their control over nobles, officers and churchmen not only through personal patronage but also through a compact set of chancelleries (*prikazy*) whose heads were directly responsible to the ruler. The whole system – civil, military and religious – was vulnerable to misappropriation on one side and rebellion on the other. Like many other forms of indirect rule, it granted enormous discretion to state officials within their own zones of control. But it created a large, cheap, relatively centralized governing apparatus.

Ivan IV was the first ruler in a long line of Muscovite princes to take the title tsar formally at his coronation. What is more, he gained the orthodox church's blessing for that title, which presumed equality with the Holy Roman Emperor. No modest claims for Ivan! In 1565, he tightened the state's structure, bringing it a bit closer to direct rule by creating the *oprichnina*: an administration of imperial bodyguards supported by lands expropriated from great autonomous lords, whom Ivan exiled to distant estates. Since the *oprichniki* had the mission to ferret out 'traitors', they became instruments of terror against free nobles in general.

Central control in such a state necessarily fluctuated with the capacity and determination of the current ruler as well as with the pressure of external war, which meant that the powers and autonomies of service nobles fluctuated dramatically. During the seventeenth century, service nobles repeatedly treated their tenures as private property by selling or bequeathing them; by 1714 the tsar was formally recognizing the *fait accompli* by abolishing the distinction between service tenures and private estates. During the later seventeenth century, furthermore, Russian rulers packed their growing armies with mercenaries. But they soon regretted the threat to their closed system; early in the eighteenth century, they returned to mass conscription for peasants and broad military obligations for the service nobility. Peter the Great levied an army of 370,000 men, Catherine a million, Alexander I (1801–25) two million (LeDonne 1991: 273). Even at the relatively peaceful moment of 1897, Russian armed forces numbered 1.1 million (Shanin 1986: I, 39). The main lines of administration laid down by the two Ivans survived even the reforms of Peter and Catherine.

The effort of drawing the means of war and conquest from an uncommercialized agrarian economy produced a bulky patrimonial superstructure.

In addition to plunging into general European wars, Peter and Catherine extended the Empire enormously to the south-east; both efforts greatly increased their need for funds and troops. Accordingly, their innovations consisted chiefly of regularizing the sort of administrative structure they had inherited, reducing the number of competing administrations, freezing the service nobility into a clearer hierarchy, endowing the state with a more extensive apparatus of domestic repression and imbuing the resulting bureaucracy with a Western European style. Perhaps the largest change occurred in state finances: expenditure on war increased from 6.9 million rubles in 1725 to 173.8 million in 1825, for a hefty 3.3 per cent annual average rate of increase over an entire century. (During the same century, rye prices were merely doubling or tripling, for an increase rate of perhaps 0.1 per cent; see Mironov 1985.) During that period, the share of state revenue from fixed taxes (capitation and quitrent) declined from 54 to 32 per cent while excise taxes rose from 46 to 48 per cent of the greatly increased total; income from state-promoted vodka sales – a monopoly, characteristically, of nobles – alone increased from 1.0 million to 128.4 million rubles, an average rise of 5 per cent per year (LeDonne 1991: 277–83).

Peter and Catherine also extended Russian-style administration to their new possessions. With the eighteenth century, the Empire imposed a relatively uniform structure through a vast territory. Since the ambient social structure continued to vary enormously from region to region within the Empire, this meant necessarily that the Empire's actual operation also varied: from the north-west zones where merchants provided substantial imperial revenue and wielded considerable power in local affairs to those of the south-east where military governors in alien and uncommercialized zones either ruled by naked force, struck deals with local headmen, or both.

The Polish state operated quite differently, to the point of eventual suicide. Landlords in both Russia and Poland raised grain on large estates, which with sixteenth-century population growth and prices rises gave them substantial opportunities for profit. But Polish-Lithuanian landlords had greater access to Western

European markets through such ports as Danzig. They built a manorial economy that eventually undercut previously prospering cities as independent political actors and centres of internal trade. They excluded peasants and Polish merchants from the grain trade, dealing directly with foreign merchants. They prospered on their export revenue, imported western goods and treated the state as their plaything.

The 'republic of nobles' that formed in Poland gave representation to that privileged tenth of the population, which offered them the means both to fortify their control over the peasantry and (from 1572 onward) to make the monarchy the nobility's elected instrument. They rendered serfdom fiercer and more general as the process continued. Meanwhile nobles' private armies, cheaply manned by their own subjects, greatly outnumbered the crown's armed force. Although the recurrent three-way split in Polish politics – king, magnates, lesser nobles – gave frequent opportunities for the king to ally with lesser nobility from the later sixteenth century, it undermined every royal effort to create reliable, centralized fiscal and military systems.

Responding to the threats of Tatar, Cossack and Ottoman horsemen, furthermore, Polish armies emphasized cavalry long after both Russian and Western European armies had moved massively toward infantry and artillery; that arrangements accentuated the autonomy and self-financing of the individual warrior and his retinue while making it difficult for any king to buy a replacement force. In the long run, the presence of weak, contested kingship and the absence of a significant national army made Polish territory a plum ripe for plucking by the expansive armed forces of its Swedish, Russian, Austrian and Prussian neighbours. First the Polish-Lithuanian Empire contracted, then during the eighteenth century Poland disappeared chunk by chunk as a separate state.

The grain of Russia's sixteenth-century landlords had no access to Western European markets. English merchants controlled the Arctic port of Archangel, founded in 1584, which in any case exported fur and timber from the north, not grain from southern plains. Instead, landlords shipped their products to Russia's own cities, precisely where tsars had entrenched themselves. Intervening brutally in markets and landownership, Russian rulers seized for themselves and their war-making enterprises the gains from sixteenth-century population increases and price rises. By the time of seventeenth-century contraction and eighteenth-century involvement in European trade, they had thoroughly subjugated the nobility – indeed, created a new nobility heavily obligated to government service. By frequently collecting taxes in grain rather than money, they reduced the involvement of landlords and peasants in commerce while assuring food supplies for their cities, armies and officials.

During the nineteenth century, however, the process reversed. From Paul I (1796–1801) onward, tsars worked to create an autonomous bureaucracy and military organization, increasingly free of aristocratic patronage. A formidable non-noble administrative class, among whom only the highest ranking could hope for ennoblement, grew up to run the country from day to day. The process worked only too well; it left the aristocracy to administer its land and enjoy its income while separating from the state and losing its commitment to regional administration; tsars unwittingly neutralized three centuries of extraordinarily effective co-optation. As a result, Russian monarchs lost a crucial clientele without containing its power or discontent.

Tatar states that ringed Russia's south-east had a very different sort of organization: supple, segmented, connected by tribal identities and patron–client chains. In many respects, they consisted of nothing but their formidable cavalries writ large. To a large extent, furthermore, the armies simply aggregated kin groups and patron–client chains. Mongols (of whom the Tatars were first a subdivision, then a residue) supported their mobile armies by exacting tribute from nearby agrarian peoples, taxing transit trade and supplying protection to long-distance merchants. Krim Tatars prospered by capturing and shipping slaves (often, in fact, Slavs) for the Turkish and Italian markets. Ready to retaliate against insubordination but not to set up a substitute administration, they ordinarily relied on rulers of subject peoples for the collection of their taxes. They created little central structure, which offered them great flexibility but also made them vulnerable to secession and to struggles over succession. As parasites, they prospered when the caravan trade quickened and when adjacent grain-producing states became stable, productive and docile. Russians finally drove them back and absorbed their remainders by a combination of superior military might, tighter central administration, divide-and-conquer alliances and shrewd deal-making with local potentates.

During the 1250s Mongol invaders, with help from Alexander Nevsky, had established suzerainty over Muscovy. The Golden Horde, as Russians called them, collected their tribute for two centuries. By 1438–41, the Horde was splitting into separate Khanates of Sarai (the Mongol capital), Kazan, Astrakhan and the Crimea, the latter soon becoming a dependency of the Ottoman Empire. With Russian expansion and battles among the remaining Mongols, only the Krim Tatars survived the reign of Ivan the Terrible as a distinct political entity; Catherine the Great finally incorporated their lands as well in 1783. From that point on the Empire's major European territorial gains came at the expense of Poland and the Ottoman Empire.

War and Rebellion, Rebellion and War

Everywhere in Europe the transformation of states resulted chiefly from war and preparation for war. Nowhere was the connection more evident than in Russian imperial expansion. Until well into the nineteenth century the Russian state spent the bulk of its income on military force. The two Ivans, Peter, Catherine, Alexander and the tsars in between them used that armed force to put down their Russian rivals, conquer adjacent peoples and hold off enemies based in Europe or the Middle East. During only twenty-nine years of the century beginning in 1492, for example, was the Muscovite state *not* at war with an external foe.

By comparison with later military efforts, those sixteenth-century wars cost fairly little to pursue. Nevertheless, they drove the fundamental recasting of the Russian state that occurred from Ivan the Great to Ivan the Terrible. In the effort to conquer and to hold their conquests, sixteenth-century tsars inadvertently con-structed a massive, expansible system of patrimonialism at the top, indirect rule in the middle, a growing class of serfs under control of state-backed landlords at the bottom. Subsequent wars trans-formed that structure chiefly by thickening it.

Despite the importance of struggles among Sweden, Poland and Muscovy, sixteenth-century wars in the region intersected little with military confrontations farther west; they formed a separate complex whose main axes ran south and east from Warsaw. Although Mediterranean powers were already battling with the expansive Ottomans, for example, Eastern European states played no part in the major European wars between 1495 and the 1560s, which centred on the contest between Spain and France for Italian territory. During the same time, Muscovites were fighting not only their western neighbours but also the Tatars and Cossacks who resisted their south-eastward expansion, as Polish forces were also battling powers to their south: Moldavians, Turks and Tatars.

During the later seventeenth century, however, both the Russian and the Ottoman Empires became much more heavily involved in European wars. Russia joined its first European alliance in 1680. By 1682 it had banded together with Austria, Poland, Venice and the German states against its long-time foe, the Ottomans. Peter the Great's famed westernization of Russia included acceleration of the Empire's implication in Western European diplomacy and belligerency, not to mention nuptial politics; up to Peter's generation, Russia's royal families married almost exclusively into other Russian, Polish or Byzantine families, but from the next generation onward tsars became in-laws, then descendants, of many families based farther west, especially in German states.

By the 1730s, Russia had become a regular participant in Europe's more general wars, which *ipso facto* made the wars even more general. With its greatly expanded and westernized armies, Russia became a valuable ally and a fearsome enemy. In the same process, Poland, Sweden and the Ottoman Empite (although not the surviving Tatars) also plunged, or were dragged kicking and screaming, farther into wars originating to their west. On the way, Poland disappeared as Sweden lost its hold on Slav-inhabited lands.

War and revolutionary situations overlapped. Repeated Cossack rebellions against Poland between 1590 and 1734 greatly resembled Tatar resistance to Russian expansion a bit farther east, with the crucial difference that the Cossacks had prospered under Polish hegemony as mercenaries and as raiders on Turks or Tatars, but fought back when the Poles tried to trim their autonomies and subordinate their war-making to Polish armies. Cossacks presented a classic frontier problem to the Polish and Russian states. A composite people bringing together nomads, escaped serfs and freebooting soldiers, they became skilled warriors against the

Table 6.1 *International wars in Russia and adjacent regions, 1492–1992*

Date	War
1491–1502	Crimean Tatars vs. Kazan Tatars
1492–4	Muscovy vs. Lithuania
1495–6	Muscovy vs. Sweden
1497–9	Poland-Lithuania vs. Moldavia, Turks, Tatars
1500–3	Muscovy, Tatars vs. Poland-Lithuania, Livonian Order
1506–7	Muscovy vs. Kazan Tatars
1507–8	Poland-Lithuania, Tatars vs. Moldavia, Muscovy
1510	Muscovy vs. Pskov
1512–22	White Russian War
1521–4	Crimean and Kazan Tatars, Cossacks vs. Muscovy
1527–31	Poland vs. Moldavia
1532–3	Holy Roman Empire vs. Poland-Lithuania, Moldavia
1534–7	Muscovy vs. Poland-Lithuania, Tatars
1547–52	Muscovy vs. Kazan
1552–6	Russian conquest of Kazan, Astrakhan
1554–7	Muscovy vs. Sweden
1557–82	Livonian war
1563–70	Denmark, Poland, Lübeck vs. Sweden
1569	Turkey vs. Russia in Astrakhan
1570	Muscovy vs. Novgorod
1571–2	Crimean Tatars vs. Muscovy
1578–84	Muscovy vs. Siberian Tatars
1583–90	Polish–Turkish war

Date	War
1710–11	Russo–Turkish war
1716–17	Russia vs. Khiva
1722–4	Russia vs. Persia
1733–5	War of the Polish Succession
1734–9	Russia, Austria vs. Turkey
1740–48	War of the Austrian Succession
1741–3	Russo-Swedish war
1756–63	Seven Years War
1768–72	War of Confederation of Bar
1768–74	Russo–Turkish war
1781–2	Russia vs. Crimea
1787–92	Ottoman War
1788–90	Russo-Swedish war
1792–3	Russia, Prussia vs. Poland
1796–7	Russia vs. Persia
1799–1801	War of the Second Coalition
1803–15	Napoleonic Wars
1804–13	Russia vs. Persia
1806–12	Russo–Turkish war
1808–9	Russo-Swedish war
1821–4	Russian intervention in Moldavian, Wallachian war vs. Ottoman Empire
1821–9	Russian intervention in Greek war vs. Ottoman Empire
1826–8	Russia vs. Persia
1827	Navarino Bay
1828–9	Russo–Turkish war
1832–9	Russia vs. Circassians

1586–7	Muscovy vs. Siberian Tatars
1587–8	Austro-Polish war
1591–8	Crimean Tatars vs. Muscovy
1600	Poland vs. Moldavia, Wallachia
1600–14	Poland vs. Sweden
1605–6	Crimean Tatars vs. Muscovy
1611–18	Poland vs. Russia
1613–17	Sweden vs. Russia
1616–17	Poland vs. Turkey
1617–18	Poland vs. Sweden
1618–21	Polish–Turkish war
1621–2	Poland vs. Sweden
1625–7	Turkey, Tatars vs. Poland, Hungary
1625–9	Poland vs. Sweden
1631–4	Turkey, Tatars vs. Poland, Hungary
1632–4	Russia vs. Poland
1632–41	Crimean Tatars vs. Russia
1637–8	Cossacks vs. Crimean Tatars
1638	Denmark vs. Poland
1654–6	Russia, Cossacks vs. Poland
1658–61	Transylvania vs. Poland, Tatars, Turkey
1658–68	Russia, Cossacks vs. Poland
1672–6	Turkey, Tatars, Cossacks vs. Poland
1677–81	Turkey, Cossacks vs. Russia
1682–99	Turkey vs. Austria, German states, Poland, Venice, Russia
1687–9	Russia vs. Crimean Tatars
1700–21	Great Northern War
1839–40	Russia vs. Khiva
1847–53	Russia vs. Kazakhs
1848	Russian intervention in war of Moldavia, Wallachia vs. Ottoman Empire
1853–6	Crimean War
1855–9	Russia vs. Circassians
1857–8	Russia vs. Georgia
1864	Russia vs. Georgia
1865–8	Russia vs. Bokhara
1865–9	Russia vs. Khokand
1873	Russia vs. Khiva
1873–6	Russia vs. Khokand
1875–8	Russian intervention in Bosnian, Bulgarian rebellions vs. Ottoman Empire
1877–8	Russo-Turkish war
1877–81	Russia vs. Turcomans
1904–5	Russo-Japanese war
1914–18	World War I
1918	Soviet–Finnish war
1918–20	Soviet–Polish war
1919	Latvia, Estonia vs. Germany, Russia
1919–27	Polish-Lithuanian war
1939	Russo-Japanese war
1939–40	Soviet–Finnish war
1939–45	World War II
1956	Soviet intervention in Hungary
1979–85	Soviet intervention in Afghanistan

dreaded Turks and Tatars, and therefore useful to both Poland and
Russia. But in their zones of contested sovereignty, or no sovereignty at all, the more prosperous among them claimed the right
to hunt, fish, own land, avoid external taxes, bear arms and
conduct warfare on their own; in Russia or Poland, such claims
constituted self-designation as noble. Hence ambivalent Russian
and Polish policies: encouraging Cossacks to raid their enemies,
attempting to subordinate them to national authority, denying
their claims to special status when they came under national
authority. As Poland colonized the rich-soiled Ukraine for noble-
run agricultural estates during the sixteenth century, the policies
generated war after war, rebellion after rebellion.

The vast Cossack uprising of 1648–54 against Poland led to the
formation of a nominally independent Ukraine governed by
Cossacks, then (as Polish forces gained) produced a Cossack–
Russian accord placing the Ukraine under Russian suzerainty. In
1667, after further Russian–Polish–Cossack battles, the likely
happened: Russia and Poland partitioned the Ukraine, hence the
Cossacks, between them. Thenceforth both Russia and Poland had
to deal with Cossack resistance to central control. When, for
example, the Polish national assembly (*Sejm*) declared the autonomous Cossack army dissolved in 1699, Polish attemps to
implement that decision incited a major rebellion in 1704. All these
armed conflicts walked drunkenly along the line between war and
revolution.

Cossacks figured regularly in those movements in ways that
resemble contemporaneous conflicts on South and North American frontiers, where agents of European powers battled not only
resistant indigenous populations but also rival claimants to the
territory and renegades from their own camp who sought autonomy beyond the imperial span of control. Because of their
military prowess, Russians often relied on Cossacks as they moved
out across Siberia and into the south-east. As the central Russians
sought to settle landlords and peasants on the territories Cossacks
had helped them claim, Cossacks typically resisted the encroachment. But poorer Cossacks, including newcomers who had fled
from regions of serfdom, often sought to set up farms against the
will of richer Cossacks, who drew their wealth from fishing and
raiding, and who reasonably feared that extensive agriculture
would bring in Russians, landlords and serfdom. Stenka Razin led

Table 6.2 *Revolutionary situations in Russian states, 1492–1992*

1537	Gentry rebellion in Poland
1577	Poland vs. Danzig
1591–3	Cossack rebellion vs. Poland
1597–9	Cossack rebellion vs. Poland
1598–9	Polish rebellion, Swedish intervention
1598–1613	Time of Troubles: Muscovite rebellion, intervention by Poland, Sweden, Cossacks
1606–8	Gentry rebellion in Poland
1630	Cossack rebellion vs. Poland
1637–8	Cossack rebellion vs. Poland
1648–54	Cossack rebellion vs. Poland, Tatar intervention
1650	Novgorod, Pskov vs. Russia
1664–6	Lubomirski revolt vs. Poland
1667–71	Cossacks (Stenka Razin) vs. Russia
1668	Cossack rebellion vs. Poland, Tatar intervention
1674–81	Bashkir rebellion vs. Russia
1682	*Streltsy* rebellion in Moscow
1699	Lithuanian peasants vs. Poland
1705–11	Bashkir rebellion vs. Russia
1707–8	Bulavin (Cossack) rebellion vs. Russia
1734	Cossack rebellion vs. Poland
1735	Bashkir rebellion vs. Poland
1751–3	Peasant revolt in Russia
1754–5	Bashkir rebellion vs. Russia
1768–9	Haïdamak insurrection vs. Poland in Ukraine
1768–71	Polish civil war (Russian, French, Austrian intervention)
1773–5	Pugachev revolt vs. Russia
1794–5	Polish rebellion
1830–1	Polish rebellion
1863–4	Polish rebellion
1905	Russian Revolution
1916	Kirghiz vs. Russia
1917	Russian Revolutions
1917–21	Russian civil war, broad international intervention
1990–1	Separation of republics from Soviet Union

a group of poorer 'Naked' Cossacks. Razin's rebellion of 1670 followed his band's successful raids on Persia, across the Caspian Sea from its Don base. Razin's troops soon held Astrakhan, Saratov and Samara, and were beginning to gather force for a march on Moscow. Then the tsar sent an army to the Volga. It defeated Razin's forces and drove him into flight, whereupon Cossack leaders obligingly turned him over to Muscovite officials for eventual execution in Moscow.

Similar conflicts pitted Cossacks against the expanding Empire for another century or so. In 1707–8 Kondrat Bulavin emulated Stenka Razin in leading poor Cossacks against their richer neighbours and against troops Peter the Great had sent to the Don; Kalmucks and imperial forces collaborated in putting them down. In 1773–5, Cossack Emelian Pugachev identified himself as tsar Peter III, friend of the oppressed including Old Believers, miraculously preserved despite widespread belief in his death. Pugachev led a great rebellion that eventually connected Cossacks, Bashkirs, Old Believers, small farmers, serfs employed in factories and other serfs on the estates that were beginning to spread through the south-east. Pugachev's programme of freeing the peasantry made his revolt exceptional, but it also steeled the determination of Catherine the Great to exterminate him. As Pugachev's military campaign faltered, fellow Cossacks saved their own skins by turning him over to imperial troops; he died on the Moscow executioner's block in 1775. Meanwhile, Bashkirs repeatedly rebelled against imperial attempts to tame them. During the eighteenth century, Poland encountered similar challenges from Cossacks and Haïdamaks in Ukraine. Thus both Russia and Poland put down rebellion after rebellion on their frontiers well into the eighteenth century.

Both Poland and Russia also experienced important rebellions much closer to the centres of their polities. In 1537, for instance, the increasingly prosperous Polish gentry rose against king Sigismund the Old's attempts to maintain a royal military policy in the war against Muscovy, forcing him to confirm the Nothing New (*nihil novi*) decree, that the Polish government would undertake no innovations whatsoever without the full consent of the gentry's Chamber of Deputies, the Sejm's increasingly dominant component. Since the Chamber of Deputies had adopted a *liberum veto*, which essentially required unanimous consent on every measure the king proposed, the decree paralysed reform of any kind. The successful gentry rebellion weakened an already faltering crown, thereby accentuating the differences between centralization in Russia and decentralization in Poland.

Centralization did not occur without struggle in Russia. The greatest crisis of the sixteenth century arrived at its very end, in the famous Time of Troubles (1598–1613). Taxes and conscription for the long Livonian War (1557–82) had bled peasant villages, many of whose inhabitants had fled to freer lands farther south-east. That flight in turn diminished revenues of the great landlords (boyars), who agitated for compensation and repression. During the tenure of the incompetent Fedor I (1584–98), successive regents Nikitin Romanov and Boris Godunov had to hold off bids for power by the great families of Belsky, Shuisky and Mstislavsky; Godunov had many of them executed or exiled. At Fedor's death without an heir, tsarina Irene abdicated, which produced an acute succession crisis. After extensive negotiations and endorsement by the Zemsky Sobor (approximately an Estates General, but without the long prior history of its Western European counterparts) Godunov became tsar. The boyars went into opposition as Godunov turned to both preventive and retaliatory persecution, but by no means eliminated their political influence.

In that same period, disastrous harvests produced bands of marauding countrymen, urban residents fought over the dwindling food supply, and a pretender to the throne (the false Dmitry, posing as the son of Ivan IV whose murder Godunov had probably incited in 1591) appeared with military support from boyars and Polish nobles. Dmitry began the parade of fourteen serious pretenders during the seventeenth century. Many discontented subjects of the tsar, including Donetz Cossacks, joined the pretender's army in its march on Moscow. Faced with disintegration of his own armed force and attack by his enemies, Boris Godunov died in 1605. Despite widespread awareness of his false credentials, the pretender became tsar.

Not for long. Russia's boyars rose against tsar Dmitry in 1606, killing him, burning his body and – just to be sure – shooting his remains from a cannon. Although Basil Shuisky then claimed the throne, his coup generated resistance on the small scale and the large. Durable rebellions arose throughout the Empire. At one point, a rebel army led by former serf Ivan Bolotnikov menaced

Moscow before its remnants fell back to Tula, where Shuisky besieged them into defeat. A second false Dmitry also led an army toward Moscow, but with less success than the first.

Shuisky's effort to re-establish control precipitated a war, Polish intervention, his downfall and the establishment of the long-lived Romanov family on the Russian throne. Shuisky enlisted military support from Sweden's Charles IX in return for renunciation of Russian claims on Livonia, which then brought Poland to war against Russia. Polish forces took Moscow, a council of boyars recognized Polish king Sigismund as tsar and different segments of the Empire fell to Swedish, Cossack and Polish forces. Under ecclesiastical leadership, however, Cossacks and Russian townsmen allied to raise an army against the Polish conquerors of Moscow. They re-established Russian control. In 1613, another Zemsky Sobor elected boyar Michael Romanov tsar. Tsar Michael inherited the job of taming his fellow boyars (now decimated by fifteen years of civil war), driving out the Swedes and Poles and restoring imperial power in the hinterland. In essence he and his successors traded even greater concessions of power over the peasantry to the nobility for military and administrative co-operation with the crown.

Difficult successions continued to provide opportunities for the opening of revolutionary situations. The *streltsy* ('shooters' or musketeers) were elite infantrymen garrisoned in Moscow and other major cities who augmented their meagre military incomes with civilian employment. At the death of twenty-year-old tsar Fedor in 1682, notables including the orthodox patriarch passed over Fedor's sister Sophia and brother Ivan in favour of their ten-year-old half-brother Peter. But Sophia allied with aggrieved *streltsy* to raid the imperial palace, where they successfully called for Ivan to be named tsar with Sophia regent. Then the *streltsy* not only insisted that the government give a hearing to complaints of their favourite religious dissidents, the Old Believers, but began preparing to use their force to seize power. Sophia broke with them, calling out militiamen and imperial troops to counter a coup. She ruled on her brother's behalf for seven years.

By then, able younger brother Peter was approaching his majority and a likely coup of his own. Sophia's agents plotted to kill him beforehand, but Peter got wind of the conspiracy in time to act first. In 1689, his partisans (who naturally included members of great noble families) arrested Sophia and brought their candidate to power. The new tsar grew into one of the most influential of all: Peter the Great. He ruled until 1725, facing major rebellions of Bashkirs and Cossacks on the imperial frontiers, but no major internal challenge except for a recurrence of *streltsy* militarism in 1698. In war, on the other hand, he was involved for almost his entire tenure, battling with Turks, Swedes and Persians, not to mention the warriors of Khiva and Bukhara in Central Asia. Peter's expansion of the state's war-making capacity augmented the incentives for internal rebellion as it diminished rebellion's prospects for success.

In many respects, seventeenth- and eighteenth-century rebellions strengthened the Russian crown as they weakened the Polish crown. The differences lay in two essential facts: first, that during those two centuries Russian tsars always triumphed over their rebels, and used each occasion to decimate yet another set of potential opponents, while in Poland rebels repeatedly gained ground through alliances with some segment of the gentry and concessions from the crown; second, that the Russian nobility cast its lot irrevocably with the tsar, while in Poland the nobility sought continually to enhance its privileges and to restrain central power. Not that Russian aristocrats showed nobility of spirit that their Polish peers lacked; the control of grain trade by Polish nobles gave them leverage their Russian cousins surely envied them. In both cases, the bulk of the two centuries' larger-scale rebellions occurred chiefly in contested territories at the imperial periphery. As a result of these contrasting processes, the Russian state expanded in the eighteenth century, while the Polish state disappeared.

Built on the assumption of an autocratic tsar, nonetheless, the Russian Empire remained vulnerable to *coups d'état* by members of the ruling circle whenever a dubious succession occurred. Not only did pretenders to the throne multiply every time a tsar or tsarina died, but also great lords and elite military units such as the Guards (who drew their officers, *noblesse oblige*, from great families) plotted repeatedly to place their candidates on the imperial throne. At Peter's death, imperial guards passed power to a junta of Peter's new nobles, who ruled in the name of Peter's widow Catherine and then of their son Peter II. Guards and grandees similarly intervened at Peter II's death before coronation in 1730, helping Peter I's niece Ann to the throne.

Yet again in 1742 a coalition of Guards and great lords awarded Peter I's daughter Elizabeth the crown, as after Elizabeth's death in 1762 an officers' revolt against designated successor Peter III brought his wife in as tsarina Catherine II. She reigned until 1796, becoming known through vigour, intelligence and longevity as Catherine the Great. Then, after five years of struggle with great nobles, her son and successor Paul lost his life in a coup carried out with the consent of his own successor Alexander I. Thus the eighteenth-century Empire displayed a stunning combination of military expansion, administrative consolidation, state intervention, outstanding rulers and great vulnerability in the state's very centre at each succession.

Eighteenth-century successions caused even greater vulnerability in Poland, but there a combination of Polish lords and foreign potentates, including the Russian monarch, typically intervened to choose the new king. Eighteenth-century Polish kings included Augustus, Elector of Saxony, who defeated the French prince of Conti for the post; wealthy Polish nobleman Stanislas Lesczynski, scion of an old Polish gentry family; Augustus III, son of the older Elector; and Stanislas Poniatowski, candidate of Catherine the Great, who beat out the Czartoryski family and suffered their opposition throughout his reign. Meanwhile Russia posed as protector of Poland's orthodox subjects as Prussia claimed a special interest in Poland's Protestants. Since the Polish crown was advancing the rights of its own Uniate church (orthodox in ritual, but affiliated with Rome), both protectors had reasons for alarm. In any case, the civil war of 1768–71, during which a gentry confederation based in the town of Bar rose against the king and his efforts to strengthen the crown, attracted (or at least justified) the further intervention of Prussia, Russia, then Austria. As a consequence, Poland lost major segments of its lands to the north, east and south, including much of Pomerania, Little Poland, Ruthenia, Byelorussia, Livonia and Vitebsk. By then Russia dominated Eastern Europe.

Poland still had more to lose through Russian intervention. In 1791, at royal insistence, the Sejm of shrunken Poland adopted a centralizing constitution that immediately alienated part of the nobility. Organized as the Confederation of Targowica, noble leaders invited Catherine of Russia to send in troops. She promptly did, occupying Warsaw and checking the crown's feeble forces. King Stanislas went over to the conservative confederation. That brief civil war led to the second partition of Polish lands among Russia, Prussia and Austria in 1793. Soon after, Thaddeus Kosciuszko (a veteran of the American Revolutionary War) led a reorganized army on behalf of the abortive new constitution, just rescinded by a frightened Sejm. On behalf of the nation, the rebel forces daringly but vainly declared war against both Prussia and Russia. Prussian and Russian forces did not take long to reply by defeating the Poles and seizing Kosciuszko. This time the three-way partition among Austria, Prussia and Russia left no Polish territory independent. Poland disappeared except as a memory, a nationalist programme, and a set of administrative subdivisions within newly enlarged, newly adjacent empires.

Nineteenth-century Consolidation

In the process, Russia became much more heavily involved in the politics of Western Europe. The Napoleonic Wars themselves implicated Russia deeply in Western European affairs, and Western Europeans in Russian politics; the duke of Richelieu, for example, first served as a Russian officer and governor-general of southern Russia, then became Louis XVIII's chief minister at the Restoration, when Russians were occupying France. During the occupation, furthermore, cultivated francophone Russian officers (as well as bequeathing the Russian word *bistro*, 'quickly', to the French language) established durable ties with Parisian salon life. With the important exception of the Crimean War, which again pitted Russia against France, nineteenth-century Russian forces did not make war against Western European armies; instead they became the battering ram that jarred the Ottoman Empire's northern provinces. While West European powers captured colonies overseas, Russia fought chiefly to extend its own frontiers southward and eastward.

No one could claim that Russia or Poland's ghost faced the nineteenth century calmly, but openly revolutionary situations became rare after 1775; indeed, the only major revolutionary situations between then and 1905 were Polish insurrections against

Russian rule in 1794–5, 1830–1 and 1863–4. The attempted Russian officers' coup of December 1825 has attracted wide attention because it involved a secret society of reformist aristocrats, but the open revolt consisted of no more than brief military face-offs in St. Petersburg and Kiev. The Decembrist revolt took place, like its eighteenth-century predecessors, during an interregnum. When Alexander I died suddenly, his brother and designated successor Nicholas hesitated to take the crown because of his own notorious unpopularity in the officer corps; the officers meant to strike in favour of his reluctant brother Constantine before Nicholas assumed office. That was the last serious attempt of landlords and officers to seize power at a disputed succession. Like many of his ancestors, Alexander II was to die as a result of assassination in 1881, but Alexander fell to the bombs of Populist activists, not his fellow aristocrats.

Polish patriots, on the other hand, watched their Russian rulers closely for signs of vulnerability. The first great nineteenth-century Polish rebellion took place in 1830, when reactionary Nicholas I proposed to send the Polish army to suppress the recent revolutions in Belgium and France. Liberal conspiratorial societies had been active in Poland since the end of the Napoleonic Wars. When Nicholas ordered his mobilization, their members had already been planning an insurrection to begin with Warsaw's infantry cadets. They therefore had to strike before they had completed their preparations. Cadets attacked the palace of the Grand Duke (Nicholas' brother Constantine), and gained substantial popular following. The rebels managed to establish an Administrative Council, then a Provisional Government, which declared the dethroning of the Romanovs. After international diplomatic pressure in favour of the Poles, incessant manoeuvring among Polish factions and six months of battles with Russian troops, however, the revolutionary regime collapsed. Russia restored its rule, integrating Poland much more thoroughly into its own administrative system.

Despite the formation of National Committees and sporadic uprisings in the Austrian and Prussian segments of former Polish territory, the revolutions of 1848 passed without significant popular collective action in Russian Poland. Coming to power in the midst of the disastrous Crimean War, Russia's Alexander II (1855–81) extended his liberalizing efforts from emancipating

Russian serfs in 1861 to restoring a number of Polish liberties in 1862. While Polish moderates collaborated with the tsar's programme, active nationalists (Reds) demonstrated for more, especially agrarian reforms. Alexander's government decided to draft activists, who were disproportionately students, into the Russian army. The new mobilization order incited the rebellion of January 1863. This time nobles were little involved; the insurrection had a broad popular base and connections through the intelligentsia, but lacked a central military command. As a result, Russian forces prevailed after fifteen months of guerilla warfare. Russia replied with even greater repression and incorporation than in 1831.

Within Russia itself, the nineteenth century boiled with revolutionary ideas and conspiracies, but none of them split the polity as earlier succession crises had. Repression and censorship worked for a time, neutralizing the grandees who aspired to power, holding down the Cossacks and the numerous minorities who were being incorporated into the Empire, fragmenting the peasantry, deflecting the intelligentsia into conspiracies or silence. As in other settings where grievances are deep, repression fierce and dissident organization thin, urban opponents of the regime took to assassinations and clandestine attacks on property. Such terrorist acts exposed the regime's vulnerability while avoiding face-to-face, force-to-force confrontations with authorities.

Peasants, it is true, attacked landlords and officials at an increasing pace, especially after the emancipation of 1861. But even the most determined peasant rebels did not coalesce into major regional rebellions, ally themselves with other dissidents who already possessed a national communication structure, or gain access to serious weapons on their own. Despite the hopes of conspirators, even Alexander II's assassination by members of People's Freedom in March 1881 called up no popular revolution. On the contrary, it stimulated an unprecedented wave of repression, including settlement laws and government-inspired pogroms that wiped away the public rights, often the very lives, of Russian Jews.

Alexander II's reforms did not accomplish what the tsar's advisors intended, but they had profound effects on Russian politics from the 1860s onward. They moved Russia toward direct rule by wiping out nobles' administrative powers and creating alternative institutions in direct contact with higher state officials. The emancipation of serfs freed household workers (whose owners often hired them out to factories and shops) without land. Estate peasants received the opportunity to buy half the land they tilled, not on their own account but on behalf of a commune which, under the supervision of state agents, controlled land use and periodically redistributed the land in proportion to household size. The creation of hierarchies of regional assemblies, *zemstvos*, put a quasi-representative apparatus into place. Reorganization of the courts established a much more complete judicial system, also extending from local to national level. Communes, regional assemblies and courts provided an unprecedented basis for direct intervention in local affairs from the top down, for political mobilization from the bottom up. The continued importance of landlords, many of them now possessing half of a commune's land in fee simple and hiring former serfs to work it at starvation wages, fed local conflicts to bursting.

During the quarter-century after Alexander II's assassination, Alexander III and Nicholas II presided over great contradictions: on one side, rapid industrialization, swift population growth, vigorous urbanization, extensive proletarianization of the rural population, political mobilization through the *zemstvos* and the universities; on the other, expanded repression and censorship, limitation of the *zemstvos'* power, forced Russianization of ethnic and religious minorities, new privileges for nobles. Flowing together, the two currents issued in a raging torrent.

At the very end of the 1890s arrived a series of challenges to the state from students, peasants, then workers. Between 1899 and 1901, confrontations between students and public authorities at the universities of St. Petersburg and Kiev stimulated national waves of student strikes and demonstrations as well as the assassination of the minister of education. In 1902 peasants attacked noble estates in 175 communes of the Ukraine, upon which tsarist authorities sent 837 peasants to prison and assessed the guilty villages collectively with a collective fine of 800,000 rubles (Shanin 1986: II, 11). In 1903, a wave of industrial strikes brought out exceptional numbers of workers in southern Russia, ending with the army's occupation of the oil fields. These strikes sufficed to swell the number of workers charged with 'crimes against the state'; the total number charged with such crimes quintupled between

1884–90 and 1901–3, as the proportion of those charged who were non-agricultural workers rose from 17.2 to 50.3 per cent (Shanin 1986: II, 25–6). Not only intelligentsia but also peasants and workers were aligning themselves visibly against the regime.

Prospects of Revolution

Eleven years after serf emancipation and eight years after the *zemstvo* and judicial reforms, in 1872, French liberal intellectual Anatole Leroy-Beaulieu made the first of many trips to Russia for a survey of political and social life he would report first in multiple issues of the *Revue des Deux Mondes* and then in *L'Empire des tsars et les Russes* (three volumes appearing in 1881 to 1889). As he was working on his reports, the French visitor witnessed a brutal, pivotal Russo-Ottoman war, the introduction of universal military service, the rise of labour unions, strikes and revolutionary associations, repeated attacks against officials including the assassination of tsar Alexander – in short, widespread domestic conflict, and grounds for much more. As the book version of his observations was appearing, moreover, he could see the massive reaction that would fortify revolutionaries and reformists in their opposition to the regime. Yet if his analysis incorporated a teleology, it was not of revolution, but of liberal individualism.

Like many observers today, Leroy-Beaulieu saw the present and future of Russia chiefly in terms of obstacles to liberalization: an entrenched bureaucracy, a rural commune (*mir*) that blocked the peasant's rational use of his land, religious discrimination, the weakness of civil liberties. Anticipating observers of the 1990s who perceived the Communist Party's destruction as the start of a long, dangerous process of readjustment, he saw the emancipation of serfs as a necessary first step toward a progressive society, but a step making more urgent the reorganization of economic and political institutions. He also portrayed individualism and industry as spreading rapidly in Russia, hastening the country toward the model of Western Europe. Leroy-Beaulieu died in 1912, having known the Revolution of 1905 (indeed, having attended the Duma of 1906), but he did not live to see World War I and the Revolutions of 1917.

Nevertheless, Leroy-Beaulieu did recognize the strength of radicalism and the possibility of revolution in Russia: 'What above all has promoted the development of radicalism is the moral repression, the intellectual poverty and deprivation that are inherent in the political regime' (Leroy-Beaulieu 1990:827). Since he saw no chance that the intelligentsia's 'missionaries' would join forces with workers and peasants, however, he envisioned a popular revolution quite differently. Given the influence of the *mir*, it would consist of savage revenge:

> In that agrarian socialism, the provinces would again see the bloody Jacquerie of Pugachev. Among the most ignorant and credulous people of Europe, a revolution would probably exceed in barbarity all our Terrors and Communes. (p. 841)

Drawing directly on the French revolutionary model, Leroy-Beaulieu ticked off the reasons why no popular revolution would occur: too big an empire, too scattered a population, too strong a bureaucracy, too few big cities, no rebellious populace in the capital (p. 843). More suprisingly, he held out the alternative possibility that a series of nationalist revolutions would recast the heterogeneous elements of the Russian Empire as a federation, perhaps even as a federated appendage of the United States (pp. 865–8). Finally he held out the prospect of a liberal revolution from above that would pre-empt a much more dangerous reactionary revolution from below:

> The West had its revolution in the French Revolution; all the German and Latin peoples felt its influence to some degree, adopted its doctrines, experienced its goods and evils. Our revolution was more or less the redemption of old feudal Europe; but one can say that patriarchal eastern Europe, the Orthodox Slav world is still waiting for its revolution, or what will take its place; where will the initiative come from, if not from Russia? Thus seen, a Russian revolution could be history's greatest event since the French Revolution, and its complement at the other end of Europe. (p. 890)

Leroy-Beaulieu wrote in the 1880s, two decades before the Russian Revolution of 1905.

What were the grounds for expecting revolution, of whatever sort, in that Russia of the 1880s? They echoed Tocqueville on Old

Regime France, saying essentially that the Empire had alienated much of its former mainstay, the nobility, without creating an alternative base of political support; that the end of serfdom had given nobles incentives to dissolve their ties of obligation and control, if not of exploitation, with a rapidly proletarianizing peasantry; that peasants themselves, the bulk of the Russian population, were accumulating powerful grievances against both nobles and rulers; that in St. Petersburg and Moscow connected industrial proletariats and bourgeoisies were forming and chafing under the regime's restriction of civil liberties; that a vast, if poorly connected, network of revolutionary associations was attracting many members of the intelligentsia and some members of the former ruling classes; in short, that the proximate conditions for revolutionary situations were forming, namely: (1) the appearance of coalitions of contenders advancing exclusive competing claims to control of the state; (2) commitment to those claims by a significant segment of the citizenry; (3) incapacity or unwillingness of rulers to suppress the alternative coalition and/or commitment to its claims. Of these conditions, most lacking was a blow that would weaken and discredit the state, thus making the revolutionary alternative seem not only desirable but credible.

In general, three further circumstances promote the proximate conditions for revolutionary situations: increasing discrepancies between what rulers demand of their best-organized subjects and their own capacity to compel compliance; attacks on major identities and their perquisites within the subject population; diminution of rulers' power in the presence of well-organized competitors. In later nineteenth- and early twentieth-century Russia, all three occurred: state demands for taxes and conscripts rose with the Crimean, Ottoman and Russo-Japanese Wars, as repression tightened after Alexander II's assassination, but with the nobility's alienation state capacity to enforce control actually declined. Attacks on distinctive identities occurred in the non-Russian regions as well as in the persecution of Russian Jews. The most dramatic changes concerned the visible capacity of the state; it plummeted.

The push off the precipice resulted from Russia's spectacularly losing participation in two wars, the first with Japan, the second with a coalition centred on the German Empire. Not the beginnings, but the ends, of those two wars brought the collapse of the tsarist state.

The 1905 Revolution

It is tempting to treat the Russian Revolution of 1905 as a mere prelude to 1917. If the Revolutions of 1917 had not occurred, however, today's histories of Russia might well have treated 1905 as a great moment of decision. The war and revolution of 1904–6 marked the limits of Russian imperial expansion, exposed the vulnerability of the tsarist state, established workers as major political actors, introduced the soviet as a form of revolutionary government, publicized the general strike as an effective means of popular anti-state action, identified Bolsheviks, Mensheviks and Social Revolutionaries as credible challengers to the existing power, created a kind of national assembly where only an occasional Zemsky Sobor had ever met, then stimulated significant steps toward full-scale capitalism.

The 1905 Revolution took its immediate impulse from imperial expansion and a failed war. By the late nineteenth century, Russian imperial forces were advancing deep into Asia, constructing a trans-Siberian railroad, brushing Afghanistan, establishing themselves along China's northern border, penetrating Manchuria, threatening Korea and therefore clearly entering the space in which an expansive Japan and a weakened China were competing for control. Playing the usual divide-and-conquer game, Russia aligned itself loosely with China against Japan while cooperating with Germany and Great Britain in the penetration of China. Russia's drive toward the Pacific met Japan's own effort to build an Asian empire; the result was war. To the surprise of Russians and other Europeans, the Japanese fleet trounced the Russian navy. The Russian government lost credit, revolutionaries assassinated interior minister Plehve, a national congress of *zemstvos* met to call for a national assembly and the concession of civil liberties, and demands for government liberalization arose widely in the land.

On 22 January 1905 – Bloody Sunday – tsarist troops fired on a workers' procession, led by orthodox priest Gapon, on their way to petition the tsar. The movement spread, augmented by multiple strikes. Mutinies broke out in the army and navy, demands for autonomy in non-Russian provinces more vocal, and peasants once again attacked landlords, until (in October 1905) a vast general strike shut down much of European Russia. In St. Petersburg, a worker's soviet coordinated the strike. The tsar's concession first of a consultative assembly (Duma), then of more extensive representative institutions and civil liberties, co-opted some of his opposition while making the Social Democrats (both Mensheviks and Bolsheviks) the state's most visible enemies. At prime minister Witte's arrest of the St. Petersburg soviet, workers in Moscow rose to fight imperial troops in the streets, but lost their bid for power.

The ultimate return of tsarist forces to power relegated the events of 1905–6 to the category of failed rebellions. But observers at the time saw 1905 as a major revolutionary crisis. In January 1905, no less an observer than V. I. Lenin wrote from exile in Geneva:

> The working class has received a momentous lesson in civil war; the revolutionary education of the proletariat made more progress in one day than it could have made in months and years of drab, humdrum, wretched existence. The slogan of the heroic St. Petersburg proletariat, 'Death or freedom!' is reverberating throughout Russia. Events are developing with astonishing rapidity. The general strike in St. Petersburg is spreading. All industrial, public and political activities are paralysed. (Lenin 1967: I, 450)

Lenin went on to detail revolutionary activity in Moscow, Lodz, Warsaw, Helsinki, Baku, Odessa, Kiev, Kharkov, Kovno, Vilna, Sebastopol, Revel, Saratov and Radom. When Lenin drew the 'Lessons of the Moscow Uprising' in August 1906, it is true, he concluded

> the December action in Moscow vividly demonstrated that the general strike, as an independent and predominant form of struggle, is out of date, that the movement is breaking out of these narrow bounds with elemental and irresistible force and giving rise to the highest form of struggle – an uprising. (I, 577)

Lenin concluded that the proletariat had to arm itself for the next revolutionary opportunity. This time, he said, the workers (read: the Bolsheviks) were not ready. The occasion had passed.

Just before the meeting of the first Duma (May 1906), the tsar had pre-empted much of its political space by issuing Fundamental Laws that amounted to limited constitutional government. Relatively conservative in composition because the radical parties had

boycotted elections, the Duma nonetheless criticized the government bitterly and dissolved without substantial accomplishment.
Meanwhile the government, operating under martial law and
backed by masses of troops returned from the Far East, began
prosecuting and executing the rebels of 1905; over a thousand died.
New prime minister Stolypin promulgated an agrarian law essentially instituting private property, checked a second Duma including more radical representatives, imposed a restricted electorate for
the third Duma and tightened repression of revolutionary groups,
but also initiated a series of liberal reforms as the economy began
to recover from a long depression.

Both repression and conspiratorial violence continued. In the
relatively peaceful year of 1908, politically motivated attacks
resulted in the deaths of 1800 officials and the wounding of another
2083 (Fitzpatrick 1982: 29). Even the assassination of Stolypin in
1911 and the participation of Russia in the Balkan wars (1912–13)
did not change the balance of power fundamentally. But the army's
massacre of strikers in the Lena goldfields (April 1912), where 170
workers died, incited yet another round of strikes, the start of a
wave that would not recede until the Bolshevik seizure of power in
1917.

Two More Revolutions

Another assassination indirectly drew Russia into a great war. As
the Ottoman Empire weakened, Austria-Hungary had been laying
hands on its Balkan territories. Austria annexed Bosnia and
Herzegovina in 1908, thus heating up anti-Austrian feeling in
adjacent Serbia and Montenegro. Russia was soon involved in
organizing alliances in the Balkans and elsewhere to block further
Austrian advances. Austria worked with equal eagerness to prevent
Serbia from extending its territory to the Adriatic, which was one
of several possible outcomes of the Balkan wars that broke out in
1912 and 1913. One month after Gavrilo Princip, Bosnian agent of
the Serbian Black Hand, assassinated archduke Franz Ferdinand
(28 June 1914), Austria declared war on Serbia. Russia mobilized
its troops almost immediately, which in turn led Germany to
declare war against Russia. The cascade toward World War I had
begun.

World War I repeated some of the revolutionary effects of the Russo-Japanese war in Russia and elsewhere in Europe. It devastated much of the European continent: 9 million deaths in battle, 20 million combatants wounded, millions more killed and wounded among civilians and more than 300 billion US dollars (1918 style) in material losses. It brought not only the Russian Revolutions of 1917 but also the disintegration of the Russian, German, Austro-Hungarian and Ottoman Empires, the establishment of an independent Poland, Finland, Latvia, Estonia and Lithuania, plus numerous other changes of boundaries and rulers. Although Scandinavia and the Iberian peninsula avoided direct military action, the searing breath of war left no part of Europe untouched. The depth and breadth of wartime mobilization produced large expansions of state bureaucracies and state power, including power to requisition, conscript and tax. All states ran up enormous burdens of debt, not to mention overpowering commitments to veterans and other war-justified claimants on the state; all states failed to meet some of their commitments, and therefore felt their citizens' wrath.

The partition of Poland twelve decades earlier meant that the Russian Empire shared long frontiers with Germany and Austria-Hungary. The three powers fought across those frontiers for the next four years. Most of their battles took place on former Polish territory, especially the portion Russia had taken during the eighteenth century. Before the armistice of December 1917, neither German nor Austrian forces had penetrated the Russian heartland. But in Poland and the Baltic, they battered Russian armies. Russian defeats of 1915 in Galicia and Bukovina first signalled Russia's military vulnerability. In 1916, German occupiers announced the formation of an independent Polish state, and in March 1917 the new Russian provisional government actually recognized Poland's independence. The army was suffering defeat after defeat, and the Empire was beginning to disintegrate.

Industrial conflict registered the dissatisfaction of Russia's workers with the war and the regime. In 1914, almost thirty times as many Russian workers struck as in 1910; in 1915, the level fell by more than half, only to regain great heights in 1916. Judging from the compilations of Diane Koenker and William Rosenberg (1989), 1917 surely surpassed 1914. Russian increases outshadowed those of any other major European country, even Germany, where 1919 brought almost fourteen times as many strikers out as 1910.

Worker action played a crucial part in the struggle of 1917. In Petrograd (which St. Petersburg had become at the beginning of the war) workers struck massively, then a general mutiny of the capital's troops began. The Duma replied to an imperial order for its dissolution by declaring a provisional government. Tsar Nicholas abdicated in favour of his brother Michael, who quickly abdicated in his turn; a provisional government staffed by conservatives and liberals suddenly found itself in charge of the threatened state. The Petrograd soviet of workers and soldiers soon challenged the government's authority, using its extensive influence in factories and the army to block central control and installing elected committees as counter-authorities. In April and May, radical leaders including Lenin and Trotsky returned from their diaspora.

A first attempt by the Bolsheviks to seize power in Petrograd (July 1917) failed, sending Lenin back into exile, this time in nearby Finland rather than distant Switzerland. The provisional government split over how hard a line to take against the Bolsheviks, with Alexander Kerensky (prime minister) dismissing general Lavr Kornilov (commander in chief). Kornilov unsuccessfully ordered his troops to take Petrograd. From then on, the Bolsheviks stole support steadily from the discredited provisional government. On 6 November (24 October in the old Russian calendar), the Bolsheviks struck against the government and won. On the following day, the All-Russian Congress of Soviets ratified the Bolshevik coup; in alliance with Soviet Revolutionaries, Bolsheviks took over the state.

They had their work cut out for them. The war continued, counter-revolutionaries were arming, and the new government was trying to implement rapid collectivization of land, capital and industry, beginning with the immediate partition of great estates. In many regions, peasants anticipated the government by seizing land on their own. Elections to a constituent assembly later in November returned a large majority of Social Revolutionaries, but when the assembly met in January 1918 Red troops immediately dissolved it by force. To the extent that anyone commanded in Russia, it was henceforth the Bolsheviks, who soon styled themselves the Communist Party.

As the Bolsheviks conducted peace talks at Brest-Litovsk, major segments of the Empire declared their independence: Ukraine,

Estonia, Finland, Moldavia and Latvia. At the treaty's signature, Russia lost Lithuania and Transcaucasia as well. By the end of the year Cossacks were allied with the counter-revolutionary White army against the Bolshevik state. As the Allies and the Entente continued their war, multiple powers entered other parts of the Empire: American, French and British forces in Murmansk, Archangel and Vladivostok, Japanese in the Far East, Turks in the south, Germans on many sides. Perhaps the most bizarre incursion brought in 100,000 Czech troops. Unable to break through Austrian lines from the east, they headed eastward across Siberia in an effort to return to Europe via Vladivostok. First, however, they seized a number of towns along the Trans-Siberian Railway, then declared war on Germany from Russia's interior. (That declaration of war gained them recognition from the British and the Americans, thus cementing their claims to an independent post-war state.) During 1918, Georgia, Azerbaijan and Armenia joined the ranks of self-declared independents. The Empire had essentially shrunk to Russia; even portions of Russia were in revolt.

Over the next four years, Trotsky's Red armies struggled to regain control of imperial territory. They did not win back Finland, the Baltic states or Poland, but they did eventually gain victories in most of the other territories the Empire had held in 1914. A war with Poland over Ukraine (April–October 1920) and an uprising of sailors at Kronstadt (February–March 1921) were the last great internal military challenges. The Polish war cost Russia the western halves of Byelorussia and Ukraine. Russia's communists rebuilt the state by means of armed struggle and fundamental reorganization of the economy. Indeed, they had an advantage that became a problem: with the revolution and civil war, they built a governmental structure that consisted essentially of a vast army – over five million men in 1920 – penetrated by a highly centralized Party. Demobilization therefore posed a serious threat to the entire communist system of rule. The communists solved their problem, to the extent that they solved it, by substituting the civilian bureaucracy, with its vast numbers of pre-revolutionary functionaries, for the army. They again inserted a tightly disciplined but tactically supple Communist Party into that bureaucracy.

Civil war and an Allied blockade combined to devastate both agricultural and industrial production. The number of industrial workers dwindled from 3.6 million in 1917 to 1.5 million in 1920 (Fitzpatrick 1982: 85–6). By 1921, Lenin and his collaborators undertook essentially to arrange a new deal with peasants; the New Economic Policy imposed a grain tax but left cultivators free to sell the rest of their surplus and to acquire farms of their own. At the same time, the state sought to stabilize its currency. In retrospect, NEP looks a lot like the 'market socialism' many East Europeans were advocating in 1992, except that the communists held tightly to central controls over manufacturing, distribution and, especially, finances.

The contrast with Germany's contemporaneous economic crisis clarifies what was happening. Whatever crisis the Soviet Union faced in the 1920s, it was the crisis of a socializing economy; whatever crisis Germany faced, it was the crisis of a capitalizing economy. 'Capitalist economies,' Edward Nell has argued, 'characteristically operate with a margin of excess, not merely reserve, capacity, while socialist economies suffer under pressure of excess demand' (Nell 1991: 1). Katherine Verdery, synthesizing a good deal of work in and on Eastern Europe, helps explain Nell's distinction by saying that 'socialism's central imperative is to increase the bureaucracy's *capacity* to allocate, and this is not necessarily the same as increasing the amounts to be allocated' (Verdery 1991: 421).

Thus the attachment of access to housing, food, consumption goods and privileges to membership in administrative and productive organizations follows directly from the system's premise; it differs fundamentally from the capitalist assumption that individual owners of wealth have the right to dispose of it as they see fit. Although neither Nell nor Verdery says so, the distinction stems directly from the historical conditions under which capitalism and socialism took shape: the first in merchants' seizure or creation of productive means in competition with other merchants, the second in a state's capture of productive means from capitalists. In this light, we can see both NEP and the relative liberalization of the German economy after the great mobilization of World War I as steps away from central control over bureaucratic capacity to allocate.

For the six years that it lasted, NEP produced a substantial economic recovery. It ended with Stalin's takeover in 1927, his expulsion of Trotsky, his promotion of forced-draft industrialization and the consequent formation of a much bulkier civilian administration. With that takeover, Stalin began something of a revolution from above, with no more than a glimmer of a revolutionary situation – that is, of an effective split within the Soviet polity. Stalin and his collaborators had such a strong grip on the Party apparatus that they could stage repeated purges between 1929 and 1938 without inciting open rebellion. The rapid growth of a police force, including a deadly, politicized secret police, reinforced control from the centre.

In the Empire's breakaway states, the period from 1918 to 1921 similarly prolonged the revolutionary struggles of 1917. Germany had occupied Latvia, Lithuania and Estonia through much of the war, Poland became a major battleground, while Finland remained mostly *hors de combat*. At various moments soon after the Bolshevik seizure of power, all five declared their independence of Russia. From the treaty of Brest-Litovsk to German surrender, Latvia, Lithuania and Estonia maintained precarious existences under German 'protection'. With the Germans defeated, Russian forces sought to recapture all three, but gave up in 1920. Russian and international recognition were not enough, however, for Lithuania, which was soon at war with Poland over possession of Vilna; that war did not end until 1927. After initial experiments with land redistribution and democratization, all three also eventually experienced right-wing coups, although in Estonia the dictatorial regime came late (1934–6) and did not last long.

After German control through much of the war, the Polish state acquired fuller independence when Germany surrendered in 1918, and under Pilsudski's direction strove immediately to recapture adjacent territories that had once lived under Polish rule: Galicia, Posen, Lithuania, Silesia and elsewhere. That irredentism brought the new Polish leaders into war with Lithuania (1919–27) and with the Soviet Union (1920). In 1926, Pilsudski led a right-wing coup, establishing a government that endured, with many zigs and zags, until the German invasion of 1939.

In Finland, finally, a major civil war between Whites and Reds cracked the country open in 1918. A German invasion helped the Whites drive out the Reds. By 1919 Finland and the Soviet Union were briefly at war over Karelia. Like its Baltic neighbours, Finland undertook redistribution of land and democratization during the 1920s only to generate vigorous right-wing reaction.

Although Finland's versions of a military coup failed (1930, 1932), pressure from successive authoritarian-nationalist movements split Finnish politics well into the 1930s. The political contrast between the Soviet Union and the newly independent states beyond its north-east frontiers grew ever sharper. As a result, the occupation of half of Poland by the Soviet Union (1939), the defeat of Finland in the Soviet–Finnish war (1939–40) with its subsequent Finno-Russian accommodation, and the military alliances followed by outright absorption into the Soviet Union of Latvia, Lithuania and Estonia (1939–40) caused brutal shifts in the characters of those states.

Consolidation and Collapse

Under Stalin, the Soviet Union fashioned a fascinating composite. In some respects, it mimicked the Russian Empire's structure: substantial centralized direct rule in Russia itself, now pushed even more aggressively to the level of the individual commune, continued indirect rule in most of the non-Russian republics, now mediated by Communist Party functionaries and gradually modified by the flow of Russians into positions of bureaucratic, professional and industrial command. Outside of Russia itself, the vast majority of the population spoke Russian as a second language, or not at all (Laitin, Petersen & Slocum 1992: 141).

Agricultural collectivization, implantation of heavy industry and reorganization of distribution all built their own vast organizations, still monitored and connected by the Communist Party apparatus. In the 1930s, the system consolidated, with Party officials acquiring privileges, powers and manners that set them off from the rest of the population. The vicious purges of 1937 and 1938, however, demonstrated the compulsion that lay behind consolidation; Stalin was still eliminating potential challengers to his personal control. With German remilitarization looming, furthermore, the Soviet Union began devoting more of its industrial expansion to military production.

World War II had enormous but ambivalent effects on the Soviet state. On one side, the loss of 7 million lives, the destruction of 60 per cent of the country's industrial capacity and the deep incursion of German troops into Soviet territory constituted terrible disruptions of the political machine. On the other, the extraordinary mobilization for war, the ultimate victory over Nazi power and the extension of Soviet influence into Central Europe reinforced the state's already great prestige and scope. Through its coerced post-war accords with former Axis allies Hungary, Bulgaria and Romania, as well as with Axis victims Czechoslovakia and Poland, the Soviet Union extended its power farther westward than the tsars had ever accomplished; the formation of the Warsaw Pact as a counter to NATO in 1955 simply consolidated the Soviet military hold on Central Europe.

Within Soviet politics, the military gained as well. Experiences of the civil war and war communism (1917–21) had already set a precedent for massive military presence in civilian life, but subsequent efforts at economic mobilization had enhanced the power and separateness of Party cadres. The campaigns of World War II, however, increased collaboration between Party commissars and military officers; the mutual suspicion of Party and army that had characterized the 1930s declined. Reorganized under a Ministry of the Armed Forces and claiming a major share of the national budget, the military emerged from the war stronger than before.

The military revival rested, however, on a major effort in creating Soviet economic infrastructure. The Soviet Union's post-war reconstruction almost without foreign assistance constitutes one of the all-time exploits of state power anywhere; within a few years, on the ruins of a pulverized economy, the Soviets built an effective system of military production capable of launching satellites and matching American arms. That the effort solidified the power of military men and strangled the civilian sector should not blind us to the immensity of the rebuilding.

The Cold War with the United States and its allies shaped the possibilities for revolution facing the post-war Soviet Union. For many years, the Soviet Union's contact with revolutionary situations consisted of external interventions, either in its Eastern European satellites or in states outside of Europe. Of the former, the most extensive were the use of Soviet troops to put down dissidents in Hungary, Czechoslovakia and Poland. Of the latter, the most extensive and devastating was the indirect confrontation with the United States in Afghanistan, beginning with Soviet assistance in the left-leaning military coup of 1979 and continuing with the American provision of aid to a variety of Afghan rebels against the military government. Although the rebels could not win, they did not lose either. The Soviet military suffered an expensive stalemate similar to the one their American enemies had endured in Vietnam. Before the 1988 signing of peace agreements in Geneva, the Soviet Union was maintaining between 100,000 and 120,000 troops in Afghanistan, without gaining on the foes of what was by now almost a Soviet puppet regime.

After the death of hard-liner Leonid Brezhnev in 1979 and the short reigns of Yuri Andropov and Constantin Chernenko over the next six years, Mikhail Gorbachev came to the head of the Communist Party, hence *de facto* to the head of the state, in 1985. He soon announced a programme of *glasnost*, of liberalizing public life, which took such forms as releasing celebrated dissident prisoners (for example Anatoli Shcharansky and Andrei Sakharov) in 1986 and accelerating exit visas for Jews (almost none in 1985, 1000 in 1986, 20,000 in 1988, 60,000 in 1989). In 1987, Gorbachev added to his political liberalization a programme of *perestroika*, restructuring of the economy to reorient it from military to civilian production and greatly increase its productivity.

More guardedly, Gorbachev pushed the state toward shrinking its military establishment, reducing its military involvement outside the USSR and ceasing its violent repression of organized demands for autonomies – religious, ethnic and political – within the Soviet Union. Gorbachev made a series of bids for popular support for his programme, culminating in the creation in 1989 of a huge Congress of People's Deputies. The Congress was, within limits that still guaranteed Communist priority, to elect a new Supreme Soviet. Gorbachev appealed for international aid and support by publicizing his political and economic liberalization, opening the country to joint ventures and (in 1990 and 1991) collaborating with the American-led alliance against Iraq.

The attempt to liberate the economy's potential by reducing central controls over production and distribution promoted the creation of many small enterprises, a frenzied search for foreign capitalists as collaborators and the emergence from underground of informal circuits of exchange – black markets, grey markets, personal networks and barter arrangements – that had previously risked prosecution. But it also generated enormous resistance by producers to delivering goods for what remained of the official distribution system, plus a massive diversion of government-owned stocks and facilities into profit-making or monopoly-maintaining private distribution networks to the benefit of existing managers, quick-thinking entrepreneurs and members of organizations having preferential access to desirable goods, facilities or foreign currencies. Barter among firms, coupon systems that guaranteed members of privileged organizations access to goods and services, reliance on friends, family and co-workers for the acquisition of scarce commodities all particularized distribution just as the government claimed to be generalizing it via the creation of a national market. As a result, the capacity of the central state to deliver rewards to its faithful followers deflated visibly from month to month.

On the political front, a parallel and interdependent collapse of central authority occurred. As the results of Gorbachev's economic programme alienated not only producers who had benefited from the emphasis on military enterprise, but also consumers who did not have ready access to one of the new distribution networks and officials whose previous powers were under attack, his political programme opened up space for critics and rivals such as Boris Yeltsin, who, from a Moscow base, rose to control the Russian federation. Gorbachev's own effort to check the threatened but still intact military and intelligence establishments through conciliation, caution and equivocation encouraged defections of reformers without gaining him solid conservative support. Simultaneously, moreover, he sought to amass emergency powers that would free him to press the economic transformation. That brought him into conflict with rival reformers, political libertarians and defenders of the old regime alike. Although demands for guarantees of religious and political liberties arose almost immediately in 1986 and 1987, nevertheless, it was the rush of nationalities to assure their positions vis-à-vis the emerging new regime that destroyed the old regime.

We must remember the USSR's ethnic variety. Like its tsarist predecessor, the communist state had followed an ambivalent policy toward mobilized ethnic minorities: seeking priority for Russian language, Russian nationals and Russianizers among minorities, but also giving official recognition to linguistic and cultural minorities, assigning many of them distinct political subdivisions and even governing through minority leaders who cast their lot with the communists. As of the 1980s, the official

Soviet roster of nationalities included 102 different categories. It by
no means exhausted the languages or distinctive cultural traditions
existing somewhere within its territory. At the 1989 census, just
over half the USSR's population counted as Russian, about the
same proportion as lived in the Russian republic.

The complexity began with the 5 million Russians who lived
outside their 'home' republic, generally occupying positions of
command and privilege, and the 5 million non-Russians residing in
the Russian republic. Almost every ostensibly national subdivision
shared that heterogeneity, the extreme being such republics as
Latvia, where only 52 per cent of the population counted as ethnic
Latvian and the census registered 34 per cent as Russian. At the
other extreme, the Jewish autonomous region of Birobidzhan, on
the Chinese border some 800 kilometres inland from Sakhalin,
housed only 20,000 of the USSR's roughly 1.8 million Jews.

Official statistics, to be sure, simplify a complex, fluid situation.
Despite the fact that passports carried one of 102 designations,
through the play of marriage and migration millions of Soviet
citizens personally identified themselves with more than one
official nationality or none at all, and outside of Russia most
people lived multiple lives, in only some of which one salient
ethnic identity prevailed (see Comaroff 1991). Nevertheless, the
system gave substantial rewards to regional leaders who could
establish themselves credibly as authentic representatives of the
Kirghiz, the Uzbeks, the Estonians or some other recognized
nationality. Ethnicity took on greater crispness as a political fact
than as a daily experience.

Russia's communists had dealt with their non-Russian regions in
the classic style of indirect rule: co-opting regional leaders who
were loyal to their cause, integrating them into the Communist
Party, recruiting their successors among the most promising
members of the nationalities but training them in Russia, dispatch-
ing many Russians to staff new industries, professions and administrations, promoting Russian language and culture as media of
administration and interregional communication, granting regional
power-holders substantial autonomy and military support within
their own territories just so long as they assured supplies of state
revenue and conscripts, striking immediately against any individual or group that called for liberties outside of this system.
The system could operate effectively so long as regional leaders

received powerful support from the centre and their local rivals had no means or hope of appealing for popular backing.

That strength of the system proved its downfall. Gorbachev and his fellow *glasnost'chiki* simultaneously promoted the opening of political discussion, reduced the military's involvement in political control, tolerated alternatives to the communist connecting structure, made gestures toward truly contested elections and acknowledged their diminished capacity to reward their faithful collaborators. As that happened, both regional power-holders and their rivals suddenly acquired strong incentives to distance themselves from the centre, to recruit popular support, to establish their credentials as authentic representatives of the local people, to urge the priority of their own nationalities within the territorial subdivisions of the USSR they happened to occupy and to press for new forms of autonomy. For the Baltic republics and those along the USSR's western or southern tiers, furthermore, the possibility of special relations with kindred states outside the Soviet Union – Sweden, Finland, Turkey, Iran, even the European Community – offered political leverage and economic opportunity the Union itself seemed decreasingly capable of providing.

In political subdivisions containing more than one well-organized national population, threats mounted rapidly to those who lost the competition for certification as authentic regional citizens. Those who moved first could gain more. Escalation began, with each concession by the central government giving new incentives and precedents for further demands by other nationalities, increasingly threatening any connected population that shared a distinct identity but failed to mobilize effectively. As early as 1986, demands for autonomy and protection arose not only from Estonians, Latvians, Lithuanians and Ukrainians, but also from Kazakhs, Crimean Tatars, Armenians, Moldavians, Uzbeks and Russians themselves. Within such heterogeneous regions as Nagorno-Karabakh, a primarily Armenian enclave within Azerbaijan, militants of neighbouring ethnicities battled for priority, and did not scruple to kill. In addition to Azerbaijan, Moldavia, Georgia and Tadjikistan grew mean with intergroup conflict. Between January 1988 and August 1989, ethnic clashes claimed 292 lives, leaving 5520 people injured and 360,000 homeless (Nahaylo & Swoboda 1990: 336). The situation recalled the Empire's disaggregation in 1918.

Gorbachev's 1990 proposal of a new union treaty, with greater scope for the fifteen republics but preservation of a federal government's military, diplomatic and economic priority, simply accelerated the efforts of each potential national actor to assure its own position within (or, for that matter, just outside) the new system. When Gorbachev sought validation of his plans in a referendum of March 1991, the leaders of six republics (Latvia, Lithuania, Estonia, Moldavia, Armenia and Georgia, all of which had started the process of declaring themselves independent) boycotted the proceedings, as the results for the rest confirmed the division between Russia and the non-Russian portions of the tottering federation.

In the face of ethnic disaggregation, economic collapse and undermining of the old regime's powers, many observers and participants in the Soviet scene feared a bid of the military, intelligence and Party establishments to reverse the flow of events. It happened. The critical moment came in August 1991, when a junta backed by just those elements sequestered Gorbachev at his Crimean holiday retreat on the eve of his signing yet another union treaty for the nine republics that were still collaborating with the central state. Drawn especially from the military, intelligence and police administrations, plotters declared the seizure of power by a shadowy Emergency Committee; its control of the state, such as it was, lasted only three days.

During the abortive coup, president Boris Yeltsin of the Russian federation braved the army's tanks and spoke to crowds in Moscow, calling for a general strike against the Emergency Committee. Several military units defected to Yeltsin's side, setting up a defensive line around the Russian republic's Moscow headquarters. The defection and defence shattered the junta's resolve. The attempted coup broke up without armed combat. Gorbachev's captors released him.

On his return, Gorbachev faced a wave of demands for accelerated reform, renewed efforts of organized nationalities to depart from the Union, intensified rivalries from Yeltsin and his counterparts in other republics, and utter collapse of the Kremlin's authority. Resigning as Party head, Gorbachev suspended Party activities throughout the USSR. Over the next four months Yeltsin sought to succeed Gorbachev, not as Party secretary but as chief of a confederation maintaining a measure of economic, military and diplomatic authority. Even that effort ended with the dissolution of the Soviet Union into an ill-defined and disputatious Commonwealth from which the Baltic states absented themselves entirely, while others began rushing for exits.

Between 1986 and 1992, Russia and its neighbours underwent one of Europe's more peculiar revolutions: the shattering of an empire and the dismantling of its central structure without direct impact of war. Burgundian, Spanish, Ottoman, Austro-Hungarian and even Russian Empires had exploded beofre, but always under the immediate pressure of armed combat from outside and within. The costly stalemate in Afghanistan, itself a product of a hugely expensive Cold War with the United States, provided the closest equivalent to those earlier empire-ending wars. The spectacle of a United States enjoying both guns, butter and open political discussion as it bombarded Iraq in 1991 accentuated the widespread sense of the Soviet state's inadequacy, just as the impending expansion of the prosperous European Community increased the attractiveness of departure from the Soviet Union to those segments that might have something to trade farther west. The peculiar form of the 1986–92 Russian revolutions, like those of all revolutions we have surveyed in Europe from 1492 onward, depended intimately on the distinctive organization of the Soviet state.

Unlike the dynastic, patron–client and communal revolutionary situations that recurred in Russia and its neighbours every decade or so between 1550 and the Napoleonic Wars, unlike the class-coalition revolutions that rent the Russian Empire in 1905 and 1917–21, the revolutionary situations of Gorbachev's era came closest to national revolutions. National revolutions – both revolutionary situations and revolutionary outcomes – became the prevalent forms in Europe after 1815, and have not yet run their course today. For a politician to claim that he or she represents a coherent, historically distinct people that has received unjust treatment by an existing state and therefore deserves a state of its own constitutes the single most successful basis for recognition and aid from outsiders. Not only leaders of non-Russian states but also Russia's Boris Yeltsin himself made just such a claim against the Communist Party and the coercive apparatus it had put in place.

The difference between Russia's experience and run-of-the-mill national revolutions lies in two elements: first, that in the Soviet Union a revolutionary situation grew directly from the central power's efforts to reform itself and change its position in the international arena; second, that the opposition of ordinary citizens to *nomenklatura* took on some features of class war. To the extent that the Russian revolutions of 1986–92 constituted class struggle of workers against privileged officials, however, we must conclude that, as of 1992, the counter-revolution had regained the upper hand. For everywhere in the Soviet Union's debris, officials who under the old regime had held power courtesy of the Communist Party were now either exercising it in the name of national sovereignty or using their skills, connections and access to goods for the advancement of new careers as entrepreneurs. Russia's revolutions had not yet ended.

7

Revolutions Yesterday, Today and Tomorrow

Back to Eastern Europe

Whether the Eastern European struggles and transformations of 1989 to 1992 constituted genuine revolutions has excited an impressive volume of debate. 'The breakdown of the communist regimes in Eastern Europe,' intones S. N. Eisenstadt,

> has been one of the more dramatic events in the history of mankind, certainly one of the most dramatic since the end of the Second World War. What is the significance? Are these revolutions like 'the great revolutions' – the English civil war, the American, French, Russian, and Chinese revolutions – which in many ways ushered in modernity, creating the modern political order? Are they likely to lead – after a possibly turbulent period of transition – to a relatively stable world of modernity, with liberal constitutionalism heralding some kind of 'end of history'? Or do they tell us something of the vicissitudes and fragilities of modernity, even of democratic-constitutional regimes? (Eisenstadt 1992: 21)

Eisenstadt replies to his stirring questions with a resounding maybe: the fall of Eastern European regimes certainly resembled classical revolutions in generating rapid, far-reaching social change, in combining popular uprisings with ineffectual centralized efforts at reform, in featuring intellectuals and in arriving at times of general breakdown in social order. But they lacked multiple features of the past's great revolutions: the vindictive violence, the class base, the charismatic vision, the faith in politics as an instrument of constructive change and the resistance of old power-holders to removal.

Ultimately, says Eisenstadt, the new revolutions embodied 'rebellions against certain types of modernity which negated in practice other more pluralistic elements of modernity, while officially instituting certain central components of their premises' (p. 33). Translation: Eastern European citizens liked the idea of industrialization, but disliked the communist way of going about it, especially its political restrictions. Why it took Soviet citizens seventy years to act on their dissatisfaction, Eisenstadt does not say.

In the perspective of 500 revolutionary years, the collapse of Eastern European regimes loses some of its close-up magnitude; that half-millennium brought Europe collapses and upheavals aplenty. Eastern Europe alone saw the shattering of great Polish-Lithuanian, Mongol and Ottoman Empires, not to mention sweeping realignments of sometimes imperial Sweden, Hungary and Russia. Nevertheless, Eisenstadt is absolutely right to reject simple analogies between 1989's events and the major revolutions of England, France or even an earlier Russia; social conditions, states and the international system have changed far too much for a repetition of the old scripts. Whatever else the histories in this book have taught, that lesson should be almost self-evident.

Given this book's concepts, do Eastern European events of 1989 qualify as revolutions? Four answers should now be clear. First, the question is not so pressing as it first seemed, since in each country the events of 1989–92 obviously had something revolutionary about them; how much is a matter of degree rather than of kind. Second, we greatly need a distinction between revolutionary situations and revolutionary outcomes; without some such distinction, recent Eastern European transitions will only baffle us. Third, in most of Eastern Europe the *outcomes* of 1989 were definitely revolutionary, since transfers of state power to substantially new ruling coalitions occurred almost everywhere; the real questions concern the depth of the revolutionary situations. Fourth, some do qualify, some don't. If we mean to ask for each East European state whether there occurred a forcible transfer of power over a state in the course of which at least two distinct blocs of contenders made incompatible claims to control the state, and some significant portion of the population subject to the state's jurisdiction acquiesced in the claims of each bloc, then the scorecard looks something like this:

Country	Revolutionary situation?	Revolutionary outcome?	Revolution?
Albania	marginal	yes	marginal
Bulgaria	marginal	marginal	marginal
Czechoslovakia	yes	yes	yes
East Germany	yes	yes	yes
Hungary	yes	uncertain	uncertain
Poland	marginal	yes	marginal
Romania	yes	doubtful	doubtful
Soviet Union	yes	yes	yes
Yugoslavia	yes	yes	yes

The judgements pose greater problems than one might have thought. Bulgaria, for example, appears as 'marginal' across the board because the country most closely approached a revolutionary situation in the hunger strikes of May 1989 and the mass exodus of Muslims from May to August of that year; touched on a revolutionary outcome with the establishment of recognized opposition groups; and flirted with armed struggle in confrontations between troops and demonstrators, all of which happened at the edge of revolution. Yugoslavia, Hungary and East Germany, furthermore, experienced very different outcomes, the first splintering (despite Serbian resistance) into component republics, the second combining the dissolution of its old rulership with an uncertain constitution of the new, the third merging incompletely into its rich, powerful neighbour, the German Federal Republic. All these transformations occurred somewhere in revolutionary terrain, but by no means in exactly the same corners of that terrain. Nor did they all seem equally revolutionary to observers and participants.

The Soviet Union was not the only European state that fractured in the 1990s. Yugoslavia, the state glued together from remnants of the Ottoman and Austro-Hungarian Empires after World War I in a deliberate attempt to contain Serbian expansionism, was seeing its predominantly non-Serbian segments secede one by one. The process had its ironies, as each departure of a non-Serbian republic threatened the remainder with greater domination by Serbia. Thus after Slovenia and Croatia had fought their way out by battling both (predominantly Serbian) Yugoslav army troops and ethnic Serbian irregulars, then by attracting intervention from Western European states and the United Nations, Bosnia and Herzegovina began to bid actively for outside recognition while Serbian and Croatian militants began trying to carve out their own autonomous territory within that small country-in-the-making as well. The Yugoslav experience and dissolution in Czechoslovakia established that national revolutions were still quite possible in Europe.

The once mighty Soviet Union broke up into a debilitated but probably curable Russia and fourteen republics. Three of those republics (Latvia, Lithuania and Estonia) fled almost immediately to the embrace of their Northern European neighbours, while the rest varied enormously in both their likely viability as independent states and their eagerness to bolt from the Commonwealth. In 1992, the former components of the Soviet Union faced momentous, interlocked questions: what would they do with the insistent demands of their own ethnic minorities – often including previously powerful Russian minorities – for protection or their own autonomy? How would they recast their disintegrated communist economies, most of them so strongly bound to Russian markets? How could such entities as Georgia, Tadjikistan, Uzbekistan and Azerbaijan survive a world of armed, rapacious states?

The comparative study of European revolutionary situations offers no crisp answers to these questions about the future. But it does place them squarely in context: emphasizing how common such national revolutions have been over the last two centuries; relating their prevalence to the consolidation of states that occurred so widely in Europe after 1750; suggesting that the new states' manner of acquiring (or, for that matter, failing to acquire) military capacity will shape them as strongly as their attempted solutions to economic problems; noting that the multiplication of sovereignties in Eastern Europe runs against the most recent trends toward formation of larger international compacts, detachment of capital from sovereignty and internationalization of economic activity in Western Europe and elsewhere.

Rules of Revolution?

Do the 500 years of revolutionary experience we have surveyed yield any general lessons about the conditions for revolution? Not many: at half-millennial scale, the history of revolutionary processes tells us much about the mechanisms of political change, but rebuts all neat formulations of standard, recurrent conditions for forcible transfers of state power. Instead, we have learned chiefly about how the conditions for revolution varied and changed between 1492 and 1992. At an extremely abstract level, we might nevertheless risk a few separate generalizations about revolutionary situations and revolutionary outcomes.

According to the chronologies I have assembled, revolutionary situations appeared most frequently in one or more of three circumstances: (1) when discrepancies increased sharply and visibly between what states demanded of their best-organized citizens and what they could induce those citizens to deliver; (2) when states made demands on their citizens that threatened strong collective identities or violated rights attached to those identities; and (3) when the power of rulers visibly diminished in the presence of strong competitors.

A revolutionary situation combining the first two formed in northern England of 1536, for example, when Henry VIII's suppression of the monasteries, seizure of their riches and incorporation of local parishes into the new state church incited a great Catholic rebellion called the Pilgrimage of Grace. Eastern Europe of 1989 illustrates the third circumstance, the visible diminution of rulers' power. But so did the recurrent disputed successions of the sixteenth and seventeenth centuries, when the appearance of a youthful or manifestly incompetent heir to a throne invited rival lineages to bid for royal power.

When did revolutionary situations lead to revolutionary outcomes? Especially in the third case, when a state's access to coercion had significantly and visibly diminished. A case in point is the successful rebellion of Portugal in 1640, which took place as Castilian overlords were weakened by revolt in Catalonia and war with France. While Castile eventually managed to reassert control in Catalonia, Portugal (fortified by colonial revenues and English support) remained independent from that time forward. A state's access to coercion can also diminish drastically through defeat in war, defection of its armed forces or collapse of its finances.

By what processes did revolutions occur? Broadly speaking, by the opening and closing of a clear split in the polity such that significant numbers of citizens had to choose between conflicting demands for loyalty and compliance, such that many constituted interests were newly at risk. How these revolutionary processes unfolded depended, however, on the current character of the state, of organized coercion, of prevailing beliefs, of political organization outside the state and of the international system. In 1514, as we have seen, the Hungarian Cardinal Primate Tamas Bakocz received the Pope's authorization to organize a crusade against the advancing Turks. When no great lords volunteered but many peasants did, the Cardinal put the force under command of a professional soldier, Gyorgy Dozsa. Dozsa turned peasants against lords when the crusaders received no supplies or financial support for their effort; a Jacquerie ensued in which whole regions essentially declared themselves exempt from noble rule. That the largely unarmed peasants lost to the warrior nobility and consequently suffered even deeper subjugation than before does not gainsay the revolutionary character of their action.

This sort of general, mutinous rising of the commons represented an entirely different path to a split in the polity and its forcible closing from the organization of an abortive but bloodily repressed insurrection by the conspiratorial United Irishmen in 1798, which differed in turn from the massive, revolutionary takeovers of Russian metal-working factories by workers during the spring of 1917. Yet all three shared the mobilization of a connected opposition to government action, the forcible seizure of territory and facilities within the jurisdiction of the state, a claim (however temporary, tenuous or localized) of alternate governmental authority and a struggle with previously constituted authorities to maintain that alternative base of power.

What, finally, determined the character and extent of change in citizens' lives as a consequence of revolution? They depended chiefly on three factors. First, social differences between those who ruled before it began and those who ruled once it ended; the greater the differences, the greater the changes in everyday life. The displacement of nobles and clergy in the French Revolution of 1789–99 wrought far larger consequences than the relatively minor shifts of governing personnel in 1830's July Revolution. Second, the extent of transformation depended on the depth of cleavage that appeared during the revolution; a completely sundered polity, on the average, produced greater changes in subsequent life. Even though the existing monarchy regained power, for example, the depth of division in France's Fronde (1648–53) greatly affected post-Fronde life, as the losing parties gave up much of their autonomous power. Third, the degree to which struggles during the revolutionary situation themselves reorganized social life substantially affected what was to follow. In particular, political institutions formed in the course of revolutions had an enduring effect on the aftermath; in the English Revolution of 1640, for all the dictatorship of Cromwell and all the restoration of monarchy in 1660, the central place of parliament in the struggles left it in a definitively stronger position vis-à-vis the sovereign than it had occupied under the Tudors or Stuarts.

We must always recall how much the rules of revolution changed over time. The histories we have parsed show that the conditions and consequences of revolutionary situations (deep divisions over control of state power) and of revolutionary outcomes (effective transfers of state power) changed in partial independence of each other. Revolutionary situations sometimes occurred widely in times and places where revolutionary outcomes remained rare, and large transfers of state power (by no means always, as we shall see, revolutionary) sometimes became relatively common where and when revolutionary situations did not often occur. Europe's seventeenth century, for example, erupted repeatedly in revolutionary situations, but in almost all of them previously established rulers managed to resume power after a bloody period of multiple sovereignty. The seventeenth-century successes of Dutch and Portuguese rebels were remarkable exceptions in a time of failed revolutions.

In the 1640s, France's Fronde and Catalonia's rebellion provide cases in point. During the Fronde, popular coalitions seized power and introduced large changes in Bordeaux and other cities, but eventually Louis XIV's mother Anne of Austria, their minister Mazarin and the grandees who had defected from the crown reconciled their differences and squeezed out all capacity for popular resistance. In Catalonia, with French help, regional power-holders established sovereignty for a dozen years, but eventually returned to Castilian hegemony at the cost of Roussillon's and Cerdagne's cession to France as well as of diminished provincial privileges. Even in Portugal, which did achieve durable independence, the revolution of 1640 greatly resembled a standard succession struggle among rival noble claimants to a throne.

In fewer instances did revolutionary outcomes occur in the absence of revolutionary situations. Large transfers of power certainly occurred without revolutionary situations, but either they passed through decades of social change and struggle (as in the rise of British capitalists to power) or they took place regionally rather than on a national scale while national authorities engaged in debilitating battles (as when Portuguese peasants and artisans seized land and formed autonomous cooperatives while military–civilian factions fought over the state during the 1970s). For lack of rapidity and/or generality, such transfers fail to qualify as revolutionary.

Nonetheless, five non-revolutionary situations did sometimes produce revolutionary outcomes: (1) the conquest of an existing state by another very different state, as when Mongols overran Muscovy; (2) a general war's settlement, as when the 1815 Congress of Vienna restored France's Bourbon monarchy and its aristocracy; (3) intervention of powerful outsiders in national politics, as in the Bulgaria of 1919, when Alexander Stamboliski and his Agrarian National Union came to power through elections protected by the victorious Allies of World War I, then proceeded to attack the power of landlords; (4) a ruler's sudden, deliberate and thorough reorganization of power, as when Mustapha Kemal undertook to secularize and westernize Turkey during the 1920s; (5) a dominant class coalition's withdrawal of support from a state, as when the Italian and German bourgeoisies tolerated fascist seizures of power by more or less legal means. In all five cases, a top-down imposition of force rapidly displaced power to a new ruling coalition. The Turkish case actually illustrates a combination of all five, if we include the dismemberment of Turkey in and after World War I as well as the Soviet Union's crucial protection for the Turkish reforms of the 1920s. Similarly, Bulgaria's peaceful revolution of 1919 issued directly from struggles occasioned by ending World War I on the losing side. Romania, having switched opportunely to the winners, did much better. In all of these circumstances, war and military power loomed very large.

The histories demonstrate, in fact, that the organization of military force mediated effectively between revolutionary situations and revolutionary outcomes: challengers to existing rulers who actually lacked the capacity to seize power often produced revolutionary situations when rulers overreached themselves, but no one seized state power without gaining effective control over military force. Peasant revolts occurred repeatedly in Europe, but they almost never maintained themselves unless they allied with magnates or municipalities that had their own armed forces. Since the organization of military force has its own history, one intimately connected with the changing organization of states in general, the likelihood and character of revolution altered in step with the transformation of European states.

Even these generalizations are thin, frail, ephemeral: suffering exceptions, distant from the realities they claim to represent, timeless and pathless when the essence of revolutionary processes consists of paths in time. The real regularities lie not in these recitations of universal conditions for revolutionary situations or revolutionary outcomes but in the mechanisms that move national politics closer to or farther from vulnerable states and divided polities. Most of the relevant mechanisms form part of the process by which states change, whether or not they approach revolution: mechanisms of succession, mechanisms of extraction, mechanisms of co-optation, mechanisms of war-making, mechanisms of conflict resolution. Remember the proximate conditions, still true by definition, of revolutionary situations and outcomes:

Revolutionary Situation	*Revolutionary Outcome*
1 The appearance of contenders, or coalitions of contenders, advancing exclusive competing claims to control of the state, or some segment of it.	1 Defections of polity members.
	2 Acquisition of armed force by revolutionary coalitions.
2 Commitment to those claims by a significant segment of the citizenry.	3 Neutralization or defection of the regime's armed force.

Revolutionary Situation	*Revolutionary Outcome*
3 Incapacity or unwilling- ness of rulers to suppress the alternative coalition and/or commitment to its claims.	4 Control of the state apparatus by members of a revolutionary coalition.

Over and over we have watched the mechanisms of change in states affecting both the likelihood of and the path to all these proximate conditions, just as they affected the character of routine politics and the long-term shift from communal, patron–client, and dynastic revolutionary situations to revolutionary situations based on nationalism and on class coalitions.

Five Centuries of Revolution

Look back one last time. As a rough indication of revolutionary rhythms over the half-millennium we have been surveying, table 7.1 presents for each major region the number of years per half-century in which at least one revolutionary situation was open. The figures simply sum up the implications of the chronologies presented earlier; in principle, a 'revolutionary situation' was an occasion on which some domestic opponent(s) of the previously existing power controlled at least one major region or subdivision of the state for a month or more. Beyond that minimum, the figures make no allowance for the conflicts' scale, casualties or long-range consequences; the Irish revolt of Sir Cahir O'Doherty (1608) counts the same as a full year of the French Revolution.

Let us give these rough numbers no more respect than is their due. We could greatly inflate these totals, especially for the earlier centuries, by including every interstate war in which one of the belligerents claimed that another was already subject to its jurisdiction, that the war therefore actually involved suppression of a rebellion. Before 1700 or so, as we have seen, the lines among interstate wars, civil wars and revolutionary situations blurred, for two related reasons: many jurisdictions overlapped in territory,

Table 7.1 Years in revolutionary situations by region and period, 1492–1991

Period	Low Countries	Iberia	Balkans and Hungary	British Isles	France	Russia	Total
1492–1541	23	9	9	19	0	1	61
1542–1591	26	6	6	28	22	2	90
1592–1641	19	3	12	13	26	22	95
1642–1691	2	27	23	20	25	24	121
1692–1741	1	14	19	3	5	10	52
1742–1791	9	2	3	2	5	12	33
1792–1841	8	36	34	6	10	4	98
1842–1891	0	22	21	0	4	2	49
1892–1941	0	36	16	6	0	7	65
1942–1991	0	2	16	23	2	2	45
Total	88	157	159	120	99	86	709

and most of the time someone was contesting most claimed jurisdictions in some regards. Including wars of conquest with disputed territories among revolutionary situations would no doubt increase the totals in Iberia more than in the Low Countries, France or Britain, in the Balkans more than Iberia, in Russia even more than the Balkans. With these important qualifications, the numbers identify an important part of what we have to explain: substantial inequalities in revolutionary situations among regions, great concentration of revolutionary situations in some periods of frequent challenge to state power.

We should not read the table as a measure of political conflict in general. France, for example, experienced no revolutionary situations between 1492 and 1541. But in the 1490s the French king was forcibly subduing Brittany on the claim that the duke was his rebellious vassal. During the same period, French troops busied themselves trying to conquer Italian territory for their king. Urban rebellions also recurred during the early sixteenth century, as in Agen's rising of 1514 against municipal taxes, which led to the popular proclamation of a Commune, or the great Rebeine that shook Lyon in 1529, when 'about two thousand inhabitants, most of them unskilled laborers, women, and boys in their teens, looted the municipal granary, the Franciscan monastery nearby, and the homes of several wealthy men, including that of Lyon's earliest humanist, the physician and former Consul Symphorien Champier' (Davis 1975: 27–8). The frequency of revolutionary situations in one of our regions does not represent the overall level of conflict, armed or otherwise, but the extent to which concerted challenges to state power became feasible and attractive alternatives to grudging compliance or passive resistance.

By a narrow margin, the Balkans had the most revolutionary years in our set: 159 to Iberia's 157. In those two regions, almost a third of all years between 1492 and 1991 contained revolutionary situations. Even the Low Countries experienced revolution about one year out of six. But in the Balkans and Iberia, revolutionary situations remained common into the 1930s; in the Low Countries, they had almost disappeared by the time other countries formally recognized the independent Dutch Republic at the Treaty of Westphalia (1648).

In the Low Countries, the vast majority of revolutionary situations over the entire period resulted from confrontations between burghers who were jealous of their liberties and royal or aristocratic powers who sought to impose something more like monarchical control; almost none conformed to the classic image of revolution as the attempt of subordinated classes to wrest control of the state away from their oppressors. Except in the service of sixteenth- and seventeenth-century dynasties, furthermore, military seizures of power played no part in the Low Countries' revolutionary history. The Low Countries moved decisively from multiple communal, patron–client and dynastic revolutionary situations preceding 1648 to a handful of class-coalition and national revolutions thereafter.

In Iberia, on the other hand, revolutionary situations rarely opened up between 1492 and the 1640s, then multiplied toward the end of the Thirty Years War. Despite fluctuations, they remained frequent into the twentieth century. In this regard, Iberia and the Balkans resembled each other. They followed quite a different pattern from the Low Countries, France and (with Irish struggles as one important qualification) the British Isles. In those three regions, the formation of the early modern state generated revolutionary situations in roughly one year out of four, after which such situations became much rarer, if sometimes more acute. The extreme case was the Low Countries, where very few open splits in either major polity formed after 1640. France took an intermediate position, with a great concentration of revolutionary years during the sixteenth and seventeenth centuries, but major revolutions during the eighteenth and nineteenth centuries. Britain's temporal pattern would greatly resemble the Low Countries', were it not for the eternal struggle of England with Ireland, a struggle persisting to the present.

Russia followed a more distinctive path of rising frequencies for revolutionary situations during the seventeenth century, persistence in the eighteenth century, rarer but acute splits thereafter. The apparent pacifism of Russia during the sixteenth century is, to be sure, partly illusory, since Muscovy and its neighbours spent that century in nearly incessant wars of conquest and defence. As Ivan the Great and his successors created a Russian Empire, the proportion of their armed struggle that they aimed at formerly acquiescent subjects rather than at vulnerable neighbours increased significantly. As always, nevertheless, the qualification leads us exactly where we want to go: to the recognition that changes in

European states and state systems deeply affected the form and incidence of revolution.

One feature of these histories is puzzling. Remember that the classification of revolutionary situations as communal, patron–client, dynastic and so on arrays connections within their social bases along two dimensions: direct vs. indirect social relations, shared territory vs. shared interest. Given increases in the scale of the states, we are not surprised to find indirect connections among revolutionary actors becoming more prevalent. But we might also have expected the specialization of state structure and the growth of interest-group politics at a national scale to reduce the importance of shared territory as a basis of revolutionary solidarity.

The opposite happened. Although communal groups such as the local communities of religious dissidents hounded into rebellion by so many states during the sixteenth and seventeenth centuries eventually disappeared from the revolutionary scene, others claiming rights to national power on the basis of shared heritage and geographic concentration more than took their place. Right up to 1992 putatively national groups rather than class coalitions or other concatenations of interests remain the most common launchers of deep challenges to existing European rulers.

Why? The very process by which European states changed during the eighteenth and nineteenth centuries explains the renewed emphasis on territory at a national scale. Beginning with the construction of national standing armies from the resident male population at large, European rulers circumscribed their territories and the resources within them, then undertook to homogenize, discipline and rule directly their subjects. Bargaining over the supply of military means established citizenship and citizens' claims on the state, promoted the formation of interest groups devoted to exercising power over the state, and thus drew those interest groups willy-nilly into the routine games of national politics. The principles of centralized territorial administration, direct rule and cultural nationalization, on the other hand, generally excluded from national politics populations claiming common origins other than the one authorized by the state's cultural policies.

In that soil rooted paradox: the same processes made statehood more valuable, pivoted it on claims to common origin and denied it to the great majority of its potential holders. Although the advocates of most such marginalized 'parochial' identities would lose their bids for statehood, furthermore, a few would make it. The disintegration of empires and the redrawing of boundaries in ostensible attention to nationality at the ends of wars made those few all the more visible as models for the rest, especially for the intellectuals and other brokers who had much invested in their biculturalism, their existence athwart newly national and newly parochial identities. Those regional elites who could enter the national elite as equals did so, abandoning their parochial fellows in the process, but those who found themselves relegated to inferior positions on the national scene became zealous nationalists.

Despite the recent surge of state-seeking nationalism, nevertheless, a number of changes point toward a longer-term *decline* in nationalism. The most important is the shrinking capacity of European states to sustain the dramatic circumscription of capital, labour, goods, services, money and culture that began occurring so widely 200 years ago. After two centuries in which they did succeed remarkably in monitoring, capturing and storing resources within well-defined borders, Western states in general are finding it increasingly difficult to maintain control of migrant workers, capital, drugs, technologies and money. All of them are internationalizing and becoming exceedingly mobile.

The European Community is compounding that difficulty for its members by actually promoting free movement of capital, commodities and labour, establishing a common currency and pressing them toward uniform welfare policies. In the longer run, these pressures will undermine the autonomy and circumscription of individual states, make it extremely difficult for any state to carry on a separate fiscal, welfare or military policy, and thus reduce the relative advantage of controlling the apparatus of a national state. It is quite possible that the many activities states bundled together in the era and aftermath of the French Revolution will again separate, with capital, for example, operating rather independently of any particular state's interests. If this happens, the incentives to both state-led and state-seeking nationalism will decline rapidly.

A conceivable result, ironically, is a proliferation of cultural particularisms, now freed from the burden of challenging state authority and seeking political autonomy. In the future, cultural pluralism may well become compatible with the devolution of economic and political power to very large units, no longer identical and no longer consolidated states as we have known them for 200 years. What some people see as an age of renewed revolutionary nationalism may well preface an age of its utter decline.

References

This list includes only items cited in the text. For a more general bibliography, see Charles Tilly, 'A Bibliography of European Revolutions, 1492–1992', Working Paper 149, Center for Studies of Social Change, New School for Social Research, September 1992.

Alefirenko, P. K. (1958): *Krest'ianskoie dvizhenie i krest'ianskii vopros v Rossii v 30–50-x godax XVIII veka.* Moscow: Nauk.

Amann, Peter (1962): 'Revolution: A Redefinition', *Political Science Quarterly* 77: 36–53.

Arendt, Hannah (1963): *On Revolution.* New York: Viking.

Aya, Rod (1990): *Rethinking Revolutions and Collective Violence. Studies on Concept, Theory, and Method.* Amsterdam: Het Spinhuis.

Aylmer, G. E. (1986): *Rebellion or Revolution? England 1640–1660.* Oxford: Oxford University Press.

Baechler, Jean (1970): *Les phénomènes révolutionnaires.* Paris: Presses Universitaires de France.

Bairoch, Paul (1976): 'Europe's Gross National Product: 1800–1975', *Journal of European Economic History* 5: 273–340.

Bercé, Yves-Marie (1974): *Histoire des Croquants. Etude des soulèvements populaires au XVIIe siècle dans le sud-ouest de la France,* 2 vols. Paris: Droz.

—— (1980): *Révoltes et Révolutions dans l'Europe moderne.* Paris: Presses Universitaires de France.

Berend, Iván & György Ránki (1977): *East Central Europe in the 19th and 20th Centuries.* Budapest: Akademiai Kiado.

Blickle, Peter (1981): *The Revolution of 1525. The German Peasants' War from a New Perspective.* Baltimore: Johns Hopkins University Press. German edition first published in 1977.

—— (1987): 'Communal Reformation and Peasant Piety: The Peasant

Reformation and its Late Medieval Origins', *Central European History* 20: 216–28.

Blickle, Peter (1988): *Unruhen in der ständischen Gesellschaft, 1300–1800*. Enzyklopädie Deutscher Geschichte, vol. I. Munich: Oldenbourg.

Bois, Paul (1981): 'Aperçu sur les causes des insurrections de l'Ouest à l'époque révolutionnaire', in J.-C. Martin (ed.), *Vendée-Chouannerie*, pp. 121–6. Nantes: Reflets du Passé.

Braddick, Michael (1991): 'State Formation and Social Change in Early Modern England: A Problem Stated and Approaches Suggested', *Social History* 16: 1–18.

Brady, Thomas A. Jr. (1985): *Turning Swiss. Cities and Empire, 1450–1550*. Cambridge: Cambridge University Press.

Brinton, Crane (1938): *The Anatomy of Revolution*. New York: Norton.

Broeker, Galen (1970): *Rural Disorder and Police Reform in Ireland, 1812–36*. London: Routledge & Kegan Paul.

Chandler, Tertius & Gerald Fox (1974): *3000 Years of Urban Growth*. New York: Academic Press.

Charlesworth, Andrew (1983): ed., *An Atlas of Rural Protest in Britain, 1548–1900*. London: Croom Helm.

Chassin, Charles-Louis (1892): *La préparation de la guerre de Vendée*, 3 vols. Paris: Dupont.

Clark, J. C. D. (1986): *Revolution and Rebellion. State and Society in England in the Seventeenth and Eighteenth Centuries*. Cambridge: Cambridge University Press.

Clark, Samuel D. & J. S. Donnelly (1983): eds, *Irish Peasants: Violence and Political Unrest, 1780–1914*. Madison: University of Wisconsin Press.

Clay, C. G. A. (1984): *Economic Expansion and Social Change: England 1500–1700*, 2 vols. Cambridge: Cambridge University Press.

Comaroff, John (1991): 'Humanity, Ethnicity, Nationality: Conceptual and Comparative Perspectives on the U.S.S.R.', *Theory and Society* 20: 661–88.

Cornwall, Julian (1977): *Revolt of the Peasantry 1549*. London: Routledge & Kegan Paul.

Cronin, James E. (1991): *The Politics of State Expansion. War, state and society in twentieth-century Britain*. London: Routledge.

Davis, Natalie Zemon (1975): *Society and Culture in Early Modern France*. Berkeley: University of California Press.

Dawson, Philip (1972): *Provincial Magistrates and Revolutionary Politics in France, 1789–1795*. Cambridge: Harvard University Press.

Dekker, Rudolf (1982): *Holland in beroering. Oproeren in de 17de en 18de eeuw*. Baarn: Amboeken.

Dietz, Frederick C. (1932): *English Public Finance 1558–1641*. New

York: Century.

Dunn, John (1989): *Modern Revolutions, An Introduction to the Analysis of a Political Phenomenon*, 2nd edn. Cambridge: Cambridge University Press.

Eisenstadt, S. N. (1992): 'The Breakdown of Communist Regimes', *Daedalus* 121(2): 21–42.

Fitzpatrick, David (1985): 'Review Essay: Unrest in Rural Ireland', *Irish Economic and Social History* 12: 98–105.

Fitzpatrick, Sheila (1982): *The Russian Revolution 1917–1932*. Oxford: Oxford University Press.

Fletcher, Anthony (1968): *Tudor Rebellions*. London: Longman.

Forrest, Alan (1975): *Society and Politics in Revolutionary Bordeaux*. Oxford: Oxford University Press.

Friedrich, Carl J. (1966): ed., *Revolution*. New York: Atherton.

Furet, François (1989): 'L'idée démocratique est l'avenir de l'idée socialiste,' (interview) *Le Monde de la Révolution Française*, no. 1, p. 28.

—— & Mona Ozouf (1989): eds, *A Critical Dictionary of the French Revolution*. Cambridge: Harvard University Press.

Gambrelle, Fabienne & Michel Trebitsch (1989): eds, *Révolte et société. Actes du Colloque d'Histoire au Présent, Paris mai 1988*, 2 vols. Paris: Histoire au Présent.

Goldstone, Jack A. (1986): 'Introduction: The Comparative and Historical Study of Revolutions', in Jack A. Goldstone (ed.), *Revolutions. Theoretical, Comparative, and Historical Studies*, pp. 1–17. San Diego: Harcourt Brace Jovanovich.

—— (1991): *Revolution and Rebellion in the Early Modern World*. Berkeley: University of California Press.

Greenfeld, Liah (1990): 'The Formation of the Russian National Identity: The Role of Status Insecurity and Ressentiment', *Comparative Studies in Society and History* 32: 549–91.

Greer, Donald (1935): *The Incidence of the Terror during the French Revolution*. Cambridge: Harvard University Press.

Griffiths, Gordon (1960): 'The Revolutionary Character of the Revolt of the Netherlands', *Comparative Studies in Society and History* 2: 452–72.

Hanson, Paul R. (1989): *Provincial Politics in the French Revolution. Caen and Limoges, 1789–1794*. Baton Rouge: Louisiana State University Press.

't Hart, Marjolein (1989): 'Cities and Statemaking in the Dutch Republic, 1580–1680', *Theory and Society* 18: 663–88.

—— (1990): 'Public Loans and Lenders in the Seventeenth Century Netherlands' in *Economic and Social History in the Netherlands*, vol. I, pp. 119–40. Amsterdam: Nederlandsch Economisch-Historisch Archief.

't Hart, Marjolein (1991): '"The Devil or the Dutch'": Holland's Impact on the Financial Revolution in England, 1643–1694', *Parliaments, Estates and Representation* 11: 39–52.

Heller, Henry (1991): *Iron and Blood. Civil Wars in Sixteenth-Century France*. Montreal: McGill-Queen's University Press.

Hirst, Derek (1986): *Authority and Conflict. England, 1603–1658*. Cambridge: Harvard University Press.

Hobbes, Thomas (1990): *Behemoth or the Long Parliament*. Chicago: University of Chicago Press. Completed about 1668; first published officially in 1682.

Hobsbawm, E. J. (1986): 'Revolution', in Roy Porter & Mikulas Teich (eds), *Revolution in History*, pp. 5–46. Cambridge: Cambridge University Press.

Hood, James N. (1971): 'Protestant–Catholic Relations and the Roots of the First Popular Counterrevolutionary Movement in France', *Journal of Modern History* 43: 245–75.

—— (1979): 'Revival and Mutation of Old Rivalries in Revolutionary France', *Past and Present* 82: 82–115.

Jessenne, Jean-Pierre (1987): *Pouvoir au village et Révolution. Artois 1760–1848*. Lille: Presses Universitaires de Lille.

van Kalken, Frans (1946): *Histoire de Belgique des origines à nos jours*. Brussels: Office de Publicité.

Kennedy, William (1964): *English Taxation 1640–1799. An Essay on Policy and Opinion*. New York: Augustus Kelley. First published in 1913.

Kimmel, Michael S. (1990): *Revolution. A Sociological Interpretation*. Philadelphia: Temple University Press.

Knecht, R. J. (1989): *The French Wars of Religion 1559–1598*. London: Longman.

Koenker, Diane P. & William G. Rosenberg (1989): *Strikes and Revolution in Russia, 1917*. Princeton: Princeton University Press.

Kossmann, E. H. (1978): *The Low Countries 1780–1940*. Oxford: Clarendon Press.

Laitin, David D., Roger Petersen & John W. Slocum (1992): 'Language and the State: Russia and the Soviet Union in Comparative Perspective', in Alexander J. Motyl (ed.), *Thinking Theoretically About Soviet Nationalities. History and Comparison in the Study of the USSR*, pp. 129–68. New York: Columbia University Press.

Laqueur, Walter (1968): 'Revolution', *International Encyclopedia of the Social Sciences* 13: 501–7. New York: Macmillan.

Lebrun, François & Roger Dupuy (1985): eds, *Les résistances à la Révolution*. Paris: Imago.

LeDonne, John P. (1991): *Absolutism and Ruling Class. The Formation of the Russian Political Order 1700–1825*. New York: Oxford University Press.

Le Goff, Jacques & Jean-Claude Schmitt (1981): eds, *Le Charivari*. Paris: Mouton.

Le Goff, T. J. A. & D. M. G. Sutherland (1984): 'Religion and Rural Revolt in the French Revolution: An Overview', in János M. Bak & Gerhard Benecke (eds), *Religion and Rural Revolt*, pp. 123–46. Manchester: Manchester University Press.

Lenin, V. I. (1967): *Selected Works*, 3 vols. New York: International Publishers.

Lepetit, Bernard (1988): *Les villes dans la France moderne (1740–1840)*. Paris: Albin Michel.

Leroy-Beaulieu, Anatole (1990): *L'Empire des tsars et les Russes*, 3 vols. Paris: Robert Laffont. First published in 1881–9.

Le Roy Ladurie, Emmanuel & Michel Morineau (1977): *Histoire économique et sociale de la France. Tome I: de 1450 à 1660. Second Volume: Paysannerie et croissance*. Paris: Presses Universitaires de France.

Lesthaeghe, Ron J. (1977): *The Decline of Belgian Fertility, 1800–1970*. Princeton: Princeton University Press.

Levy, Jack S. (1983): *War in the Modern Great Power System, 1495–1975*. Lexington: University Press of Kentucky.

Lewis, Gwynne (1978): *The Second Vendée: The Continuity of Counter-Revolution in the Department of the Gard, 1789–1815*. Oxford: Clarendon Press.

Lewis, Gwynne & Colin Lucas (1983): eds, *Beyond the Terror. Essays in French Regional and Social History, 1794–1815*. Cambridge: Cambridge University Press.

Luard, Evan (1987): *War in International Society*. New Haven: Yale University Press.

Lucas, Colin (1973): *The Structure of the Terror: The Example of Javogues and the Loire*. London: Oxford University Press.

Lyons, Martyn (1980): *Révolution et Terreur à Toulouse*. Toulouse: Privat.

MacCulloch, Diarmaid (1979): 'Kett's Rebellion in Context', *Past and Present* 84: 36–59.

McPhail, Clark (1991): *The Myth of the Madding Crowd*. New York: Aldine De Gruyter.

McPhee, Peter (1988): 'Les formes d'intervention populaire en Roussillon: L'exemple de Collioure, 1789–1815', in Centre d'Histoire Contemporaine du Languedoc Méditerranéen et du Roussillon, *Les pratiques politiques en province à l'époque de la Révolution française*, pp. 235–52. Montpellier: Publications de la Recherche, Université de Montpellier.

Manning, Roger B. (1988): *Village Revolts. Social Protest and Popular Disturbances in England, 1509–1640*. Oxford: Clarendon Press.

Markoff, John (1985): 'The Social Geography of Rural Revolt at the Beginning of the French Revolution', *American Sociological Review* 50: 761–781.

Martin, Jean-Claude (1987): *La Vendée et la France*. Paris: Le Seuil.

Mironov, B. N. (1985): *Khlebn'ie tsen'i v Rossii za dva stoletiia (XVIII-XIX vv.)*. Leningrad: Nauka.

Moody, T. W. & F. X. Martin (1987): eds, *The Course of Irish History*, revised edn. Cork: Mercier Press.

Mousnier, Roland (1967): *Fureurs paysannes: les paysannes dans les révoltes du XVIIe siècle (France, Russie, Chine)*. Paris: Calmann-Lévy.

Nahaylo, Bohdan & Victor Swoboda (1990): *Soviet Disunion. A History of the Nationalities Problem in the USSR*. New York: Free Press.

Nell, Edward (1991): 'Demand and Capacity in Capitalism and Socialism', Working Paper 22, Political Economy Program, New School for Social Research.

O'Brien, Conor Cruise (1989): 'Nationalism and the French Revolution', in Geoffrey Best (ed.), *The Permanent Revolution. The French Revolution and its Legacy, 1789–1989*, pp. 17–48. Chicago: University of Chicago Press. First published in 1988.

O'Brien, Patrick K. (1988): 'The Political Economy of British Taxation, 1660–1815', *Review* 41: 1–32.

—— (1989): 'The Impact of the Revolutionary and Napoleonic Wars, 1793–1815, on the Long-run Growth of the British Economy', *Economic History Review* 12: 335–95.

Østergard, Uffe (1992): 'Peasants and Danes: The Danish National Identity and Political Culture', *Comparative Studies in Society and History* 34: 3–27.

Palmer, R. R. (1959, 1964): *The Age of the Democratic Revolution*, 2 vols. Princeton: Princeton University Press.

Palmer, Stanley H. (1988): *Police and Protest in England and Ireland 1780–1850*. Cambridge: Cambridge University Press.

Popovsky, Linda S. (1990): 'The Crisis over Tonnage and Poundage in Parliament in 1629', *Past and Present* 126: 44–75.

Prevenier, Walter & Wim Blockmans (1985): *The Burgundian Netherlands*. Antwerp: Fonds Mercator.

Richardson, R. C. (1977): *The Debate on the English Revolution*. New York: St. Martin's.

Rosenberg, Harriet G. (1988): *A Negotiated World: Three Centuries of Change in a French Alpine Community*. Toronto: University of Toronto Press.

Rowen, Herbert H. (1972): ed., *The Low Countries in Early Modern Times*. New York: Harper & Row.

Rozman, Gilbert (1976): *Urban Networks in Russia 1750–1800 and Premodern Periodization*. Princeton: Princeton University Press.

Rule, James B. (1989): *Theories of Civil Violence*. Berkeley: University of California Press.

—— & Charles Tilly (1972): '1830 and the Unnatural History of Revolution', *Journal of Social Issues* 28: 49–76.

Russell, Conrad S. R. (1982): 'Monarchies, Wars, and Estates in England, France, and Spain, c. 1580–c. 1640', *Legislative Studies Quarterly* 7: 205–20.

—— (1990): *The Causes of the English Civil War*. Oxford: Clarendon Press.

—— (1991): *The Fall of the British Monarchies 1637–1642*. Oxford: Clarendon Press.

Scott, William (1973): *Terror and Repression in Revolutionary Marseilles*. New York: Barnes & Noble.

Shanin, Teodor (1986): *The Roots of Otherness: Russia's Turn of Century*, 2 vols. New Haven: Yale University Press.

Stone, Lawrence (1972): *The Causes of the English Revolution, 1529–1642*. London: Routledge & Kegan Paul.

Sugar, Peter F. (1990): ed., *A History of Hungary*. Bloomington: Indiana University Press.

Swanson, Guy E. (1967): *Religion and Regime. A Sociological Account of the Reformation*. Ann Arbor: University of Michigan Press.

Tarrow, Sidney (1989): *Struggle, Politics, and Reform: Collective Action, Social Movements, and Cycles of Protest*. Occasional Paper No. 21, Western Societies Programme. Ithaca: Center for International Studies, Cornell University.

—— & Sarah Soule (1991): 'Acting Collectively, 1847–49: How the Repertoire of Collective Action Changed and Where it Happened', unpublished paper presented to the Social Science History Association, New Orleans.

Thompson, E. P. (1972): 'Rough Music: Le Charivari anglais', *Annales; Economies, Sociétés, Civilisations* 27: 285–312.

Tilly, Charles (1982): 'Britain Creates the Social Movement', in James Cronin & Jonathan Schneer (eds), *Social Conflict and the Political Order in Modern Britain*, pp. 21–51. London: Croom Helm.

—— (1984): 'Demographic Origins of the European Proletariat', in David Levine (ed.), *Proletarianization and Family History*, pp. 1–85. Orlando: Academic Press.

—— (1986): *The Contentious French*. Cambridge: Harvard University Press.

—— (1991a): 'From Mutiny to Mass Mobilization in Great Britain, 1758–1834', Working Paper 109. Center for Studies of Social Change, New School for Social Research, March.

Tilly, Charles (1991b): 'Revolution, War, and Other Struggles in Great Britain, 1789–1815', Working Paper 127. Center for Studies of Social Change, New School for Social Research, September.

Tracy, James D. (1985): *A Financial Revolution in the Habsburg Netherlands. Renten and Renteniers in the County of Holland, 1515–1565.* Berkeley: University of California Press.

Trotsky, Leon (1932): *The Russian Revolution.* New York: Simon & Schuster.

Underdown, David (1985): *Revel, Riot, and Rebellion. Popular Politics and Culture in England 1603–1660.* Oxford: Clarendon Press.

Verdery, Katherine (1991): 'Theorizing Socialism: A Prologue to the "Transition" ', *American Ethnologist* 18: 419–39.

de Vries, Jan (1984): *European Urbanization 1500–1800.* Cambridge: Harvard University Press.

Wallerstein, Immanuel (1974–89): *The Modern World System,* 3 vols to date. New York: Academic Press.

Watkins, Susan Cotts (1990): *From Provinces into Nations.* Princeton: Princeton University Press.

Winter, J. M. (1986): *The Great War and the British People.* Cambridge: Harvard University Press.

Wuthnow, Robert (1989): *Communities of Discourse. Ideology and Social Structure in the Reformation, the Enlightenment, and European Socialism.* Cambridge: Harvard University Press.

Zagorin, Perez (1982): *Rebels and Rulers, 1500–1660,* 2 vols. Cambridge: Cambridge University Press.

Index

257